THE BEDFORD SERIES IN HISTORY AND CULTURE

Andrew Jackson vs. Henry Clay

Democracy and Development in Antebellum America

Harry L. Watson

*University of North Carolina
at Chapel Hill*

BEDFORD/ST. MARTIN'S   Boston   •   New York

This book is dedicated to my own teachers, Bob Wiebe and Jack Thomas.

For Bedford/St. Martin's
History Editor: Katherine E. Kurzman
Production Editor: Sherri Frank
Marketing Manager: Charles Cavaliere
Editorial Assistant: Jen Lesar
Production Assistant: Deborah Baker
Copyeditor: Rosemary Winfield
Text Design: Claire Seng-Niemoeller
Indexer: Steve Csipke
Cover Design: Richard Emery Design, Inc.
Cover Art: Andrew Jackson (detail) 1845 by Thomas Sully. Andrew W. Mellon Collection, © 1997 Board of Trustees, National Gallery of Art. [Henry Clay] *The Father of the American System* (detail) by John Neagle. Courtesy of the Abraham Lincoln Foundation of the Union League of Philadephia.
Composition: ComCom
Printing and Binding: Haddon Craftsmen, Inc.

President: Charles H. Christensen
Editorial Director: Joan E. Feinberg
Director of Editing, Design, and Production: Marcia Cohen
Managing Editor: Elizabeth M. Schaaf

For information, write: Bedford/St. Martin's, 75 Arlington Street, Boston, MA 02116 (617–399–4000)

ISBN-10: 0–312–11213–0 (paperback)
     0–312–17772–0 (hardcover)
ISBN-13: 978–0–312–11213–4

Acknowledgments
    Andrew Jackson, "Division Orders to Tennessee Militia," March 7, 1812. Reprinted from *The Correspondence of Andrew Jackson,* edited by John Spencer Bassett, by permission of the Carnegie Institution of Washington. Copyright © 1926–1935 Carnegie Institution of Washington.
    "The Hunters of Kentucky." Reprinted from *Andrew Jackson: Symbol for an Age,* by John William Ward. Courtesy Oxford University Press.

Foreword

The Bedford Series in History and Culture is designed so that readers can study the past as historians do.

The historian's first task is finding the evidence. Documents, letters, memoirs, interviews, pictures, movies, novels, or poems can provide facts and clues. Then the historian questions and compares the sources. There is more to do than in a courtroom, for hearsay evidence is welcome, and the historian is usually looking for answers beyond act and motive. Different views of an event may be as important as a single verdict. How a story is told may yield as much information as what it says.

Along the way the historian seeks help from other historians and perhaps from specialists in other disciplines. Finally, it is time to write, to decide on an interpretation and how to arrange the evidence for readers.

Each book in this series contains an important historical document or group of documents, each document a witness from the past and open to interpretation in different ways. The documents are combined with some element of historical narrative—an introduction or a biographical essay, for example—that provides students with an analysis of the primary source material and important background information about the world in which it was produced.

Each book in the series focuses on a specific topic within a specific historical period. Each provides a basis for lively thought and discussion about several aspects of the topic and the historian's role. Each is short enough (and inexpensive enough) to be a reasonable one-week assignment in a college course. Whether as classroom or personal reading, each book in the series provides firsthand experience of the challenge—and fun—of discovering, recreating, and interpreting the past.

Lynn Hunt
David W. Blight
Bonnie G. Smith
Natalie Zemon Davis
Ernest R. May

Preface

The Americans who lived between the War of 1812 and the territorial crisis of 1850 experienced a generation of rapid and complex change. Under the influence of new inventions in transportation and communication, the economy quickened significantly. Thousands of Americans crossed the Appalachian Mountains and founded new communities in the Ohio and Mississippi valleys. Factory production gathered strength in the Northeast, and slavery extended its reach across the South. White men demanded the end of all limitations on their own political rights, and religious movements fed hopes of moral regeneration and social reform.

Andrew Jackson and Henry Clay were the two most outstanding American political leaders of this busy era. They had much in common with each other, but they were bitter personal and political rivals whose wide-ranging conflicts illustrate many of the changes and choices that faced the United States in their lifetimes. Because their competing aspirations also inspired the country's two leading political parties, the conflict between Jackson and Clay also gave major direction to the lives and decisions of most of their fellow Americans.

This book focuses on the relationship between Andrew Jackson and Henry Clay and especially on tension they perceived between "democracy," or the movement for equality and popular rule by the majority of all white men, and the contemporary economic development of the United States. This conflict framed political debate for the pre–Civil War generation. It also led to the creation of political structures like political parties and mass political campaigning that shaped the way that Americans would respond to future events and emergencies like the secession crisis and that continue to dominate its process of government today.

The controversy over democracy and development was not the only debate or dilemma that faced the United States in this period. In part, the debate that preoccupied Andrew Jackson and Henry Clay became so absorbing because it enabled Americans to evade or avoid other debates that were at least as important but less amenable to peaceful solutions.

Principal among these other controversies was the question of slavery and its place in American life, a question that could not be solved within the political structures that Jackson and Clay created. Sensing that this was true, politicians of the 1820s, 1830s, and 1840s tried to keep disagreements over slavery out of their debates, even though the underlying controversy was too important and too urgent to remain hidden for long.

This book necessarily follows a similar strategy. It attempts to introduce students to the subjects that major American politicians debated vocally and endlessly—tariffs, internal improvements, and especially banking. These subjects are worth treating because they were important to contemporaries and they had significant consequences for the future. An exclusive focus on the issues that later eclipsed them can distort our understanding of the age. The book therefore skirts the subjects that Jacksonian politicians tried to avoid, especially slavery, not because the subject is unimportant but because it is too important to dispose of in a work of this size. When the urgency of the slavery question made it impossible for politicians to avoid, it appears in this book as well.

Specialists will also notice there is little here on other important contemporary problems such as evangelical reform, gender issues, or immigration. Political movements such as Antimasonry, which did not deeply involve the two principals, are also neglected. The closely related issues of Indian removal and geographical expansion receive attention but do not form the crux of the argument because they were not the central focus of political controversy between Jackson and Clay. The book does not even treat every facet of the lives of Henry Clay and Andrew Jackson but concentrates on their relationship with each other and their clashing political movements. My hope is to give students a sample of how the clashing perspectives of two individuals shaped and exemplified the major issues of contemporary national politics—the preservation of the union, federal commitments to banking, tariffs, and internal improvements, and the egalitarian tone of national political culture. That is plenty for one short book.

ACKNOWLEDGMENTS

I would like to thank Charles Christensen of Bedford Books for the idea of this book and my patient and gracious editor Katherine Kurzman for her help in completing it. I am also grateful to an unusually perceptive group of readers who have made numerous valuable suggestions: Marilyn Baseler, David W. Blight, Paul Finkelman, Michael F. Holt, Robert T. Mackenzie, Robert V. Remini, Charles Sellers, Thomas P. Slaughter, and Pershing Vartanian. Their careful criticisms have helped the book in many ways; while I have not followed them all, I have consistently benefited from rethinking the issues they have raised.

Harry L. Watson

Contents

Illustrations

Andrew Jackson
vs. Henry Clay

Democracy and Development
in Antebellum America

PART ONE

Introduction:
Old Hickory, Prince Hal,
and the World of
the Early Republic

Andrew Jackson (1767–1845) and Henry Clay (1777–1852) were American political leaders who had much in common. Both men came of age in the generation following the American Revolution and dominated national politics in the generation following the War of 1812. Both men were born in South Atlantic seaboard states and crossed the mountains to begin their careers on the trans-Appalachian frontier—Jackson in Tennessee and Clay in Kentucky. Both became southern planters and slaveholders who were dedicated to preserving the federal Union, despite the growing tension between North and South. Each one was also a lawyer who devoted himself to electoral politics and used the War of 1812 as a springboard for his political ambitions. Only Jackson served as president of the United States, but Clay sought the office avidly, repeatedly, and almost successfully. Both men were long-standing leaders of their respective parties and played major roles in the creation of America's two-party system, yet both men occasionally deplored the influence of political parties on American public life. Despite their similarities, however, Andrew Jackson and Henry Clay heartily despised one another and thought the other was his total opposite in politics, morals, and personal characteristics.

Clay and Jackson were too young to take any part in the writing or ratification of the U.S. Constitution, but they flourished in the period following its adoption, when political leaders struggled to implement its practical details. These were the years when the majority of white men became eligible to vote, and Clay and Jackson won political office by appealing to ordinary voters' demands for recognition and respect. Their careers also spanned an era of significant geographical and economic expansion, as tens of thousands of settlers crossed the Appalachians and established America's hold on the land between the mountains and the Mississippi. (See Figure 1.) The steam engine was harnessed to railroads and paddle wheels, new canals and turnpikes stretched across the wilderness, and the factory system began its rapid growth. Southern plantations burgeoned in an effort to supply the new spinning machines with cotton fiber, and the labor of African American slaves was demanded more than ever.

Superficially, at least, Henry Clay and Andrew Jackson both endorsed the movements in their lifetimes for increased democracy and economic development. Neither man favored either property requirements for the right to vote or restrictions on new technology. Fundamentally, however, both Clay and Jackson shared a suspicion with many thousands of Americans that the political and economic changes of their era were in subtle competition with each other. Jackson and his supporters tended to think that the growing wealth and power of the business community might erode the equality and independence of ordinary citizens. Alternatively, Henry Clay and his followers often wondered if strict deference to the uninformed opinions of ordinary voters might somehow undermine the businesses that generated U.S. prosperity. In other words, in an age of democracy and economic development, Andrew Jackson and his supporters feared that democracy might suffer at the hands of development, while Henry Clay and his admirers worried that the opposite might be true. Despite their other similarities, these different reactions to the changing patterns in American life put Henry Clay and Andrew Jackson into serious conflict with each other. The rise and evolution of their conflict brought permanent changes in American politics and became key aspects of America's transformation from a modest set of Atlantic settlements into a raucous electoral democracy and the world's most powerful industrial economy.

Henry Clay and Andrew Jackson also diverged in the roads they took to national prominence. Like most of his contemporaries in public life, Clay made his mark in civilian politics, building a long and distinguished record in the Kentucky legislature, the U.S. House of Representatives, the diplomatic service, the cabinet, and finally the U.S. Senate. He was a

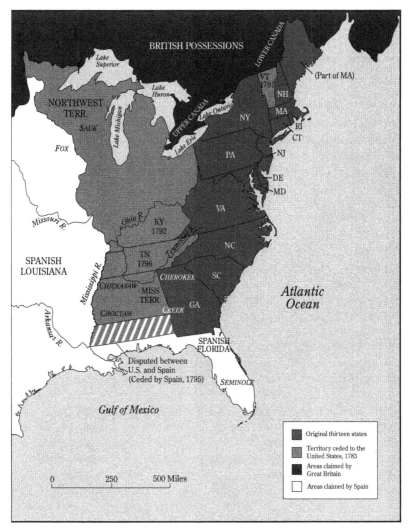

Figure 1. The United States, Shortly After Independence

On the eve of the nation's birth, the country's prosperity was far from assured. The thirteen original colonies lined the Eastern seaboard, their expansion limited by the continued presence of European powers and hostile Indian tribes to the North, West, and South.

brilliant orator whose command of language let him dominate every legislative chamber he ever entered and left audiences awestruck in an age when the standards of speechmaking were already high. He was also blessed with a complementary talent in private negotiations—in the subtle arts of compromise, maneuver, and consensus building. Clay became famous as a legislative craftsman and dealmaker who could balance competing factions and fashion a bill to allow each special interest just what was needed to obtain its consent and no more. His skill in both the public and the private dimensions of parliamentary leadership made him a superior power in the U.S. Congress for most of his political career.

Andrew Jackson's career was quite different. Though he too had dabbled in legislative politics, Jackson built his fame as a powerful general who triumphed over "savage" Indians and seasoned British veterans alike. While Clay was famous for negotiation and compromise, Jackson gave commands and backed them with force. While Clay was the ultimate Washington insider, Jackson posed as the outsider on horseback whose strong will and political independence gave him the moral authority to lead the nation. Jacksonians tended to think that Henry Clay could destroy the republic by giving in to corruption, while Clay supporters felt that Jackson could do the same thing by unleashing a military despotism. In short, each man's supporters thought him ideal for the presidency precisely because they saw him as radically different from his opponent.

Clay's and Jackson's disagreements over democracy and development were intimately connected to other American disputes, especially those connected with slavery and geographical expansion. Cotton grown by slaves was the most valuable export of the antebellum United States, and factories for spinning and weaving it were among the most important fruits of economic development. Growth of the textile industry led to geographical expansion, as southerners pressed for more lands suitable for growing cotton with slave labor. The pressure for more slave territory brought southerners into conflict with antislavery northerners and touched off furious conflicts that the political party system of Clay and Jackson could hardly mediate.

Slavery was obviously connected to the issue of race, and both were directly linked to the question of democracy. For centuries, white Americans had used the color of Africans as a badge of enslavement. By the beginning of the nineteenth century, they were also accustomed to regard blackness as a mark of moral and intellectual inferiority, as a justification for enslavement, and as an excuse for numerous other forms of racial discrimination. Most American states did not permit African American men to vote, for example, even when they were not slaves. Whites who demanded their own political rights often appeared to think that political equality was the most fitting barrier between black and white. In effect, democracy itself became an aspect of racial identity.[1] The same set of issues had a deep impact on Native Americans. While whites did not usually enslave Indians in the nineteenth century, they included them in some of the same color prejudices they felt about Africans. The assumption that Indians could never share equal rights with white people encouraged white Americans to call for the seizure of Indian lands. Native Americans in the southern states owned excellent cotton territory through the 1830s, and the pressures of economic expansionism, racial inequality, and democratic (or demagogic) politics fed powerful popular demands for their expropriation. Andrew Jackson was the primary leader of this movement, and his campaign for Indian removal tied the movements for economic development, territorial expansion, racial discrimination, white democracy, and the spread of slavery tightly together.

With the partial exception of Indian removal, however, the questions of race and expansion were not central to the dispute between Andrew Jackson and Henry Clay. The two men clashed instead over tamer matters like taxes, public works, and above all, banking policy. Unlike slavery, these seemingly mundane questions were not too explosive to address in national political circles. Unlike geographical expansion and racial prejudice, they were controversial enough to create lasting political divisions. In complex ways that I hope to explain in this book, they were also deeply important to antebellum white Americans. While the issues of slavery, racism, and conquest were also deeply important to these Americans, they did not form the cornerstone of contemporary debate because politicians worked hard to keep them at the margins of political discourse.

Eventually, particularly in the 1850s, the issues of Jacksonian debate were at least partially resolved, and the hidden questions of slavery and expansion pushed forward almost unavoidably. When they did so, the party structures created by men like Clay and Jackson collapsed, and civil war soon followed. The political creations of Clay and Jackson continued to be important in the crises over secession and war, however, because these structures had so long shaped the ways that Americans thought and acted about the matters most important to their public life.

This book focuses on the issues that Jackson and Clay did debate and not on the issues they tried to avoid. Readers must always bear in mind, however, that other burning questions always smoldered in the minds of

---

[1]Winthrop Jordan, *White over Black: American Attitudes toward the Negro, 1550–1812* (Chapel Hill: University of North Carolina Press, 1968); David R. Roediger, *The Wages of Whiteness: Race and the Making of the American Working Class* (London: Verso, 1991).

antebellum Americans, sometimes flaming out despite the efforts of politicians to keep them smothered. In the long run, the differences that politics obscured were just as important to national debate as the differences that politics magnified.

Most voting Americans seemed to agree that Clay and Jackson were completely different, and there were very few Americans of the antebellum era who admired both Clay and Jackson or claimed to recognize their common qualities. For adherents of Andrew Jackson's Democratic Party, "Old Hickory" was the honest, courageous, and patriotic defender of traditional republican virtues, while Henry Clay was a corrupt and devious libertine who would turn the country over to corporate financiers. To Clay's admirers in the newly founded Whig Party, on the other hand, "Prince Hal" was a glamorous and dedicated statesman who cherished the Union and its prosperity and fought ceaselessly against the tyrannical ambitions of the "military chieftain" they called "King Andrew the First." Carrying these rival images into countless electoral battles, the Democratic and Whig Parties campaigned furiously against each other for about twenty years, from 1834 to the mid-1850s, and in some states down to the Civil War itself. Americans who carried on this electoral combat gradually established a system of two competing political parties as the enduring norm of American public life.

SOCIAL CHANGE AND THE MARKET REVOLUTION

The political careers of Andrew Jackson and Henry Clay unfolded within a period of critical social and cultural change that swept the United States in the generation following the American Revolution. By comparison to the world of Jackson and Clay, the world that colonial Americans had lived in seemed, in retrospect, to be stable and circumscribed. Colonial settlements had not extended far beyond the Atlantic seaboard, partly because bad roads and primitive technology limited their ability to expand and partly because both hostile Indians and British imperial policy discouraged migration beyond the Appalachian Mountains. Many white Americans lived on small farms that were gradually getting smaller as a growing population pressed against a fixed supply of land. In the South, a few plantation owners held large tracts of land along the banks of navigable rivers and streams and profited from the labor of growing numbers of African slaves. Inland communities like the one that Andrew Jackson grew up in were populated by yeoman farmers and their families, who owned small plots and tilled them with their own hands.

In North and South alike, commerce grew out of the export of products from the fields and forests near navigable waters. Towns grew up where merchants collected local products like flour, rice, tobacco, tar, lumber, hides, salted meat, and codfish and shipped them abroad in exchange for consumer goods from Europe. Throughout the backcountry, however, the high costs of overland transportation put limits on the spread of commerce. In these isolated districts, settlers might take a small surplus to a distant market once a year or so but otherwise produced what they needed at home or bartered with their neighbors. This economy grew steadily in the colonial period but not so rapidly that social stability was overturned.

In many colonial communities, a few families had managed to control the best lands or other economic resources in the early days of settlement and had managed to stay on top of local society for several generations. Whether they were southern slaveholders or simply the most prosperous farmers and merchants in the northern colonies, well-established colonists formed a gentry or upper class that dominated local society. These families frequently intermarried with one another and used their wealth and educational advantages to build a reputation for culture, refinement, and public service. Their ranks included the most distinguished lawyers, doctors, and ministers in the colonies, as well as the most prominent merchants and landowners, and they provided services for their neighbors in return for deference, respect, and political office. In most colonies, leadership by prominent local gentlemen like George Washington, Thomas Jefferson, John Hancock, or John Adams had been essential to the success of the American Revolution.

Like all societies, colonial America experienced its own dynamics of evolution and change, even within its seemingly stable and elitist framework. Change began to accelerate in the 1790s, however, and accelerated further after 1815. Cultural and political developments from the American Revolution had a significant impact, but the most powerful transformations began in the U.S. economy. The success of the industrial revolution in Great Britain had inspired American imitators, and restrictive imperial economic policies no longer stood in their way. Ambitious entrepreneurs launched successful experiments in factory production, especially of cotton cloth. Canals reached into the interior and invited farmers to produce more crops for sale to urban and foreign markets. The invention of the steamboat and later the railroad created even more opportunities for cheaper transportation and gave a powerful boost to the culture of cotton and use of slave labor. Businessmen eagerly promoted the spread of banks and paper money to finance the new developments, and reformers created public schools and other educational institutions to enable citizens to take full advantage of them. Historians have come to call this period of increased commercial activity the "Market Revolution."

In fact, the Market Revolution was a specific instance of what economists call "economic development," referring to changes in society that bring more sophisticated technology, faster transportation and communication, more efficient business institutions, and a better-educated workforce to the processes of economic production. Properly speaking, economic development not only results in growth, or a higher level of raw economic output, but also in the production of more sophisticated goods and services than before.

The prospect of economic development held momentous consequences for newly independent Americans. Abundant new chances for wealth and opportunity offered the possibility of higher standards of living for consumers and producers alike. For some Americans, the stable and deferential villages of the eighteenth century had been stifling traps. Limited economic opportunities kept a few families in security at the top, but a significant number of young people found it harder and harder to improve themselves or even to replicate the social and economic status of their parents.[2] For these frustrated citizens, the coming of the Market Revolution and the opening of western lands could offer the chance to cross the mountains for a fresh start, to move to town and learn a remunerative trade, or to cultivate a new crop and ship a profitable surplus to a previously unattainable market. In turn, these new opportunities could upset the frozen social and political hierarchies of the colonial era, giving newly prosperous citizens a chance to claim their own share of social recognition, to win public office perhaps, and to claim the equality with established families that the American Revolution had supposedly promised to everyone.[3]

More ominously, however, the Market Revolution also presented dangers for Americans, threatening economic bust as well as boom and fostering the growth of large enterprises that seemed to threaten far more harm to some citizens than they promised in rewards. In many ways, the conflict between Andrew Jackson and Henry Clay reflected this tension between the perceived costs and benefits of economic development.

The specific opportunities offered by the Market Revolution varied considerably from region to region and between the different levels of

---

[2]Kenneth A. Lockridge, "Land, Population and the Evolution of New England Society, 1630–1790," *Past and Present* 39 (1968), 62–80.

[3]Gordon S. Wood, *The Radicalism of the American Revolution* (New York: Knopf, 1991).

society. Western New York, for example, had not been settled by white Americans for more than about a generation before it felt the impact of the Erie Canal, the largest and most significant transportation project of the era. Begun by the state government in 1817, the canal connected the Great Lakes to the Hudson River at Albany in 1823 and thereby funneled all the products of the upper Midwest down to New York harbor. Even before completion, farmers along the path of the canal were expanding their production of wheat, which millers in towns like Rochester and Utica would grind into flour and ship to eastern customers. Toll revenues on the canal grew so large that the project became self-financing, with income from the eastern portions paying for construction of the unfinished segments to the west. The expansion of western trade turned New York City into the urban powerhouse of the nation and enabled it to replace Philadelphia as America's largest city. A subsidiary string of smaller towns grew up along the canal itself, each one creating new opportunities for lawyers, ministers, storekeepers, schoolmasters, bookkeepers, newspaper editors, clerks, construction workers, and roustabouts.[4]

The Erie Canal unquestionably brought prosperity to adjacent communities. It also brought together people who might otherwise have preferred to remain apart, such as churchgoing townspeople with strong roots in the culture of Puritan New England, and rowdier, hard-drinking canal workers who didn't much care for the strait-laced moral conventions of their employers. It likewise brought the circulation of new books, newspapers, and magazines to affluent families along the way and inspired them to replicate the idealized portraits of genteel respectability they found there. It loosened apprentices and journeymen from the immediate supervision of their masters, but it did not erase the masters' nagging conviction they were responsible for the conduct of their workers.

Intangibly, the Canal's manifest success fostered a belief among propertied families along its banks that all things were possible, that the world could be improved, that wicked people could become good, and that good people could become perfect. Beginning in the late 1820s and climaxing in a massive revival in Rochester in 1831, the middle and upper classes of western New York became seized with religious fervor in a startling series of evangelical meetings led by the handsome professional revivalist Charles Grandison Finney. The middle- and upper-class Protestant women of places like Rochester took the lead in transforming their

---

[4]George Rogers Taylor, *The Transportation Revolution, 1815–1860* (New York: Holt, Rinehart, and Winston, 1951), 32–36.

children, their husbands, and their churches, and their husbands continued their work by pressing for the reformation of the unruly employees who made the mill wheels turn. The workers who joined churches and abandoned their licentious behavior found favor with their employers and moved up the economic ladder. Those who refused these changes usually kept on moving, and soon western New York had become famous as a center for moral reform and perfectionist theology. Admirers of the moral as well as the economic effects of the Market Revolution found the "burnt-over district" of western New York a model for the transformation of the whole nation. Later in the 1830s, when it came time for citizens to sort themselves out into political parties, the voters of western New York turned overwhelmingly to Henry Clay and the Whigs.[5]

Matters turned out differently in the little coastal town of Lynn, Massachusetts. The inhabitants of Lynn had long been in the habit of making shoes for sale in Boston and other nearby markets, particularly during winter evenings when farming was impossible. After 1814, when local merchants acquired enough capital to form their own bank, and when transportation networks broadened to take in a wider circle of customers, the organization of shoemaking changed significantly. Local capitalists would buy up large quantities of hides or other raw materials and pay a skilled worker to cut them up into shoe parts. They distributed the pieces to local men, women, and children, each of whom would specialize in stitching together a different component. The completed shoes could then be shipped in barrels by steamboat, canal boat, and wagon train to customers all over America and sold for much lower prices than the cost of a custom-made shoe prepared by a skilled local artisan. By 1837, Lynn manufacturers "sold one pair of shoes for every 2.5 white females (the great bulk of the customers were white) in the United States."[6] In the process, Lynn had become an important industrial center. Its manufacturers became quite wealthy; work was created for Boston merchants, bankers, ship owners, and their employees; full-time shoe workers became important customers for the food crops of local farmers; and consumers all over the country gained the opportunity to become decently shod at lower prices.

At the same time, almost no one in Lynn knew how to make a whole shoe anymore. Control of the business had shifted from the individual artisan in his shop to the merchant capitalist who owned the leather and

[5]Paul E. Johnson, *A Shopkeeper's Millennium: Society and Revivals in Rochester, New York, 1815–1837* (New York: Hill & Wang, 1978).
[6]Alan Dawley, *Class and Community: The Industrial Revolution in Lynn* (Cambridge, Mass.: Harvard University Press, 1976), 26.

paid the wages. A community of independent artisans in command of their own families and workshops had become a society of bosses and lifelong wage earners. Many of the new workers were women and children who no doubt enjoyed the opportunity to earn their own wages and thus gain a little autonomy from husbands and fathers. These workers had relatively low skills, however, and their piecework wages were also low. If they objected or went on strike, they could easily be replaced. Both in Lynn and out in the hinterland, moreover, the change could leave skilled adult male shoemakers stranded. A few could adapt to the luxury market for customers who could still afford to pay hand-made prices, but many were left with ruined businesses, irrelevant skills, diminished self-respect, and perhaps most galling of all, enfeebled authority over their wives and children. For them, the Market Revolution brought a loss of independence, a decline in status, and a potential receptivity to political movements that could promise them a restoration of both, at least on the symbolic level. In the heyday of Whig and Democratic rivalry, Lynn voters thus gave their support to the followers of Andrew Jackson.[7]

Far away from Massachusetts and New York, farmers in the southeastern states faced very different conditions from the shoemakers of Lynn and the millers of Rochester. Soil and climate gave southerners an advantage in the production of crops that would not grow in Europe or the North, and colonists had learned long before that products like tobacco and rice could grow there very profitably with the labor of slaves. The success of English textile mills had produced a tremendous demand for new sources of fiber, and a hardy, upland variety of the cotton plant grew well in a broad crescent of territory that stretched from the North Carolina–Virginia border southwestward to the Mississippi River and beyond. Unfortunately for growers, no one knew how to separate upland cotton's lint from its seeds. In 1793, when a Connecticut tutor named Eli Whitney devised an engine or gin to perform this job quickly and cheaply, the path was opened for a southern version of the Market Revolution.

In the decade following 1790, southern production of cotton increased from 3,000 bales annually to 73,000.[8] Farmers raced to fling the seeds into ground and reap the bounty of high prices and ample harvests. Georgians stepped up their demands for Indian land sales, and back-country farmers cherished sudden aspirations to planter status. All they

[7] Ibid., 68.

[8] J. William Harris, *Plain Folk and Gentry in a Slave Society: White Liberty and Black Slavery in Augusta's Hinterlands* (Hanover, N.H.: Wesleyan University Press [University Press of New England], 1985), 14.

needed were slaves to perform the backbreaking labor of plowing, planting, weeding, and picking the crop, but plenty of workers were available in the old and crowded plantations of the Chesapeake Bay region. Under the new U.S. Constitution, moreover, Congress had no power to interfere with the international slave trade until 1807, and eager slavers kept the sea-lanes of the notorious Middle Passage busy with their infamous traffic.

Whitney's invention therefore touched off a feverish search for cotton lands and cotton hands. Native Americans were compelled to supply the former, and Africans and African Americans, the latter. One of the primary incentives for General Andrew Jackson's later Indian conquests was the Cotton Kingdom's appetite for new territories. The cotton boom likewise wrenched apart thousands of black families as slave traders put together shipments of prime field hands for purchasers in the southwest. Even white families mourned to see their loved ones depart for the fever-ridden cotton frontier. As one North Carolinian begged in an 1839 letter to his brother in Alabama, "This letter is to say to you leave Mobile and come home. Once more I say come home, your home is here if you have a home in this world. But sir for me to write and fear that I am writing to a dead man and that man my brother."[9] Farm wives wept especially bitter but helpless tears at their husbands' decisions to move their families to the wilderness.[10]

The cotton frontier continued to grow as the English and American textile industry expanded, but wild swings of the business cycle imposed a boom-and-bust rhythm on the plantation South that was as unfamiliar as it was frightening to the first generation of participants. One particularly dramatic collapse came in 1819, when a spectacular rise in the price of cotton and cotton lands was followed by a disastrous collapse. William Harris, a small planter of Madison County, Alabama, left a vivid record of what the Panic of 1819 meant to him in a series of letters to his brother. Harris had moved from Virginia to Madison County in 1819 and had borrowed the enormous sum of $26,000 to purchase a plantation. Almost immediately, cotton prices slumped, the harvest failed, and Harris was lucky to sell his land for less than half of what he paid. The experience devastated his self-esteem. "The embar-

[9]Willie Fuller to Jones Fuller, October 5, 1839, quoted in Harry L. Watson, *Jacksonian Politics and Community Conflict: The Emergence of the Second American Party System in Cumberland County, North Carolina* (Baton Rouge: Louisiana State University Press, 1981), 48–49.

[10]Joan E. Cashin, *A Family Venture: Men and Women on the Southern Frontier* (New York: Oxford University Press, 1991).

rassment of mind I have suffered for some time . . . ," he wrote his brother, "causes reflections which almost unmans me, those *feelings* I hope you never may experience. . . . If I had never left Virginia, I might perhaps been better off . . . and it grieves me to think that I have, perhaps, to go still farther." Harris was not mistaken. Still in debt after the loss of his land, he managed to start again on a rented farm, but he never found a permanent place in Madison County. In 1825, he moved again to seek elusive success in Tennessee.[11] Citizens who remained in Madison County developed the unshakable conviction that a sinister coalition of merchants, bankers, speculators, and political insiders they called "the royal party" had conspired to bring on the panic or at least to exploit it to aggrandize themselves at the expense of innocent and hardworking pioneers. For the remainder of the antebellum period, they expressed their convictions in solid support for the Jacksonian Democratic Party.[12]

Like William Harris and his brother, ordinary Americans of the early nineteenth century became painfully aware that the Market Revolution held special dangers as well as opportunities. A farmer's experiment in market agriculture might fail, leading to the loss of his land and treasured independence. Mass production might destroy the jobs of skilled artisans. In either case, the loss of a farm or workshop could lead to a perceived loss of equality and a social descent into the ranks of permanent wage laborers. The New England farmers' daughters who stitched shoes in Lynn or eagerly took positions in the region's new textile mills may have welcomed the freedom that a regular pay envelope brought them. Men who were brought up to think of independence, property ownership, and manliness as part of an inseparable package, however, were less likely to be satisfied by the new arrangements. A more powerful business cycle, moreover, would create depressions and recessions that could bring bankruptcy and ruin to thousands of families through no fault of their own, while the rise of powerful corporations could overwhelm the political strength of ordinary voters. Voting Americans therefore experienced the changes of the Market Revolution with a mixture of pleasure and anxiety, and they passed along their ambivalence to their politically elected representatives.

[11]William Harris to Frederick Harris, April 25, 1821, quoted in Daniel S. Dupre, *Transforming the Cotton Frontier: Madison County, Alabama, 1800–1840* (Baton Rouge: Louisiana State University Press, 1997), 59.
[12]J. Mills Thornton III, *Politics and Power in a Slave Society: Alabama, 1800–1860* (Baton Rouge: Louisiana State University Press, 1978), 7–20.

POLITICS IN THE EARLY REPUBLIC

Nineteenth-century Americans were very proud to call their form of government "republican," but the political creed they inherited from the revolutionary generation had been a product of the more stable social and economic world of the eighteenth century. Derived from political principles dating back to the Greeks and Romans, to the Italian Renaissance, and to English radicals of the seventeenth century, republican thinking predicted an eternal warfare between the forces of "liberty" and "power" or "despotism." To preserve liberty, republicans believed that government must be strictly limited and never used for the personal benefit of individuals, or the favored few would use power to perpetuate themselves in office and exploit the helpless majority. Republicans opposed monarchy and aristocracy because these forms of government encouraged the few to take liberty and property from the many, as Britain's colonial tax policies had seemed to prove.

Republicans feared that a nation could succumb to tyranny if its leaders and citizens put personal advantage before the common good. "Virtue" was the special word that republican political thinkers used to denote a devotion to the common good, and they took it for granted that political parties could never embody political virtue. By definition, partisans were in politics for selfish reasons and could never put the common good ahead of their own personal goals. In a truly virtuous republic, disinterested leaders would confer about the public welfare and reach consensus without scheming or trading favors to build a majority behind one set of policies or leaders. Traditional thinking thus assumed that a good republic would be a small, relatively homogeneous society with no sharply clashing interests. Government would rest on the consent of all men who were independent enough to exercise good judgment and self-control, but major offices would belong to the small number of wealthy and well-educated men whose distinguished wisdom, virtue, and independence would best enable them to perceive the common good.

Almost no Americans thought of themselves as democrats when the Constitution was adopted. Eighteenth-century political thinkers associated this word with direct rule by the people themselves, without the use of elected representatives. New Englanders had practiced this kind of government in their town meetings, and it had existed in the city-states of ancient Greece, but nobody thought it practical in a country the size of the United States. Revolutionary Americans also worried that a purely democratic government would be too unstable, too impulsive, and too insensitive to the rights of property. To make sure that government would represent only the will of responsible people, state constitutions often restricted the political rights of those who were thought to be too weak to be wise or virtuous. Excluded groups typically included children, paupers, insane persons, criminals, servants, African Americans, women, and propertyless white men.

During the post-Revolutionary decades, many white men began to resent these restrictions on their own political rights. As the implications of Jefferson's Declaration of Independence sank deeper, these citizens demanded equality in more and more areas of public life. If all men were equal, they argued, ordinary men were just as likely to possess virtue as their leaders. Ambitious politicians were often inclined to agree, especially when they thought that their own faction would benefit from a wave of grateful new voters. After the beginning of the nineteenth century, state governments began to abolish property requirements for the right to vote and hold office, to expand the number of elected offices, and to adopt public policies designed to increase the independence of ordinary white men. Reformers began to praise democracy as the rule of the majority, where public opinion governed with as few intermediaries as possible. Firmly aligning himself with this definition of democracy, Andrew Jackson used his "first annual message" (or State of the Union address) to emphasize what he called "the first principle of our system — *that the majority is to govern.*"[13]

Beyond its formal, constitutional meaning of "majority rule," *democracy* in the early nineteenth century also came to mean a pattern of public customs and attitudes that expressed respect for the tastes, values, and decisions of the mass of ordinary white men, regardless of their incomes, education, or family backgrounds. The *Democratic Review,* which became the leading ideological journal for Jackson's Democratic Party, celebrated respect for majority opinion as "that high and holy *democratic principle.*" Its editor, John L. O'Sullivan, defined *democracy* as "that universal and unrelaxing responsibility to the vigilance of public opinion which is the true conservative principle of our institutions."[14] The widespread prevalence of this kind of democratic equality became a distinctive feature of American antebellum culture, prompting comment by Americans and Europeans alike. Most famously, perhaps, it inspired the French traveler

---

[13] Andrew Jackson, "First Annual Message," December 8, 1829, in James D. Richardson, comp., *A Compilation of the Messages and Papers of the Presidents, 1789–1897,* 10 vols. (Washington, D.C.: Government Printing Office, 1897), 2:448.

[14] "Introduction," *United States Magazine and Democratic Review* 1, no. 1 (October 1837), 1–15.

Alexis de Tocqueville to compose his classic 1835 analysis, *Democracy in America.* "Among the most novel objects that attracted my attention during my stay in the United States," he wrote, "nothing struck me more forcibly than the general equality of condition among the people." Because all white men were considered equal in American culture, Tocqueville worried, it was difficult if not impossible for individuals to escape from the "tyranny of the majority."[15]

As they fought for popular rights, most early nineteenth-century political reformers continued to exclude women and African American men from their definition of "the people." Sometimes, as in the New York constitutional convention of 1821, conservatives were willing to preserve suffrage for black men who met a property requirement, while "democrats" (who later became followers of Andrew Jackson) disenfranchised blacks just when they abolished property requirements for white men.[16] In other words, early nineteenth-century advocates of democracy tended to oppose inequalities of economic class but embraced inequalities of race and gender. Andrew Jackson became a strong supporter of this kind of democracy, but it was a very different notion of democracy than the one that prevails among most Americans today.

Despite ardent hopes for a harmonious republic, post-Revolutionary experience showed that America was far more complex and contentious than the republican vision anticipated. Much to their chagrin, Americans of the late eighteenth century discovered that they did not share a consensus about the common good or the proper means to achieve it. Signs of dissension appeared even before the adoption of the federal Constitution, as rival leaders tried to advance the interests of their own states and sections above others'. Nor did the adoption of the Constitution put an end to disagreement. Early in George Washington's administration, bitter disputes broke out between the followers of Secretary of the Treasury, Alexander Hamilton and Secretary of State Thomas Jefferson.

Known as "Federalists," Hamilton's followers venerated President Washington and supported a strong central government. Hamilton worried that the United States could not survive if its foreign and domestic creditors questioned its ability and willingness to pay its debts from the American Revolution. As secretary of the treasury, he struggled to guarantee a steady supply of revenue to the government, to make regular payments on the interest of the national debt, and to win the support of the wealthy

---

[15]Alexis de Tocqueville, *Democracy in America,* trans. Henry Reeve, rev. Francis Bowen, and ed. Phillips Bradley (New York: Knopf, 1945), 3, 254–70.

[16]Chilton Williamson, *American Suffrage from Property to Democracy* (Princeton: Princeton University Press, 1960).

people in Europe and America who owned the government's bonds. If he could convince investors that lending money to the United States was completely safe and profitable, Hamilton felt sure that government bonds would become so valuable that wealthy men would use them as capital or collateral to finance the further economic development of the country. In this sense, he said, a sound national debt was "a national blessing."[17]

Pursuing this vision, Hamilton persuaded Congress to take over the war debts of the individual states and to promise repayment at their face value, even if this meant that struggling ordinary citizens would be taxed to benefit speculators who had purchased government securities for less than their nominal worth. He also supported the creation of a powerful Bank of the United States to give guidance and stability to the economy and to create a stable, uniform paper currency. He experimented with efforts to encourage manufacturing and favored federal assistance to banking and commerce, even if that meant that well-established agricultural interests in the South and West would have to pay indirect subsidies to the urban centers of the Northeast. The U.S. Constitution does not state explicitly that Congress has the authority to create institutions like a Bank of the United States, but Federalists claimed the power anyway on the grounds that Congress has broad authority to "provide for the . . . general Welfare of the United States." Their approach to constitutional interpretation became known as "broad construction" because it allows the government wide-ranging powers derived from the spirit of the Constitution rather than its most literal language.

Inspired by Thomas Jefferson, opponents of Hamilton saw America's strength in its population of independent farmers, planters, and artisans. Calling themselves "Democratic-Republicans" to emphasize their demands for equality, Jeffersonians resisted subsidies to business interests and charged Federalists with using the power of government to enrich themselves and their friends in the nation's mercantile elite. Drawing on pre-Revolutionary republican traditions, they darkly hinted that Federalist support of a strong government, dominated by wealthy and prestigious leaders, was the opening edge for aristocratic despotism and the destruction of the Republic. Warning that Federalists' glorification of George Washington portended a return to monarchy, Democratic-Republicans insisted on a plain and simple government with sharply limited authority based on "strict construction" of the U.S. Constitution. Insofar as possible, the Democratic-Republicans argued, America should be governed

---

[17]Quoted in Stanley Elkins and Eric McKitrick, *The Age of Federalism* (New York: Oxford University Press, 1993), 116 n. 80.

by its states, which were closer to the people themselves and thus less likely to subvert their hard-won liberties.[18]

There is no getting around the fact that the labels of these early political factions are inherently confusing to contemporary readers, who are accustomed to thinking of Democrats and Republicans as political opposites. Historically, "republican" (with a lower-case *r*) is the name for the eighteenth-century political tradition that stressed opposition to monarchy, aristocracy, and all forms of arbitrary power. The republican tradition also favored representative government, equality before the law, and the supreme value of virtue and consensus in civic life. The revolutionary generation also used the word "whig" to refer to these principles, borrowing the name of the British faction that had long opposed the arbitrary power of the Crown. Both the framers and the opponents of the U.S. Constitution thought of themselves as whigs and republicans in this sense. To distinguish themselves from the Constitution's opponents, supporters called themselves "federalists" while they were campaigning for ratification. After ratification in 1789, the name "Federalist" (upper case) continued to be applied to the supporters of Alexander Hamilton and the friends of strong, centralized government in the administration of George Washington.

During the 1790s, supporters of Thomas Jefferson also upheld the Constitution, but they hated Hamilton's interpretation of it, and they chose the "Democratic-Republican" label to differentiate themselves from his Federalist adherents. Unlike modern partisans, however, Jeffersonians did not view these words as mutually incompatible, so they sometimes confused things for us even further by shortening their full name to either "Democrats" or "Republicans" whenever it seemed appropriate. The usage of these words in early American history did not correspond exactly to any modern party ideas or institutions, and students of history can only rely on the historical context to understand exactly what they mean.

Historians call the pattern of competition between Alexander Hamilton's Federalists and Thomas Jefferson's Republicans the "first American party system," even though the political groupings of the 1790s were so different from modern parties that many historians and political scientists hesitate to call them true political parties at all. Neither side fully accepted its opponent's legitimacy or even its right to exist. Each tended to think of the other as a band of conspirators plotting selfishly to destroy the republic. Each one justified its own existence by the supposedly critical need to prevent the other side from gaining power, and each hoped that

---

[18]For a detailed discussion of Federalist and Republican economic policies, see John R. Nelson, *Liberty and Property: Political Economy and Policymaking in the New Nation, 1789–1812* (Baltimore: Johns Hopkins University Press, 1987).

the disappearance of the other party would make its own existence unnecessary. In other words, Federalists and Republicans both believed that national politics should operate by consensus. After the triumphant election of President Thomas Jefferson in 1801, and even more so after the defeat of the British in the War of 1812, the Federalist Party did begin to disintegrate. The elitist tone of Federalist pronouncements had worked against it, and the party's opposition to the War of 1812 made it seem unpatriotic. By 1816, serious Federalist competition for the presidency had virtually collapsed, and local leaders found that at least nominal adherence to Republican principles was essential to electoral success.

Victorious Republicans soon found, however, that political consensus escaped them, for the underlying policy debates between Federalists and Republicans would not go away. Some Republicans came to think that the government had been too weak to fight effectively in the War of 1812. They began to support the continuation of many old Federalist policies under Republican auspices and without the elitist tone of Federalist discourse. Henry Clay became an early leader of this wing of the postwar Republican Party. Other Republicans feared these compromises with party purity and fought against them. After a period of uncertainty, Andrew Jackson became their national leader. The Democratic and Whig Parties evolved out of these enduring policy differences.

President Andrew Jackson's party kept the name "Democratic-Republican" because Jackson and his followers thought of themselves as Jeffersonians, but after some experimentation, they shortened their name to the "Democratic Party." The modern Democratic Party is the direct institutional descendant of President Jackson's organization, though the party's doctrines have changed dramatically over the intervening years. President Jackson's opponents also reached back into revolutionary history and gave themselves the name "Whig Party," but that organization came to an end in the 1850s. When it collapsed, an entirely new group called the "Republican Party" emerged and successfully elected Abraham Lincoln to the presidency in 1860. The modern Republican Party is the direct descendant of that organization. Once again, the student of history can only rely on the historical context to keep these confusing names straight.

JACKSON, CLAY, AND THE PARTY SYSTEM

Henry Clay became the leader of the Whig Party and the representative of those Americans who welcomed the Market Revolution with great enthusiasm. Responding to their wishes, Clay devoted his career to preserving the Union and promoting its development or, as he would put it, to "improvement." He wanted America to become richer, wiser, kinder, and more technologically advanced—to move beyond its pioneer days. While he also claimed to support equality and democracy, he took for granted that some Americans were more capable than others and therefore obligated to guide their countrymen to better things. To do so, they needed sturdy private institutions and strong state and federal governments. Clay believed that powerful economic institutions would stimulate commerce and manufacturing and encourage the virtues of hard work, thrift, sobriety, education, and self-control among people who might confuse liberty with license. He was especially fond of what contemporaries called "internal improvements" like canals, turnpikes, railroads, and aids to navigation. These devices increased the speed of transportation and cut its costs, enabling farmers and manufacturers to sell more at lower prices and for higher profits. As a devoted American nationalist, Clay also anticipated that internal improvements would bind the Union together, not just by uniting its regions physically but also by demonstrating that every section had something beneficial to offer the others and that the interests of all Americans were truly mutual and complementary.

In contrast to Henry Clay, Andrew Jackson's wing of the Republicans tended to think that America was already an ideal society whose political system reflected a nearly perfect balance between individual liberty, equality, and social stability. As they saw it, the proper job of a virtuous statesman was to preserve this ideal state by resisting the influence of corrupting innovations, especially from privileged institutions like banks and corporations that they found morally and socially troublesome. If there were any changes or improvements to be made in America, Jacksonians favored simple geographical expansion.[19] Beyond that, they advocated political changes to give even more liberty and political power to individual white men—expansion of the right to vote and hold office, for example, or substitution of elected offices for appointed ones.[20] Jackson did not extend his support for greater liberty beyond the circle of white men, however. He was a firm supporter of slavery, an implacable foe of Native Americans, and uninterested in the expansion of women's rights.

For Andrew Jackson, "the great body of the people" was honest and virtuous, while those who claimed the privileges of an elite were likely to be selfish and corrupt. He sought to protect what he regarded as the liberty of the many against the designs of the few by abolishing potentially undemocratic institutions like the country's largest bank, the Bank

---

[19]Major L. Wilson, *Space, Time, and Freedom: The Quest for Nationality and the Irrepressible Conflict, 1815–1860* (Westport, Conn.: Greenwood Press, 1974), 73–93.

[20]Robert V. Remini, *The Legacy of Andrew Jackson: Essays on Democracy, Indian Removal, and Slavery* (Baton Rouge: Louisiana State University Press, 1988).

of the United States, or even the Electoral College. To that end, he favored the diffusion of political power into popular hands and the expansion of individual liberty for ordinary white men. At the same time, President Jackson did not hesitate to concentrate government power in his own hands and to use it in a vigorous, even high-handed fashion. His most famous act as president was to veto a bill to recharter the Bank of the United States, a move that ultimately led to the failure of this powerful private institution.

Jackson justified this aggressive use of presidential power by arguing that the Bank was undemocratic, while he as president was the democratic instrument of majority rule. Jackson even condemned Congress as elitist because he thought its members were susceptible to bribery and more likely than the president to be the prisoners of narrow special interests. His enemies disagreed, of course, and condemned Jackson's exercise of presidential power as arbitrary and unjust. If attacks on banks and corporations brought more democracy and less development to the United States, Jackson would not complain. He had no objections to prosperity, but promoting development was ultimately less important to him than preserving what he thought of as democracy.

Unlike Jackson, Clay opposed the concentration of government power in the hands of the president, and only partly because the hands in question were never his own. He believed instead that Congress—as a council of elder statesmen, each one long tested in political leadership and deeply respected in his own state and region—was a fitter body to balance competing interests and guide the nation's destinies than a single man acting in the name of an uninformed and unreflecting popular majority. He also believed that Congress should have broad powers to encourage economic development by subsidizing internal improvements, rechartering the Bank of the United States, and imposing "tariffs," or high taxes on imports, to protect domestic industry. In effect, Clay hoped that a high tax on imported manufactures would prevent well-established foreign producers from underselling their American rivals and thus give protection or a competitive price advantage to novice American manufacturers.

Clay's most famous policy was an elaborate plan he called the "American System," which would raise tariffs, keep the price of public lands high, and use the proceeds to plan and construct a national system of internal improvements. A charter member of the American Colonization Society, he even supported the use of government funds to settle former slaves in Africa, in hopes of bringing about a slow but peaceful end to American slavery. In other words, Clay thought that a bigger, more powerful government could improve America, and he was eager to let it do so. He did not worry that all citizens might not get equal benefits from internal improvements or that privileged interests might influence the government more than others. Compared to Jackson, Clay would not leave as much power in the hands of voters, but he felt confident that the resulting improvements would be worth some sacrifices of political equality. Indeed, he argued that a growing and developing American economy created plentiful opportunities for personal advancement, eventually creating a more democratic society than the static vision of Andrew Jackson.

Henry Clay and Andrew Jackson each had a complex impact on the course of American history. Neither man completely implemented his own political program, though Jackson was more successful than Clay in the short term. As a strong president who used the veto more actively than any of his predecessors, Jackson set an example that succeeding presidents were eager to copy. He also convinced many voters that the president was a more authentic representative of the people at large than congressional representatives, whom he depicted as the prisoners of narrow special interests. Legal equality of all white men became the law of the land, and egalitarian rhetoric became a permanent fixture of American political culture. Jackson and his followers rejected equality for women, African Americans, and Native Americans, but later generations decided that the legal equality enjoyed by white men could not be denied to other adults. The Bank of the United States was never reestablished, moreover, and it was not until 1913 that the Federal Reserve System began to take over many of its earlier functions. Most important, perhaps, Jackson and his party successfully enshrined the concept of majority rule in American political culture and made democratic appeals to the people at large a permanent fixture of American politics.

Jacksonians blocked the adoption of Henry Clay's American System by the national government, but various state governments gave enthusiastic support for economic development. Even without the support of a federally sponsored American System, transportation, manufacturing, banking, and commerce all continued to expand in Clay's lifetime. After his death, the Civil War preserved the Union and put an end to slavery, though hardly as Clay had intended. After the Civil War, the victorious Republican Party also took up favorite Clay ideas like the protective tariff and the use of public lands to subsidize internal improvement and made them firm pillars of national policy for many decades. In the end, American society developed much as Henry Clay had hoped it would, though without the system of central guidance and balanced planning that he preferred.

Clay and Jackson both played significant roles in American history. Their favorite policies were not mutually exclusive, moreover, for many Americans would argue that the future brought more democracy and more development as well. Historians do not study Clay and Jackson simply to decide who was right or to find out who won or lost. Each man was influential because he spoke for a powerful vision of the American future that had deep support among different segments of American society. Each man's ideas grew directly out of the memories and the contemporary experiences of the American people. Studying Andrew Jackson and Henry Clay, we gain a better idea of the crucial choices that faced the American people in the first half of the nineteenth century. Because the choices and their outcomes were not foreordained, we can better grasp the complexity and unpredictability of the process that led to more democracy and more development in modern America.

THE MAKING OF A TENNESSEE GENTLEMAN

Andrew Jackson was born in 1767 in the Waxhaws, a frontier region on the boundary between North Carolina and South Carolina. Jackson himself always believed that his birthplace was on the South Carolina side of the line, but the exact spot remains disputed. The future president's parents were Protestant immigrants from the north of Ireland who settled with relatives in a farming community where life was hard and luxuries were scarce. Unfortunately for the family, Mr. Jackson died shortly before his wife gave birth to Andrew, the couple's third child. Elizabeth Jackson took refuge with her sister and brother-in-law, raising her three boys in their home.

Andrew Jackson grew up as a tall, gangling youth well known for his fierce pride and fiercer temper. Challenged as a child to fire an overly charged musket, he was thrown to the ground by the power of the blast, yelling in fury at the pranksters who had sought to humiliate him, "By God, if one of you laughs, I'll kill him!" Nobody cracked a smile, for Jackson's threats were instantly credible. Personal violence was commonplace on the Carolina frontier, and young Andrew Jackson grew up certain that a well-known willingness to repay violence with more violence was essential to a respected man's reputation. His mother encouraged this attitude. In a story that was repeated in several versions, she reportedly told her son, "Never tell a lie, nor take what is not your own, nor sue anybody for slander or assault and battery. *Always settle them cases yourself.*" We do not know if Elizabeth Jackson really spoke those words, but there is no doubt that Andrew Jackson did his best to live by them.[21]

---

[21]W. H. Sparks, *The Memories of Fifty Years* (Philadelphia, 1882), 147–48, quoted in Michael Paul Rogin, *Fathers and Children: Andrew Jackson and the Subjugation of the American Indian* (New York: Knopf, 1975), 44.

As a child, Jackson probably studied in a one-room schoolhouse, followed by a year or two in a local academy. His adult writings reveal that he learned to express himself with eloquence but that he never bothered with the fine points of spelling or grammar. He undoubtedly spent much time in outdoor sports—riding, hunting, and roughhousing with playmates—and performed a boy's share of labor on his uncle's farm. Childhood came to an abrupt end in 1780, when Jackson turned thirteen and the British army invaded upper South Carolina in an effort to quell the American Revolution there. Andrew's older brother Hugh joined the American forces right away and died at the battle of Stono Ferry. Andrew and his surviving brother Robert soon followed Hugh's example and joined the local guerrillas who had emerged to resist the British. The following year, both boys were taken prisoner in bitter fighting between Whig and Tory partisans. When Andrew was ordered to clean his captor's boots, the defiant youth refused this menial task, and the infuriated officer slashed his forehead with a saber. Jackson carried the scar for life.

The two young prisoners were confined with other captives in cramped and unsanitary quarters that soon fostered smallpox. Andrew and Robert were both stricken, enabling their mother to obtain their release. Returning home, Robert succumbed to the pestilence, but Andrew slowly recovered. As her last son regained his strength, Elizabeth Jackson left again, this time to nurse other captured relatives in a British prison ship near Charleston. There she contracted a fever and died, leaving Andrew Jackson the only living member of his immediate family.

In 1783, Andrew Jackson was only sixteen years old and utterly alone, but he was also a scarred and battle-tested veteran of the American Revolution. His kinfolk remained in the Waxhaws, but there are few signs that Jackson felt close to them. Attempting, perhaps, to prove his manhood and cover his grief, the youth quickly squandered his small inheritance in a few weeks of wild carousal before facing his real predicament. Many teenagers would not have been equal to the task, but Jackson pulled himself together and began the long, painful process of establishing himself. Unlike most of his male peers and relatives, however, young Jackson rejected the life of a farmer. Instead, he returned to school in the Waxhaws for a while and then taught school himself for a few sessions, until he found an opportunity to read law in the office of Spruce MacKay, a prominent attorney of Salisbury, North Carolina.

Legal training in Jackson's day was very different from what it later became. Apprentice lawyers like Jackson agreed to copy documents and help around the office of an established attorney in exchange for the privilege of reading their sponsor's law books. There is no evidence that Jackson absorbed much legal scholarship in this environment, but by 1787 he had learned enough to win permission to practice law before the county courts of North Carolina.

The young advocate's search for business was disappointing at first. North Carolina was an old state with plenty of established attorneys, while the number of paying clients was undoubtedly limited. Good fortune intervened when John McNairy, Jackson's friend and fellow law student, won appointment as Superior Court judge for Davidson County on the western side of the Appalachian Mountains. McNairy made his friend the attorney general, or county prosecutor, and the two moved west together in 1788, settling in the frontier town of Nashville in the territory that would later become the state of Tennessee.

By this time, Andrew Jackson was twenty-one years old. While traveling to Nashville, he purchased his first slave, a woman named Nancy who was a year or so younger than he. Jackson also fought his first duel, harmlessly exchanging pistol shots with an older lawyer whom he had accused of insulting him in court. Throughout the South, but especially on the frontier, the cult of honor demanded that men demonstrate their willingness to face death on the dueling grounds to defend their reputations for honesty or physical courage.[22] Dueling was illegal, but Andrew Jackson zealously supported the custom and the culture of honor that surrounded it, participating in several such encounters before he came to national political attention. Just as he came of age, then, Andrew Jackson made personal commitments to slave property and the rituals of violence, important symbolic steps for a man who intended to rise in that society and be taken seriously. He would maintain these commitments for the rest of his life.

When Jackson and McNairy arrived in 1788, Nashville was a village on the edge of the wilderness. Its few hundred inhabitants still worried about Indian attacks but threw themselves eagerly into the challenges of building a settlement. The Cumberland River gave Nashville a navigable link to the Ohio and Mississippi Rivers, and pioneers from the surrounding countryside took advantage of this opportunity to ship out quantities of furs and timber products as they cleared the forest for future plantations. The village hummed with land speculation, slave auctions, and all forms of commerce, occasionally enlivened by violent disputes between disorderly settlers. All this activity generated business for the courts, especially lawsuits over unpaid debts and criminal prosecutions

---

[22]Bertram Wyatt-Brown, *Southern Honor: Ethics and Behavior in the Old South* (New York: Oxford University Press, 1982).

for assault. Combining private practice with his duties as public prosecutor, Andrew Jackson quickly began to make his mark.

As an ambitious young man with no family, Jackson sought lodgings
with Mrs. John Donelson, the widow of one of early Nashville's most
prominent citizens and a lady with connections to all the leading figures
in the area. While in her home, Jackson formed a lifelong friendship with
another lodger, fellow lawyer John Overton, who later became one of the
wealthiest and most powerful men in Tennessee. Jackson also met Mrs.
Donelson's daughter Rachel and her husband Lewis Robards, who were
living in the Donelson home while working to establish their own farm
nearby.

The marriage of Rachel and Lewis Robards was already unhappy, and
Robards soon accused his wife of improprieties with the newcomer. In
all likelihood, Rachel and Andrew were not guilty of Robards's worst
charges, but subsequent events would prove that they were certainly
attracted to each other. Eventually the quarreling grew so bitter that
Robards left his wife and moved to Kentucky. When word arrived that he
might return and reclaim her, Andrew Jackson and a Donelson family
friend escorted Rachel to faraway Natchez so she might escape her violent and jealous partner. While there, the fugitives heard that Robards
had changed his mind and gotten a divorce, so the happy couple returned
to Nashville as Mr. and Mrs. Andrew Jackson. Unfortunately, the report
was false. Robards's divorce did not become final until after the Jacksons'
return to Nashville, which made the young couple unwitting bigamists.
To make the scandal worse, the stated grounds for the divorce were that
Rachel Robards had deserted her husband to live in adultery with Andrew
Jackson. On hearing the news, the embarrassed couple had no choice but
to marry again, but they remained hypersensitive to their technical violation of the laws of matrimony. Jackson would later be enraged by taunt-
ing reminders from his political enemies—including supporters of Henry
Clay—that he and his wife were guilty of adultery and bigamy.

For the remainder of their lives together, Rachel and Andrew Jackson
loved each other devotedly. To their great disappointment, the Jacksons
never had children of their own, but Jackson served as guardian to many
orphaned children of his deceased friends and in-laws. The couple
adopted one of Rachel's nephews in 1809 and named him Andrew Jackson, Jr. Rachel Jackson never shared her husband's taste for politics or
public life, preferring to stay in Nashville by her own hearth and family,
smoking her pipe and reading the Bible.

On his return from Natchez, Jackson resumed his law practice. His
Tennessee family and business associates had strong political connec-

tions, so it was not surprising that local voters chose the promising young attorney to represent them at the state constitutional convention of 1796. A few months later, Tennessee became the sixteenth state to join the Union and then sent Jackson to the U.S. House of Representatives. The following year, 1797, the legislature elevated him to a vacant seat in the U.S. Senate.

It was a promising start for a thirty-year-old political beginner, but Jackson soon found that he had little taste for the give and take of legislative activity. Since the new federal city of Washington, D.C., was still under construction, Congress met in Philadelphia, but Jackson the frontiersman felt out of place in the metropolis in more ways than one. Both in the House and the Senate, he occasionally spoke in defense of the particular interests of Tennesseans, but he did not take up national issues or distinguish himself in debate. It was not that Jackson was indifferent to politics, for he strongly identified with the Republican principles of Thomas Jefferson, but his powerful temper left him with no patience for the niceties of deliberation or compromise. "But Sir," he wrote to his friend John Overton, "where [sic] you where I am and See all constitutional Principles, violated and matamorphisit [sic; metamorphosed?] to Suit Party Purpose it would try your Philosophy—Particularly, when they carry objects with a silent vote [that is, without recording the vote of each member by name]."[23] Jefferson later recalled that Jackson's furious emotions actually choked him with rage when he rose to address the Senate, forcing him to sit down again in silence. Jackson's most memorable action in Congress was to vote against a resolution thanking George Washington for his services as president, on the grounds that the Federalist Founding Father had overstepped the limits of the Constitution. Expressing a strong commitment to states' rights, frugal government, and trans-Appalachian interests, Jackson clearly felt unhappy in Federalist Philadelphia, and after serving one year in the House and six months in the Senate, he gratefully resigned to resume his private life in Nashville.

Though Jackson's short career in Congress was undistinguished, his early political ideas shed light on his future principles. From the beginning, he had no patience with promises made to Indians. "Does not Experience teach us," he wrote, "that Treaties answer no other Purpose than opening an easy door for the Indians to pass [through to] Butcher our

[23]Andrew Jackson to John Overton, February 22, 1798, in Sam B. Smith and Harriet Chappell Owsley, eds., *The Papers of Andrew Jackson*, 5 vols. to date (Knoxville: University of Tennessee Press, 1980–), 1:183, hereinafter abbreviated as *Jackson Papers*.

citizens?"[24] Even before entering Congress, Jackson was strongly anti-British and furiously opposed to anything smacking of elitism. Instead of simply opposing Jay's Treaty, a 1795 commercial treaty with Great Britain which he and many Westerners regarded as excessively pro-British, Jackson denounced its approval by "20 aristocratic Nabobs" in the U.S. Senate and demanded to "have the insulting, Cringing, and ignominious Child of aristocratic Secracy removed Erased and obliterated from the archives of the Grand republick of the United States."[25] As a good Jeffersonian, Jackson associated closely with men who thought that massive popular involvement with electoral politics was the only safeguard against Federalist abuses. He undoubtedly agreed with the friend who wrote him in 1797 that "electioneering is the order of the day, and every neighbourhood is convulsed by the intrigues of rival candidates for popular favour."[26]

Significantly, Jackson's correspondent went on to praise popular democracy not because it best conformed to the innate equality of the citizens but because it inspired men of talents to seek honor and fame in public service:

> Here then is (with me) a proof of the superiority of a Republican form of Government to any other; It furnishes so great excitement to the pursuits of virtue and patriotism, and holds out to merit such certain and lasting Honors, that a spirit of emulation seems to prevade all ran[k]s of people.[27]

In other words, republicanism inspired outstanding men to compete with each other for public recognition of their superiority, while prompting less distinguished men to imitate them. In such a contest, leaders would not boast of following the voters or admit to being dominated by the popular will. On the contrary, Jackson carefully distinguished between "lasting Popularity," which was built on adherence to principle, and temporary applause, which could come from subservience to a fickle public mood. "Of all charectors on earth," he wrote, "my feelings despises a man capable of cringing to power for a benefit or an office," advising a friend to maintain his reputation for independent thought. "This is in my opinion the only road to a lasting popularity for the moment a man yields his judgt to popular whim, he may be compared to a ship without its ruder in a gale—he is sure to be dashed against a rock."[28]

[24]Andrew Jackson to John McKee, May 16, 1794, *Jackson Papers* 1:48.
[25]Andrew Jackson to Nathaniel Mason, October 4, 1795, *Jackson Papers* 1:74.
[26]William Charles Cole Claiborne to Andrew Jackson, July 20, 1797, *Jackson Papers* 1:146.
[27]Ibid.
[28]Andrew Jackson to George Washington Campbell, April 28, 1804, *Jackson Papers* 2:19.

After leaving Congress, Jackson's activities spread from politics and law to a variety of business ventures that included a plantation, a retail store, and avid speculation in frontier lands. Land was especially attractive, for it was the frontier's most abundant commodity and was bound to rise in price as the demand from new settlers increased. Fortunes could easily be won by those with the skills, capital, and connections needed to pick out promising tracts, gain title to them, and find purchasers when the price rose. Andrew Jackson may have felt rustic in Philadelphia, but in Nashville he was a promising gentleman, fiercely determined to rise above his humble origins and acquire the wealth that would establish him as a prominent member of the new state's elite. To do so, he followed the example of other ambitious men in the Southwest—plowed his legal fees into the purchase of land that he later sold to finance more speculations. On one tract, he installed a force of slaves to create a cotton plantation. Unlike many of his peers, there is no evidence that Andrew Jackson ever resorted to fraud in these transactions, but there is no doubt that he made his fortune in the land market.

Though Jackson was an active and often successful speculator, he was not successful all the time. Indeed, one reason for Jackson's unease in Philadelphia may have been his bitter experience in a failed speculation there that almost left him bankrupt. Even before he took his seat in Congress, Jackson had come to Philadelphia to find a buyer for some 50,000 acres that he held in partnership with his friend John Overton, as well as a smaller parcel that he hoped to sell on commission for another associate. The buyer he finally found for both parcels was David Allison, an urban merchant with ties to Tennessee, who bought the properties for almost $15,000 in promissory notes. Adding his signature as endorsement, Jackson then used these notes to purchase trade goods for the store he owned back home. Soon after Jackson returned to Nashville, however, David Allison went bankrupt, and Jackson himself became responsible for the whole amount plus interest. It was years before Jackson could repay this debt in full, and the experience left him with a profound distrust of paper credit. In retrospect, it is clear that Jackson should not have taken the unsecured note of a stranger for such a huge sum, but the incident also reveals Jackson's tendency to think of himself as a simple man of honor and virtue who could be victimized if he let his guard down.

Though Andrew Jackson continued to dabble in land speculation for the rest of his life, the Allison affair taught him to proceed more cautiously, seeking a safer way to make his fortune and secure his reputation. He briefly accepted a position as judge of Tennessee's Superior

Court, probably for the sake of the salary. A couple of mercantile partnerships came and went without great success, but the plantation flourished, and the family's farming operations grew steadily. Plantation life meant the purchase of slaves, and Jackson steadily bought more human property. He also did not hesitate to sell slaves, both as a punishment for disciplinary offenses and as a regular item of trade with the New Orleans market.

By 1807, Jackson let go of his stores and also his seat on the bench, joining Rachel on the plantation. In the decade after leaving the Senate, he slowly inched his way back from the brink of financial collapse and turned his plantation, the Hermitage, into a showcase estate, with dozens of slaves, ample harvests, and a stable of blooded racehorses to gratify his passion for the turf. Despite the plantation's success, the Jacksons maintained an appearance of simplicity by spending these years in a modest but substantial house of logs. It was not until 1819 that they felt sufficiently at ease with success to exchange these quarters for an imposing two-story mansion. In both settings, the Jacksons cultivated a reputation for gracious hospitality and welcomed all manner of guests and callers. These years also saw Jackson involved in a series of violent personal outbursts, as he killed one man in a bitter duel, almost fought several others, assisted friends in their own affairs of honor, and even exchanged shots in a freewheeling barroom gunfight. The puzzling combination of a genial and charming gentleman who was also a bloodthirsty ruffian with a violent temper became a part of Jackson's permanent public image.

THE GENTLEMAN BECOMES A HERO

As Andrew Jackson gradually exchanged the life of a fast-track lawyer, congressman, senator, judge, merchant, and speculator for the agrarian dignity of a gentleman farmer, he also found a political position that truly suited him. In 1802, he won election as major general of the Second Division of the Tennessee state militia and launched his improbable military career. (See Figure 2.)

Most American states had official militia organizations that nominally included all white men from teenagers to middle age, but state forces were most active in the South and West, where the danger of Indian attack or slave rebellion was quite real. Militia members met for training in their neighborhoods four times a year, and the job of supervising them was not difficult. The men elected their own local officers, and the officer corps

Figure 2. Jackson as General

Ralph Earl portrait, head and shoulders with epaulets, about 1815. Andrew Jackson was elected major general in the Tennessee state militia in 1802 and first led his troops in battle against the Creek Indians in 1813. The following year he became a major general in the U.S. Army, charged with the defense of the Gulf Coast during the War of 1812. After his victory over the British at the Battle of New Orleans in 1815, Jackson remained in the Army until 1821.

then chose the senior commanders. At the age of thirty-five, Jackson had had no military experience since boyhood, except his own militia service. It is not clear why he wanted the office of major general, but he craved it badly enough to campaign against Tennessee war hero General John Sevier, whom he defeated handily. That contest almost led to a duel between Jackson and Sevier, but more important, it set Jackson on a path that finally led to the White House.

Most militia generals treated the post as an honorary position and did not push their military adventures far beyond the parade ground. Again, Andrew Jackson was different. He took the job very seriously and trained his troops to be ready for active service. He concentrated in particular on improving their sense of discipline and railed repeatedly against the headstrong frontiersmen's lack of subordination to their commanders. He longed to lead his troops like a real general, but no war presented itself. Instead, Jackson devoted the decade before 1812 to grooming his troops and building up his plantation, while moving away from courtroom, counting house, and legislative chamber.

The United States also changed a great deal in the first decade of the nineteenth century. The Federalist Party suffered a serious setback when Thomas Jefferson won the presidency in the election of 1800, and the steady expansion of democratic political culture made it increasingly unlikely that the elitist party of Washington, Adams, and Hamilton would ever regain control of the government. After the so-called Revolution of 1800, Jefferson became the first U.S. president to be inaugurated in the raw new capital of Washington, D.C. The major public buildings were barely habitable, and most of the city was still swamp and forest, but the republic's politics would henceforth be conducted in a setting created just for the purpose.

Jefferson's triumph coincided with the intensification of a prolonged war between France, led by Napoleon Bonaparte, and a coalition of European countries headed by Great Britain. The Napoleonic wars absorbed increasing amounts of European blood and treasure, enabling American producers to benefit from high prices for their agricultural exports. In the course of the conflict's intricate diplomacy, France reacquired the province of Louisiana from Spain and then offered to sell it to the United States for $15 million. Jefferson had no constitutional authority to accept the proposal, but he suspended his strict constructionist principles long enough to snap up the bargain in 1803 and thereby double the size of the nation with the stroke of a pen.

The Louisiana Purchase did nothing to calm the wars of Europe. Each side pressured the United States to stop trading with its adversaries and outraged American national pride in the process. Seeking to punish all the belligerents, President Jefferson tried to deprive all sides of the benefits of American commerce by banning all foreign trade, but his embargo policy succeeded only in outraging those Americans who depended on international trade. The brief interruption of commerce with Britain was long enough, however, to inspire some groups of New England merchants to expand machine manufacture of textile goods, ironically promoting the very industrial society that Jefferson abhorred.

By 1812, Jefferson had left office, and his successor James Madison had spent an unsuccessful first term in seeking a peaceful way out of the crisis. British harassment of U.S. trading vessels had continued, growing so serious that many Americans clamored for war. Diplomacy had proved so ineffectual that war alone seemed powerful enough to vindicate the nation's reputation and refute the suspicion that a republic was too weak to defend itself. Land-hungry westerners like Jackson also saw war as an opportunity to invade and annex Canada and to crush the various hostile Indian tribes who took arms and encouragement from America's foreign enemies.

Shortly before President James Madison asked Congress for a declaration of war, Congress began military preparations by calling for 50,000 volunteers to join the armed forces of the United States. Jackson was delighted at the chance to restore the republic's honor in the face of Britain's insults and eagerly embraced the opportunity to form an army and lead it into battle. He responded to Congress's call for volunteers with a stirring appeal to the militiamen under his command, urging them to accept the federal offer and enroll as U.S. troops and hoping that the president would make him their commander. (See Document 1.) Jackson's proclamation passionately appealed to frontier patriotism and reminded common soldiers that liberty and equality were unattainable outside America. The address also reveals Jackson's powerful flair with words, despite his lack of formal education:

> *Who are we? and for what are we going to fight?* are we the titled Slaves of George the third? the military conscripts of Napolon [*sic*] the great? or the frozen peasants of the Russian Czar? No — we are the free born sons of america; the citizens of the only republick now existing in the world; and the only people who possess rights, liberties, and property which the[y] dare call their own.

President Madison ignored Jackson's offer, perhaps remembering his lack of military training. Months later, however, the governor of Tennessee made him commander of state troops being called to defend New

Orleans. Jackson collected his men and headed south in January 1813, only to be frustrated by an order to halt in Natchez and do nothing. Worse news arrived weeks later. The secretary of war had changed his mind; New Orleans was not in danger after all. Jackson was directed to disband his army and return home.

The order infuriated Jackson. If followed literally, it would mean releasing the soldiers without arms, pay, or supplies to drift north on their own. Stranded in the wilderness in midwinter, the men would inevitably suffer and feel betrayed. Jackson decided to disobey. Though he would always demand strict obedience to his own orders, he often bridled at the commands of others, particularly when they violated his sense of honor and justice. Instead of disbanding his army in Natchez, he would keep his men together, march them back to Tennessee under strict discipline, and disband when they arrived.

The ensuing march was a nightmare. Many of the soldiers were sick and had to be carried in wagons. Jackson and his officers gave up their own horses for the task and marched beside the men. In this ordeal, Jackson found reserves of determination and leadership that he had never shown before. Though completely inexperienced at command, he got the army home safely and won his soldiers' undying respect for the loyalty, will power, and inspiration he displayed. During this grueling march, the men began to call their commander *Hickory* for the sturdiest tree in the forest, and Old Hickory he remained for the rest of his public career.

The War of 1812 was not yet over, however, and American forces were suffering one disastrous defeat after another. In the northwest, Detroit was surrendered to the British without a shot. The invasion of Canada failed almost immediately. British raiding parties scoured the Chesapeake Bay with impunity, and ultimately torched the glorified village called Washington, D.C. Most ominously for Tennessee, Creek Indians had seized the opportunity to attack white settlements in the neighboring territory to the south. In the summer of 1813, word reached Nashville that an Indian attack on Fort Mims in present-day Alabama had resulted in the deaths of almost 250 whites, including numerous women and children. Tennessee's Governor Willie Blount asked Jackson to take charge of the military response. The invitation came at an inopportune moment, for the gun-slinging general lay wounded with an arm shattered in his most recent private quarrel. Despite his injuries, Jackson could not resist. He dragged himself from bed and began preparations for war.

The campaign that followed gave Jackson his first opportunity to lead troops into battle, and he succeeded magnificently. One faction of the divided Creeks was willing to comply with white demands for land, but a more traditional group called the Red Sticks had decided to defend their ancestral territory with force. Taking advantage of this dissension, Jackson recruited allies among the friendly Creeks and their neighbors the Cherokees, adding their strength to his own force of Tennessee militiamen. In the decisive Battle of Horseshoe Bend, Jackson's men killed some 900 Red Stick warriors, losing only seventy from their own ranks. Along the way, the determined commander learned how to stare down hungry and mutinous volunteers who threatened to abandon him when their enlistments expired.

Jackson's most brutal and audacious maneuver occurred off the battlefield at the treaty negotiations that followed the fighting. The general demanded that his Creek supporters surrender their lands and villages along with the defeated Red Sticks. Jackson's erstwhile allies were dumbfounded by this act of betrayal, for they had counted on being rewarded, not punished, for their loyalty. Too late, the friendly Creeks realized that their collaboration with the whites had actually left them friendless and therefore isolated before the Americans' insatiable land hunger. It was a classic example of the tactics of divide and conquer, but Jackson had no qualms of conscience. As a white frontiersman, he had no sympathy for the land claims of any Native American, friend or foe. Alabama contained some of the best cotton country in the world and offered a tempting invasion route for any foreign enemy who could gain a toehold in Spanish Florida. Jackson was determined to possess it for both reasons, and he left the Creeks no choice but to surrender over half their traditional domain at the Treaty of Fort Jackson. (See Figure 3.)

Jackson's victories in the Creek War finally proved his military talent to official Washington, and President Madison gave him command of all U.S. troops in the Southwest. Up to that point in the war, most land battles with the British had taken place along the Canadian border. As fighting continued, however, enemy strategists realized that America's Gulf Coast was highly vulnerable to attack. An army that captured the mouth of the Mississippi River could cripple America's western economy and use this leverage to dictate peace terms. As U.S. commander in the area, it was Jackson's job to prevent this calamity.

Jackson began by evicting a British detachment that the nominally neutral Spanish had allowed to use their fort at Pensacola, Florida. Next he turned his attention to the looming invasion of New Orleans. He rallied the city's demoralized militia, including several units of free African American soldiers, and combined them with his own army of regular U.S. troops and frontier militiamen. Repairing the city's defenses, he ordered his forces to block all routes that led to New Orleans. He even got help

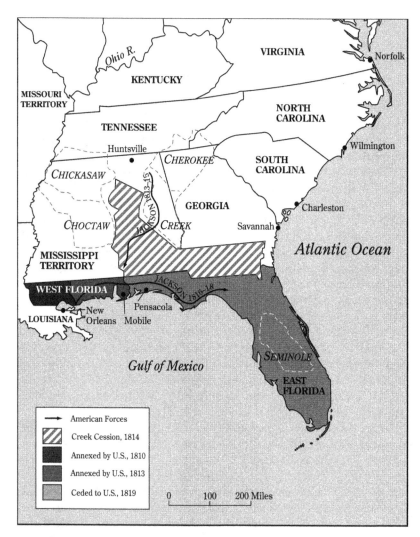

Figure 3. The Creek War and Subsequent Land Cessions

At the Treaty of Fort Jackson in 1814, Jackson compelled both the allied and the enemy portions of the Creek Nation to surrender large tracts of valuable land in the states of the old Southwest. Subsequent treaties with the Cherokees, Choctaws, and Chickasaws resulted in even further land acquisitions, as did Jackson's Florida conquests in the First Seminole War. After these losses, the so-called Five Civilized Tribes held on to their remaining lands until the 1830s, when they were forced beyond the Mississippi by Jackson's Indian removal policy.

from a band of bayou pirates, who provided valuable assistance in threading the maze of waterways approaching the city.

The British attacked in a series of advances against New Orleans, climaxing in a dramatic charge against Jackson's army on both sides of the Mississippi on the morning of January 8, 1815. Blunders and bad luck trapped the main British force underneath a murderous fire from American artillery and small arms; once again the carnage was appalling. British casualties exceeded 2,000 men, compared to seventy-one Americans. Though a series of errors on the west bank had almost led to disaster, this embarrassment was quickly forgotten amid widespread rejoicing. When the American public learned that General Andrew Jackson had saved New Orleans from the finest troops of Europe, the vanquishers of Napoleon, American honor seemed restored at last.

Ironically, Jackson's victory and Britain's bitter loss took place after the treaty of peace had already been signed in the Belgian city of Ghent. Reports of Jackson's triumph reached Washington first, soon followed by the slower-moving news from across the Atlantic. The treaty did little to resolve the causes of the war, but the defeat of Napoleon in 1814 had removed the immediate source of tension between the two belligerents. To end the War of 1812, Britain and America basically decided to stop fighting and leave their disputes to future diplomacy, with neither party making major concessions of territory or principle.

The emotional impact of Jackson's triumph completely overwhelmed the news from Ghent, as Americans celebrated a victory that seemed to prove that courage and God's blessing could enable a weak, crude republic to repel the polished forces of European monarchy. *Niles Weekly Register* set the tone of national rejoicing: "Glory to GOD, that the barbarians have been defeated, and that at *Orleans* the intended plunderers have found their grave! — Glory to *Jackson* . . . , and the hardy and gallant Tennesseans, Kentuckians and Louisianans who 'seized opportunity by the forelock' to '*demonstrate*' what freemen can do in defence of their altars and firesides. Glory to the *militia,* that . . . the boastful conquerors of the legions of *France,* have shrunk from the *liberty-directed* bullets of the high-souled sons of the west!"[29]

Word quickly spread that the victory arose from Jackson's superior leadership and from the marksmanship and heroic character of the "high-souled sons of the west," whose "liberty-directed bullets" naturally shot straighter than the missiles of despotism. In fact, American cannon fire

---

[29]*Niles Weekly Register,* February 11, 1815, p. 373.

was at least as responsible as riflemen's bullets for inflicting British casualties at New Orleans, and Jackson's own generalship was not entirely flawless. It did not matter. Jackson's reputation was seamlessly welded to the "hardy and gallant Tennesseans, Kentuckians and Louisianans" who had dominated his forces, and the commander and his men set the nation rejoicing. In the general celebration, even the helpful pirates won a share of national gratitude, but the African American militiamen who had also contributed to the victory were quietly forgotten.

The glory of the militiamen was quickly immortalized in song, and "The Hunters of Kentucky" became a national favorite. (See Document 2.) The lyrics explained that America's rough-hewn pioneers or "alligator horses" were both noble and unbeatable, while the aristocratic enemy were cowardly thieves and rapists, determined to seize the "beauty and booty" of New Orleans. The frontier general fully shared his soldiers' good qualities:

> But Jackson he was wide awake,
>   And was not scar'd at trifles,
> For well he knew what aim we take
>   With our Kentucky rifles.
> So he led us down to Cypress swamp,
>   The ground was low and mucky,
> There stood John Bull in martial pomp
>   And here was Old Kentucky.
>
> Oh Kentucky, the hunters of Kentucky!
> Oh Kentucky, the hunters of Kentucky!

Years later, the ditty still enlivened crowds at Jacksonian campaign rallies, where it emphasized the power of Jackson's frontier innocence and moral simplicity against the presumed decadence of aristocratic opponents like John Quincy Adams.[30] In an era when feminine standards of gentility and decorum were gaining in middle-class circles, the song also trumpeted the raw masculine appeal of Jackson and his movement.

Other elements of Jackson's public personality surfaced in the aftermath of the battle. The danger of invasion had apparently passed, but Jackson continued to hold New Orleans under strict martial law. When the local federal judge tried to interfere, the headstrong general clapped him into jail. Even worse, in the eyes of his critics, Jackson pressed for the trial of six militia members who had convinced their comrades that their enlistments had expired and they could go home. Convicted of

---

[30]John William Ward, *Andrew Jackson: Symbol for an Age* (New York: Oxford University Press, 1955), 13–29.

desertion and mutiny, the six received the death penalty with Jackson's approval and fell before a firing squad just as the news of victory reached the East. For the rest of his career, Jackson's reputation for military glory was closely associated with his record of strict, even violent repression of insubordination or defiance.

The coming of peace with Britain did not fully quiet the southern frontier. Powerful Indian tribes still held large sections of fertile acreage, and General Jackson threw himself into treaty negotiations to obtain their surrender. Spain still held Florida, and many of the surviving Creeks sought refuge there with their kinfolk the Seminoles. There was also a large community of armed runaway slaves in the disputed territory between Georgia and Florida who allied themselves with the Indians and attracted new escapees from Georgia plantations. Determined to eliminate these challenges to American authority, James Monroe, the new president, kept Jackson in his wartime command and ordered him to protect the Georgia frontier.

Based on Jackson's record in the War of 1812, Monroe had every reason to expect that the headstrong general would exceed his orders. Jackson had never shown any mercy to warring Indians and had conquered Pensacola once before. Nor had he ever let the letter of the law stand in the way of his objectives. If Jackson marched to the Georgia-Florida border to fight Indians and runaway slaves, he would probably pursue them across the border and take all of Florida for good measure. In fact, Jackson later claimed that he had tacit orders from Monroe to do just that.

If these were Monroe's secret expectations, Jackson lived up to them perfectly. In 1817, he launched the First Seminole War when he followed the Creeks and Seminoles into Florida. He seized the Spanish towns of St. Marks and Pensacola when he accused Spain of assisting the enemy.[31] He did not hesitate to execute prisoners of war, including two Seminole religious leaders captured by deceit and two British subjects whom he suspected of aiding the Creeks. Mission accomplished, Jackson paused for breath and calmly wrote back to Washington to inform the president of his readiness to capture St. Augustine and Cuba as well.

Jackson's high-handed actions outraged Spain and Britain and alarmed members of Congress. Jackson was following orders when he attacked the Indians, but he had no business conquering Florida when the United States and Spain were not at war. Angry voices in Washington called for

---

[31]The Second Seminole War broke out in 1837, when the remaining Florida Indians fought back against the government policy, initiated by Jackson and continued by his successor Martin Van Buren, that demanded their removal beyond the Mississippi.

an investigation, and Jackson barely escaped an official censure for his conduct. Though forced to surrender his illegal conquests, Jackson proved that the United States could capture Florida whenever it chose. In the Adams-Onís Treaty of 1819, Spain prudently agreed to sell its colony to the United States before someone decided to capture it again. Soon afterward, President Monroe signaled his approval of Jackson's actions by making him governor of the new federal territory of Florida.

By 1820, Major General Andrew Jackson had become a central figure in American public life. He had begun the previous decade as a provincial planter and an aspiring but untested leader of part-time soldiers. He ended it as the hero of his country who had scourged the nation's enemies, both "civilized" and "savage," defended its borders, and expanded its domain. Not surprisingly, Jackson began to think of himself as a national leader and even as a worthy successor to the hallowed station of George Washington himself.

Following the victory at New Orleans, Jackson began to sprinkle his correspondence with pointed allusions to his advancing age, his old-fashioned sense of virtue, and his treasured sense of personal honor. In a pair of letters to the recently elected president, James Monroe, he urged that newly acquired lands in Alabama be put on sale at once, not because they were "so well calculated for the culture of cotton" (as he told a private correspondent) but because it was important to settle the country with a loyal population who could easily rise to its defense.[32] "In this as in all my recommendations I have the public good in view," he declared.[33] In a passage that belied his later insistence on party regularity, Jackson went on to recommend a former Federalist as secretary of war, using vintage republican arguments. "The Chief Magistrate of a great and powerful nation should never indulge in party feelings," he lectured solemnly. "His Conduct should be liberal and disinterested, *always* bearing in mind that he acts for the whole and not a part of the community."[34] Upbraiding a fellow general who had dared to defend the authority of the War Department over Jackson's own prerogatives as a local commander, Old Hickory made dark threats of a duel and warned, "My notions Sir are not those now taught in modern Schools and fashionable high life; they were imbibed in ancient days."[35]

Writing in the same vein, Jackson informed the president that "it is my wish to retire from public life, for I am advancing to that age which makes

[32]Andrew Jackson to Nathan Reid, June 23, 1816, *Jackson Papers* 4:47.

[33]Andrew Jackson to James Monroe, November 12, 1816, *Jackson Papers* 4:74. See also Andrew Jackson to James Monroe, October 23, 1816, *Jackson Papers* 4:69–71.

[34]Andrew Jackson to James Monroe, November 12, 1816, *Jackson Papers* 4:75.

[35]Andrew Jackson to Winfield Scott, December 3, 1817, *Jackson Papers,* 4:157.

retirement desirable."[36] The general indeed suffered from his many wounds and illnesses, but the fifty-nine-year-old Monroe was surely not persuaded by the fifty-year-old Jackson's claims of decrepitude. Jackson's message was designed to qualify him as an honored senior statesman rather than a self-created upstart and intended to elicit a plea from the president for further public service. Monroe took the hint and lost no time in urging Jackson to stay on.

Almost inevitably, Jackson's rise to military prominence drew him into national debates, for political considerations invariably affected the careers of leading generals. As he came into conflict with cabinet secretaries and similar officeholders, the Hero of New Orleans began to suggest that Americans were ill served by their officials, that the people's virtue exceeded their leaders', and that Jackson himself was the best man to vindicate the people's rights and principles. He began by defending the rights of "the western people" to lands that had been seized from the Cherokees.[37] While professing respect for the citizens, however, he was quick to belittle their elected representatives, comparing recalcitrant Cherokees to "some of our bawling politicians, who loudly exclaim we are the friends of the people, but who, when the[y] obtain their views care no more for the happiness or welfare of the people than the Devil does."[38] By 1818, he was insisting on popular authority more strongly, calling for the retention of his Florida conquests because "the voice of the people will demand it."[39] Alert to the general's foibles, flatterers were quick to echo his opinions. How pleasing it must have been for Jackson to hear that his critics were only "designing demagogues," while "the gratitude of the American People is not to be questioned. . . . They have been with you, and will always honor and reverence the man whose life has been devoted to the interests and glory of their country."[40]

Compliments such as these fed Jackson's ambition. It is not clear when he began to think of himself as a serious contender for the presidency, but the election of 1824 offered him a promising chance to test himself against several prominent rivals. According to the custom established by George Washington, James Monroe would retire after his second term, and there was no obvious favorite to replace him. Instead, a number of secondary politicians aspired to the honor, most of them already members of Monroe's own cabinet. They included Secretary of the Treasury William H. Crawford of Georgia, once Jackson's bureau-

---

[36] Andrew Jackson to James Monroe, December 20, 1817, *Jackson Papers,* 4:162.
[37] Andrew Jackson to William H. Crawford, June 4, 1816, *Jackson Papers,* 4:38.
[38] Andrew Jackson to Robert Butler, June 21, 1817, *Jackson Papers,* 4:119.
[39] Andrew Jackson to John C. Calhoun, August 10, 1818, *Jackson Papers,* 4:233.
[40] James Gadsden to Andrew Jackson, May 3, 1819, *Jackson Papers,* 4:294.

cratic antagonist at the War Department, Secretary of State John Quincy Adams of Massachusetts, and Secretary of War John C. Calhoun of South Carolina. Henry Clay of Kentucky, Speaker of the House of Representatives, also longed for the presidency and enjoyed the support of many western leaders. All four leading candidates professed membership in the Democratic-Republican Party, all had strong support from their native regions, and all lacked broad national appeal.

Custom restrained candidates from a public avowal of their presidential ambitions, but all four candidates jockeyed discreetly among Washington insiders, hoping to win by gaining the support of established leaders. As they did so, thousands of ordinary voters came to believe that petty intrigue and corruption had taken over pursuit of the nation's highest office and looked for a fresh face to restore republican vitality. This longing for purity and change gave Andrew Jackson his great opportunity. It also brought him into direct conflict with Henry Clay, the man who became his lifelong rival.

THE WAR HAWK FROM KENTUCKY

Ten years younger than Andrew Jackson, Henry Clay had been born in 1777 in Hanover County, Virginia, a tidewater district just north of the capital city of Richmond. (See Figure 4.) Clay's father was a Baptist minister who died when Clay was small. His mother quickly remarried, and Clay grew up in a household crowded with siblings and stepsiblings. Years later, Clay was inclined to boast of his humble origins, but his parents were actually slaveholding farmers who lived in comfortable circumstances. After Clay turned fourteen, his stepfather decided to move his family to the promising young state of Kentucky and arranged for young Henry to remain in Richmond reading law. Like Jackson, Clay began by working for an established attorney, but his superior family connections enabled him to study with some of the most learned practi-

---

Figure 4 *(opposite)*.   *Henry Clay,* **by John Neagle**
Like Andrew Jackson, Henry Clay was born in the Southeast and moved west to establish himself as a lawyer and political leader. Unlike Jackson, he loved legislative politics and spent most of his career in Washington, D.C. Henry Clay's admirers commissioned this portrait in 1843, in preparation for Clay's anticipated presidential campaign in the following year. The images in the lower left-hand corner remind viewers of Clay's interest in promoting commerce, agriculture, and manufacturing, while the globe conveys his support for independence for South America, and the flag reflects his American nationalism.

tioners in the commonwealth, including Chancellor George Wythe, who had instructed Thomas Jefferson, and Robert Brooke, the attorney general of Virginia. Clay also took advantage of Richmond's opportunities by honing his oratory in a volunteer debating society and mingling with the gentlemen and jurists who gathered in his patrons' drawing rooms. Unlike Jackson, he emerged from his legal apprenticeship with a polished and urbane manner, a gift for wit and public speaking, and a sophisticated knowledge of the law, all of which he put to good use in his future career. Clay completed his studies in 1797 and received his license to practice law before his twenty-first birthday.

Like Andrew Jackson before him, the young attorney quickly decided to seek his fortune in the West. Clay followed his mother and stepfather to Kentucky, where opportunities abounded for a youth of talent and ambition. Only recently the new state had been a battleground between Indians and pioneers, but Kentucky was quickly growing famous as a land of rich soil, lush grasslands, and surging wealth, drawing ambitious new settlers from all sections of the Union.

Clay chose to settle in Lexington, county seat of Fayette County in the heart of the fabled Bluegrass region. He found the area humming with prosperity and plans for growth. The herds of deer and buffalo that had attracted Indian hunters and the followers of Daniel Boone were gone by the time of Clay's arrival. In their place, plantations were beginning to specialize in growing hemp, while local factories twisted its fibers into rope and wove them into coarse fabric. Mississippi River boats carried both products southward, to wrap and tie the cotton bales that were pouring increasingly from the plantation country downriver. The Bluegrass thus enjoyed a uniquely hybridized economy built jointly on the profits of manufacturing, interstate commerce, and plantation slavery alike. Surrounded by this symbiotic prosperity, Henry Clay quickly absorbed the lesson that the interests of manufacturing and agriculture were not mutually exclusive but complementary. It was a lesson he would seek to apply for the rest of his career.

Just as Kentucky's economy drew on a complex mixture of plantations, factories, and free labor farming, the Bluegrass state tolerated a range of opinions on slavery that would have been unthinkable further south. Slavery was vital to Kentucky society, and white Kentuckians would not give it up voluntarily, but they witnessed the advantages of free labor to the North and did not feel endangered by the relatively small number of African Americans who lived among them. Under these conditions, a limited tolerance of antislavery sentiments seemed safe. Like some of their contemporaries in Jeffersonian Virginia, a number of slaveholding Kentuckians were willing to admit that slavery was an evil and ought to be eliminated, when and if the slaveholders found it convenient.

Henry Clay's first political address put him among the moderate critics of Kentucky slavery. Using the pseudonym "Scaevola," he published an essay in 1798 calling for reform in the state constitution that would permit the legislature to abolish the institution. (See Document 3.) Characteristically, Clay appealed to his readers' emotions by describing the sensations of a slave at auction. Like Thomas Jefferson in his *Notes on the State of Virginia,* however, Scaevola also stressed the destructive impact of slavery on white men's character, industry, and economic prospects. "All America acknowledges the existence of slavery to be an evil," Clay wrote. "While it deprives the slave of the best gift of heaven, in the end [it] injures the master too, by laying waste his lands, enabling him to live indolently, and thus contracting all the vices generated by a state of idleness."

In principle, at least, Clay never abandoned his disapproval of slavery, though his own slaveholdings continued to grow. A charter member and longtime president of the American Colonization Society, he favored a vague and impractical program of compensated emancipation, with deportation of the freed slaves to new homes outside the United States. As he grew more prominent in national politics, however, and as his own plantation flourished, Clay muted his antislavery views even further. Much later in his career, Clay's moderate antislavery credentials gave him some political advantage with northerners who faintly disapproved of the institution, while allowing him to protect his relations with southerners (and with northern opponents of abolitionism) by flatly rejecting the uncompromising demands of committed abolitionists.

Though he failed to change Kentucky's slave code, Clay settled comfortably into Lexington and quickly developed a profitable law practice. Like Jackson in nearby Nashville (with whom he occasionally corresponded on business), Clay found that frontier prosperity combined with conflicting land titles, unpaid debts, personal violence, and disputed commercial dealings created plenty of business for courts and lawyers. Like most successful westerners, Clay purchased slaves and amplified his earnings with land speculation, laying the basis for a handsome fortune and a distinguished position among the first gentlemen in the commonwealth. As Henry Clay moved quickly to the top of Bluegrass society, he also courted and married Lucretia Hart, daughter of one of the town's wealthiest and most prominent families.

Lucretia Hart Clay was a quiet, domestically minded young woman, three years younger than her husband. Like Clay himself, she was never noted for physical beauty, but unlike him, she also shrank from the social limelight. The couple's family eventually included eleven children, of whom two died in early infancy. Plantation management fell to Mrs. Clay, who preferred to remain at the family homestead during her husband's frequent trips to Washington. Though Lucretia Clay remained devoted to her husband, there is little evidence that she ever took more than a polite interest in politics.

Henry Clay was a witty and popular man who blended easily in the loose, informal culture of western society. Before juries he successfully practiced the spellbinding oratory and jocular repartee that would later make him famous on the floor of Congress. Relaxing among men, he won friends as a genial lover of cards, liquor, and music, while ladies admired his gracious manners and attentive gallantry. Not surprisingly, citizens soon were mentioning his name as a possible contender for public office. Like Jackson and most of his fellow westerners, Henry Clay began his political career as a vocal supporter of President Thomas Jefferson and the Democratic-Republican Party. After his ringing party speeches brought him local renown in Lexington, Clay won election to the lower house of the Kentucky legislature in 1803.

Clay took public office at a time when partisan principles were still fairly flexible. Nationally, Federalists and Republicans had clashed over the federal government's right to promote economic development. This dispute did not settle the question of whether state governments could or should take steps that might be unconstitutional at the federal level. Though Republicans generally rejected federal assistance to economic development, they debated whether state governments should establish or subsidize banks, transportation companies, or other corporations. Henry's Clay's first major effort in the Kentucky state legislature was to come to the defense of just such a corporation, the embattled Kentucky Insurance Company.

The company had been chartered in 1802 and received a monopoly on the insurance of cargoes on the Mississippi and its branches within Kentucky. The charter also contained a couple of obscure clauses authorizing the company to make loans and issue paper currency. These provisions transformed a privileged insurance company into a highly controversial bank with enormous power over the character of money in the Kentucky economy.

For most of the period before the Civil War, the American people used many different kinds of money. The federal government itself issued some gold and silver coins, but these were scarce, so bits and pieces of many foreign currencies joined them in circulation. In the rural areas, many Americans relied on barter and did without currency most of the time. Country merchants often formalized the bartering process by offering "book credit" for a series of purchases and then canceling the debt when the customer brought in an equivalent load of product like hides or barrels of corn.

Businessmen found these makeshift arrangements were insufficient to handle a growing number of complex transactions. They wanted a flexible paper currency that could grow with the economy and facilitate commerce over long distances. They also wanted a reliable source of credit to finance the movement of their goods and commodities around the country and the trading world. The banking arm of the Kentucky Insurance Company was intended to help them accomplish both tasks.

Like other corporations in this period, most banks of the early nineteenth century got started when a group of investors obtained a corporate charter by a special act of a state legislature. The charter gave the company a legal identity separate from the individual shareholders, protecting them from unlimited liability for its debts. Drawing on the capital that shareholders paid for their stock, the bank made loans to customers and made a profit by collecting interest from the borrowers. Instead of lending specie, or metal coins that were heavy and scarce, the bank lent paper notes that carried a promise to pay a certain amount in specie to the bearer on demand. The borrower then used these notes to buy what he wished, and the notes began to circulate throughout the community in place of specie. In fact, these notes were not legal tender, so creditors could not be required to accept them. For the sake of quick, smooth transactions, however, sound bank notes circulated freely most of the time, though often at a discount that reflected the community's relative level of confidence in the bank's financial health.

In the early days of paper money banking, there were few regulations to control the volume of notes that a bank might issue. The more banks lent, the more interest they received, so bankers had a strong incentive to issue as many notes as possible. But it was also true that the more notes they issued, the more likely it became that too many note holders might come to the bank at once, all demanding specie for their paper currency. In that case, the bank could not keep its promise to redeem the notes with coin. Bankers assumed that this would almost never happen and normally lent out far more notes than they could redeem at once, but the knowledge that excessive note issue could make it impossible for the bank to keep its promises was about the only restraint on the bank's lending practices. From time to time, of course, uncertain business conditions did cause customers to demand coins instead of paper, and even the most conservative bank could run out of specie. When that happened, the bank simply suspended specie payments, refusing to honor the promises on its notes until public confidence returned. In the meantime, the bank's paper money could lose some or most of its value, and citizens who had accepted the currency could be ruined.

Kentuckians who distrusted the Kentucky Insurance Company were not ignorant or irrational. They had good reason to worry if the money economy of the state were put under the control of a single private monopoly with power to manipulate the supply of currency and thus the level of prices for lands and commodities. By flooding the state with paper, they feared that the bank could transform Kentucky from a society based on trusted personal transactions to an economy based on impersonal credit institutions. If financial trouble ever came, these farmers were certain that the Kentucky Insurance Company would have plenty of well-paid, well-trained, and highly influential friends to plead its case in the legislature and the courts. Other citizens would be left friendless, owing heavy debts and owning nothing but worthless "rags" with which to pay them.

One of those friends was Henry Clay, the new legislative representative from Lexington, in the commercial heart of the prosperous Bluegrass country. He was also a stockholder in the Kentucky Insurance Company. Despite the known risks of banking and paper currency, men like Clay were convinced that the availability of credit for new investments and a plentiful currency that could expand in volume with the needs of local business were absolutely essential for regional prosperity. When an effort began in 1804 to repeal the company's banking privileges, Clay leaped to its defense.

His chief opponent was Felix Grundy, an ambitious lawyer and politician who had already organized a strong following in the Green River country, an isolated and less fertile section of southern Kentucky where landholdings were small and commercial prospects meager. Homesteaders in the Green River basin owed the state large debts for the farms they had carved from the public domain, and Grundy had won support by protecting them from foreclosure. Grundy had little trouble persuading his constituents that the Kentucky Insurance Company was an equivalent threat to their well-being as he launched an attack on the obnoxious features of its charter.

The controversy dragged on for several years, as the company's enemies tried one tactic after another to strip it of its powers. Clay fought back brilliantly, always managing to split off just enough votes from the Green River bloc to forestall adoption of their measures. He argued over and over that banking was not dangerous, that paper money helped the whole society to prosper, and that an economy based on barter and specie alone brought poverty, not liberty, to the farmers of Kentucky. The bank's supporters finally settled the issue when they decided to make a tactical retreat. They abandoned their efforts to guarantee a monopoly of the local banking business to the Kentucky Insurance Company and chartered a number of competing banks across the state, including one in the heart of the Green River country. The tactic worked because the bank's enemies had never been quite sure if they opposed paper money banking in general or only the monopoly privileges of a specific company. Deprived of the monopoly issue, opponents lost energy and abandoned the struggle. The banking industry expanded rapidly thereafter, and Clay's larger objective, which was the growth and prosperity of the market economy in Kentucky, advanced accordingly.[41]

Perhaps the most remarkable thing about the conflict over Kentucky banking was the way it prefigured Clay's later efforts for the Second Bank of the United States. During the 1830s, President Andrew Jackson would galvanize a divided and uncertain Democratic Party by his monumental efforts to crush the BUS, while Clay's campaign to defend the Bank made him the national leader of the opposing Whigs. After moving to Tennessee and launching a new political career, moreover, Clay's antagonist Felix Grundy likewise took his place as one of the Democrats' leading spokesmen.

As he built up his legislative reputation, Clay found it necessary to fight a duel with a Federalist adversary, not only to avenge the insults he received in debate but also to prove his manhood. Unlike Andrew Jackson, however, Clay never seemed to relish dueling and escaped this encounter without serious injury. His colleagues in the legislature were not deeply troubled by this escapade; they rebuked the duelists but elected Clay twice to brief but honorific stints in the U.S. Senate to fill out the unexpired terms of resigning incumbents.

Clay's first appearance in Washington was largely uneventful, but his second interval began in 1810, when the international tension that eventually led to the War of 1812 was heating up. In the course of its long series of wars against Napoleon, Britain had resorted to economic warfare and demanded that all neutral nations stop trading with France and its allies and possessions. Insisting on its rights of free trade, the United States refused to comply. Britain also persisted in searching U.S. vessels for deserting British seamen, sometimes forcing American crewmen into British naval service in the process. Western Republicans like Clay and

---

[41]Stephen Aron, *How the West Was Lost: The Transformation of Kentucky from Daniel Boone to Henry Clay* (Baltimore: Johns Hopkins University Press, 1996).

Jackson also accused Great Britain of arming and encouraging Indian attacks on the American frontier, both among the Creeks and Seminoles of the Gulf Coast and the Shawnees of the Ohio country. Economic sanctions had been tried without success, and angry nationalists concluded that Britain wanted to return America to a sort of semicolonial status as its satellite or puppet. Tiring of fruitless diplomacy, they demanded a war to vindicate the principles of republican government, to defend the nation's honor, and to reaffirm its hard-won independence.

Still only thirty-three years old in 1810, the impetuous young senator quickly spoke up to defend America's interests and especially the young republic's fragile sense of honor. Projecting the rules of Kentucky politics into international relations, Clay took it for granted that nations, like gentlemen, must protect their reputations for manly strength and power. If the United States submitted to the insulting conduct of the British, the nation would never escape from foreign domination. The republican form of government would itself be disgraced, and the American experiment might be snuffed out. Like Andrew Jackson in the same period, Clay called imperiously for war in his first recorded speech before the Senate. (See Document 4.)

"No man in the nation desires peace more than I," Clay told his colleagues. "But I prefer the troubled ocean of war, demanded by the honor and independence of the country, with all its calamities, and desolations, to the tranquil, putrescent pool of ignominious peace." Warming to his subject, the ardent young nationalist predicted easy victory. "The conquest of Canada is in your power," he boasted. "The militia of Kentucky are alone competent to place Montreal and Upper Canada at your feet." Best of all, Clay claimed, borrowing from the language of the duel, war would restore the nation's honor and reputation: "If we surrender without a struggle to maintain our rights, we forfeit the respect of the world, and what is infinitely worse, of ourselves."

Still cautious in 1810, the Senate majority did not accept Clay's challenge, but the young orator won resounding applause from western Americans. Just as important, Clay's brief Senate service gave him a delicious taste of national fame and taught him that he was the equal, at least, of any debater in America. He loved the glamour of national publicity, the solemn approval of his colleagues on the floor, the sharp flush of satisfaction he felt from a stinging thrust of wit, the ardent admiration of the ladies in the gallery, the splendor and gaiety of social life in the nation's capital. Nothing back home in Kentucky could ever take the place of what Henry Clay loved about Washington, and he made it his business to stay there.

At this stage in his career, however, Clay felt impatient with the Senate's ponderous decorum and preferred the livelier customs of the lower chamber. When his time in the Senate grew short, he did not seek reelection but pursued and won a seat in the U.S. House of Representatives as congressman from the district around Lexington. Except for an important interval of diplomacy in 1814 and 1815, the House would be the center of Henry Clay's life for the next fifteen years.

Clay arrived in the House with a well-established reputation as a polished orator and respected political insider. His bellicose speeches in the Senate had made him the acknowledged leader of the War Hawks, a Republican faction who clamored for resistance to Great Britain. Dismayed by the passive policies of the Madison administration, the War Hawks determined to elect a Speaker of the House who was one of their own. Though he was only a freshman representative, Henry Clay won the post decisively on November 4, 1811, the first day of the Twelfth Congress, and used all his skills and influence to push the president and the Congress to accept the necessity of war. Slowly accepting the War Hawks' arguments, President Madison finally sought and received a declaration of war on Great Britain in the late spring of 1812.

Unlike Andrew Jackson, Henry Clay restricted his wartime leadership to legislative roles. Though clamoring for military action, he knew that his own gifts were in the council rather than the field, and he never doubted the superiority of civilian leadership over soldiery. Long before Jackson's victories brought the general's name to national prominence, Clay had warned against "the aggrandizement of some ambitious chief" whose martial triumphs might result in "prostrating the liberties of the country." (See Document 4.) Clay continued to support the administration's military policies, however, and no doubt groaned in near despair when the vaunted invasion of Canada collapsed and when a minor British raiding party scoured the Chesapeake and left the capital a smoking ruin. Feeble though it was, however, the United States did fight off total collapse. By 1814, moreover, Napoleon's empire was practically defeated, and the economic restrictions that provoked the war between Britain and America had no further justification. When both belligerents seemed ready for peace, President Madison asked John Quincy Adams and four other commissioners to travel to Europe and negotiate a treaty with their British counterparts. Knowing that the support of the War Hawks would be necessary to win ratification of any treaty, Madison included Clay in the delegation who joined Adams in the Belgian city of Ghent.

Adams and Clay were both fervent nationalists whose careers would be closely linked thereafter, but the two men were a very odd pair nonetheless. Though a nominal Republican, the secretary of state was the son of John Adams of Massachusetts, staunch Federalist and second president of the United States. A stern and humorless embodiment of Puritan rectitude, Adams had long diplomatic experience and a towering sense of duty. Clay, by contrast, was fun loving, exuberant, and impetuous. While he too resolved to do his duty, Clay firmly intended to enjoy himself on his first trip out of the country. Adams complained to his diary that Clay's parties kept him awake at night, while after a long night of dancing, drinking, and cards, Henry Clay sometimes found himself stumbling to bed just as John Quincy Adams was rousing himself for a few hours of predawn reading and correspondence. It is easy to imagine that the two diplomats despised each other, but they managed to work together all the same. American military failures did not give them a strong negotiating position, and the resulting treaty did not settle any of the major issues that had led to war in the first place. American sovereignty was vindicated, however, and no one rejoiced more heartily than Clay when news arrived of Andrew Jackson's stunning victory at New Orleans. "Now I can go to England without mortification," he exulted, probably never dreaming that the Hero of New Orleans would someday come between him and the White House.[42]

Returning to Congress after negotiating a commercial treaty with England, Clay became part of an extensive transformation of the Republican Party. The Federalist Party had inflicted its own political death blow by opposing the War of 1812 and even threatening the secession of its New England stronghold when the battlefield news was at its worst. In accordance with political ideals of the day, Democratic-Republicans had never endorsed the existence of a political party as valuable in itself but only as an indispensable tool to defeat a semitreasonable opposition. The collapse of Federalism seemed to open the way for an Era of Good Feelings when partisan resentments would melt away and all good Americans would join in patriotic unanimity to support the common good. More particularly, the lessons of the war had persuaded many leading Republicans that some of the Federalists' favorite measures had merit after all, including a national bank, a protective tariff, and federal aid to internal improvements. The new policies appealed strongly to Henry Clay, and the congressman from Kentucky was in the forefront of efforts to adopt them.

The first Bank of the United States had been the brainchild of arch-Federalist Alexander Hamilton. Its charter had expired in 1811, and

---

[42]Quoted in Robert V. Remini, *Henry Clay: Statesman for the Union* (New York: Norton, 1991), 126.

Clay had joined the Republican majority in voting against its renewal, probably because he thought it rivaled his favored local banks in Kentucky. Without an official bank to handle the issue of war bonds and to facilitate transfers of government funds, however, the government's financial powers had been crippled during wartime, and Clay now joined other Republican leaders in seeing the need for a replacement. Chartered in 1816, the second Bank of the United States would be the largest in the nation, with a capital of $35 million. The government would receive one-fifth of its stock and appoint one-fifth of its directors. The Bank would hold the government's money on deposit and issue a paper currency to the government's creditors and to private borrowers, which was expected to set a national standard for stability and reliability, though the currency of state banks would continue to circulate as well. Eventually, during the 1820s and 1830s, the BUS made a regular practice of collecting the paper notes of state banks and returning them with a demand for specie. State banks were then inhibited from issuing more paper than they could redeem on short notice, and the BUS exercised a kind of brake or control on the excessive issue of state bank notes. By partly controlling the volume of the money supply and seeking to regulate the quality of the currency, the BUS took on some of the functions of a modern central bank, but it did not play this role when it first began to operate.

Hamilton had also favored congressional measures to subsidize American manufactures, but congressional opponents had resisted, declaring that the Constitution gave them no power to pass such measures. By 1816, however, the experience of wartime had taught many Republicans how hard it was to supply an army and a navy without foundries and ironworks for munitions or ropewalks[43] and textile factories to make rigging, sailcloth, and uniforms. Some Republican leaders began to suggest that the United States adopt a protective tariff. When protected from foreign competition, they argued, American manufacturers could expand their operations and give the country a reliable industrial base. Once again, Henry Clay supported the new policy, well aware of the benefits that Kentucky hemp growers would receive from protection but also convinced that federal policy should encourage a harmony of interests between the farmers who grew the nation's crops and manufacturers who could process them into finished goods.

Republicans also advocated a new policy of federal aid to internal improvements. The former War Hawks were keenly aware that problems

---

[43] Ropewalks are rope manufacturers.

in transporting men and supplies had contributed to the military difficulties of the recent war. Men like South Carolina's John C. Calhoun also remembered classical warnings that a republican government was likely to fail in a far-flung country and wanted to use technology to beat the odds. "We are great, and rapidly, he was about to say fearfully growing," Calhoun reminded the House of Representatives. "Let us then . . . bind the Republic together with a perfect system of roads and canals."[44] As in the case of a bank and a protective tariff, the Constitution gave Congress no explicit authority to undertake internal improvements, and Presidents Madison and Monroe both decided that a constitutional amendment would be necessary before they could approve a building program. Undiscouraged, Clay and his ambitious counterparts looked forward eagerly to the election of a president with less cramped conceptions of constitutional interpretation.

As Clay joined his fellow congressmen in reshaping American republican values to include a leading role for the national government in promoting economic development, he also took part in another episode that powerfully shaped his relationship with the now-famous general from Tennessee. Jackson's unauthorized invasion of Florida during the First Seminole War had prompted a congressional investigation in 1818. Sticklers for discipline introduced resolutions calling for Jackson's formal censure, and Speaker Clay spoke eloquently in their favor.

Privately, Henry Clay held Indians in contempt and pronounced them not worth rescuing from extinction, but he may have seen Jackson as a rival by this point, and he certainly longed to score points against President Monroe. More seriously, he remembered that republics were traditionally unstable and prone to overthrow by popular but lawless "military chieftains." America's only defense against such a fate, he reasoned, was to insist on the supremacy of law and civilian authority, especially in the case of an otherwise popular military action against foreigners and Indians.

Clay thus put himself at the head of those who called for Jackson's censure. His speech to the House began by denying any personal animosity to Jackson or Monroe, but no one was fooled. His speech was an excellent example of Clay's grandiloquent rhetoric and invoked sympathy for the Indians and fear for the supremacy of civilian government. (See Document 5.)

---

[44]John C. Calhoun, "Speech on Internal Improvements," February 4, 1817, in Robert L. Meriwether, ed., *The Papers of John C. Calhoun,* vol. 1, 1807–1817, 23 vols. to date (Columbia: University of South Carolina Press, 1959–), 401.

They may bear down all opposition; they may even vote the general the public thanks; they may carry him triumphantly through this house. But, if they do, in my humble judgment, it will be a triumph of the principle of insubordination—a triumph of the military over the civil authority—a triumph over the powers of this house—a triumph over the constitution of the land. And he prayed most devoutly to heaven, that it might not prove, in its ultimate effects and consequences, a triumph over the liberties of the people.

The speech was a rhetorical masterpiece, but it failed to dent the general's popularity or to win passage for the resolutions of censure. Clay did win the eternal hatred of Andrew Jackson, however, and the general was fierce and unforgiving in his hatreds. The accusation that Jackson was a threat to public liberty and order had undoubtedly hit close to the bone, for Jackson thought of himself as devoted to liberty. He also struggled hard to master his own impulses and deeply resented anyone who pointed out the obvious fact that he sometimes had difficulty in doing so. Along with Clay, Jackson blamed the ambitions of Treasury Secretary William H. Crawford for the embarrassing debate, at least partly because he had tangled with Crawford long before. Later, in 1824, Clay and Crawford would both be seeking the presidency, and Jackson would enter the race against them, at least partly because he hated them both so cordially. Jackson's rivalry with Clay, in other words, grew largely out of the two men's deep ideological and policy differences, but it also emerged from their deep and powerful personal animosities.

POSTWAR PROBLEMS: BANKING PANIC AND MISSOURI CRISIS

The new program of banking, tariffs, and internal improvements was not universally popular. Like the pioneers who opposed the banking privileges of the Kentucky Insurance Company, many Americans worried about the corrupting power of monopolies and feared that the creation of a new class of moneyed capitalists based on paper wealth would undermine the moral and political fiber of the republic. Unknown to Washington insiders, General Andrew Jackson shared their views. The fears of these doubtful citizens seemed perfectly confirmed when the booming postwar economy came crashing down in the Panic of 1819.

American trade with Europe had exploded after the war as consumers sought out long-unavailable foreign luxuries and a series of poor harvests stimulated European purchases of American farm products. Banks and government land offices vied with one another to see who could offer the easiest credit terms to those who wished to buy lands from Jackson's vast new conquests, and land speculation mushroomed sharply. Inexperienced in the fluctuations of an unregulated market economy, government officials, and officers of the newly chartered second Bank of the United States cooperated merrily in feeding the boom, often profiting from banking and land speculation on their personal accounts.

The party ended abruptly, however, when the BUS had to collect enough specie to make the final payment on the Louisiana Purchase. Loans were suddenly called in, and the Bank demanded specie in exchange for its holdings of state bank notes. Suddenly deprived of credit, numerous urban businesses collapsed and discharged their employees. Thousands of borrowers could not pay their loans and lost homes, farms, and businesses to the sheriff's auction. Coincidentally, a bumper crop in Europe cut demand for American foodstuffs and drove farm prices even lower. From a heyday of prosperity and expansion, the American economy was plunged into the rigors of high unemployment, widespread bankruptcy, and the suspension of specie payments by the banks.

The panic struck in 1819, and parts of the economy continued to be affected throughout the first half of the 1820s. Fortunately, most Americans still lived on subsistence farms that provided food for their tables regardless of the level of commodity prices or the prospects for waged labor. For those who were earning wages, purchasing farms, or struggling with ambitious speculations, however, the panic revealed an ugly side of the Market Revolution. Banks demanded strict repayment of their loans but refused to honor their own obligations to pay specie. Lawsuits flourished as creditors pressed debtors and seized their lands and houses for default. At the center of everything, the Bank of the United States was the strictest creditor of all, seeking to pay its own debts by pressing state banks and private customers with equal severity. Among the many lawyers who did a handsome business suing delinquent borrowers and foreclosing lands for the BUS, Henry Clay was one of the most active, with a heavy case load all over Kentucky and Ohio. During the boom, the BUS had behaved like a private, profit-making lender instead of a public regulator, so much so that it now brushed close to bankruptcy itself. Steely-eyed management by Langdon Cheves, its second president, staved off that calamity, but the BUS made no friends for itself in the process. As one observer later concluded acidly, "The Bank was saved, and the people were ruined."[45]

---

[45]William M. Gouge, *A Short History of Paper Money and Banking in the United States* (Philadelphia: T.W. Ustick, 1833), 2:110. (Reprint, with an introduction by Joseph Dorfman, New York: A.M. Kelley, 1968.)

As if the panic were not enough to rock Americans' confidence, a political explosion soon followed it that portended even greater perils for the young republic. The controversy erupted when the territory of Missouri applied for statehood in 1819, and it exposed deep and bitter rifts over the nature of the American Union and the future of African American slavery.

At the time of the American Revolution, slavery had been legal in all the British colonies, but the greatest numbers of slaves on the North American mainland were found in the plantation colonies between Georgia and the Chesapeake. Led by Massachusetts, Pennsylvania, and Vermont, the northern states began to abolish the institution, and even some Virginians admitted the system's evils and sighed for a means to abandon it painlessly. By the time the Constitution was adopted, serious policy differences already divided the slave states from the free states, but many northerners seemed to feel that an unspoken agreement prevailed that the South would soon find a way to dismantle the system of bondage.

Instead of ebbing away, however, slavery only grew stronger. The growth of textile mills, first in Britain and later in New England, created a powerful demand for cotton, and in 1793 an inventor named Eli Whitney responded with a machine or gin to separate cotton fibers from the seeds. The same Market Revolution that spawned factories in the North soon spread cotton plantations across the South, and slave property became ever more valuable. Slavery spread westward with the frontier and took root in every new state south of the Ohio. In Kentucky, a few voices joined Henry Clay in criticizing the system, but in Jackson's Tennessee and further southward, the profits of slavery silenced all doubters.

The growth of slavery pained many northern leaders, but the political consequences were especially irksome. The Constitution's three-fifths clause inflated the congressional representation of the slave states, so the steady expansion of slavery put the North at a disadvantage in Congress and the Electoral College. In 1819, when the territory of Missouri applied for admission to the Union as another slave state, Representative James Tallmadge of New York decided to act. He offered an amendment to the Missouri bill that would require the end of slavery as a condition for the new state's admission. If Tallmadge's amendment had succeeded, it might well have set a precedent for denying the admission of other slave states, thereby excluding American slaveholders from the expanding prosperity of the frontier.

The House erupted in a furor. Southerners were enraged by what they felt was northern interference with their rights of property. Even if slavery were an evil — and some southern congressmen would no longer admit that it was — outsiders had no right to impose a solution. Missouri would become a sovereign state, they argued, and Congress had no power to dictate or restrict its institutions. Above all, they thundered, it was monstrous for free-state congressmen to prate publicly about liberty in ways that might incite the slaves to violence. "If you persist," cried one furious Georgian, "the Union will be dissolved. You have kindled a fire which all the waters of the ocean cannot put out, which seas of blood can only extinguish."[46]

Henry Clay disliked slavery, but he was also a large slaveholder himself. His instincts were to evade this quarrel and move back to the great economic questions he preferred. He spoke against the Tallmadge amendment but failed to halt its passage in the House. The Senate refused to adopt it but agreed in February 1820 to balance the admission of Missouri as a slave state with the admission of Maine as a free state, while also banning new slave states in that portion of the Louisiana Purchase lying above 36° 30′ north latitude. As Speaker, it was Clay's responsibility to get this compromise through the House, and he did so by carefully stacking the committee that considered it and allowing the bill to be broken into its component parts. While there was no majority for the package as a whole, separate majorities could be found for each one of its provisions, so the Missouri Compromise passed the House of Representatives in early March 1820.

The Missouri controversy briefly flared again the following year when the new state attempted to ban the immigration of free African Americans, but Clay once more guided Congress to a negotiated settlement that left the states in charge of their own racial policies. The two Missouri settlements launched Henry Clay's reputation as the Great Compromiser, a reputation he would extend with the settlement of the nullification controversy of 1832–1833 and the territorial crisis of 1850. At the time, however, Clay no doubt thought the sectional bitterness painful and unnecessary and regretted that the attention of Congress should be diverted from the greater interests of the country.

Meanwhile, Henry Clay had economic problems of his own. Like most other wealthy Americans, his personal finances had been seriously deranged by the recent panic, and he needed to recoup his fortunes. Resigning from Congress, he applied himself to the law and to building up his plantation at Ashland. As counsel for the Bank of the United States in 1821, he successfully defended the bank against an attack by the Ohio state legislature and won a crucial constitutional victory from the U.S. Supreme Court, in the case of *Osborn v. Bank of the United States.*[47] While

[46]*Annals of the Congress of the United States, 1789–1824,* 42 vols. (Washington, D.C., 1834–1856), 15th Cong., 2d sess., 1204.
[47]9 Wheaton 738 (1824).

he was back in Kentucky, a bitter political dispute broke out among those Republicans who sought to relieve the distress of the panic's victims by limiting the ability of creditors to sue for collection of debts. Clay tried to steer clear of this "Relief" controversy, but the debate was strongly reminiscent of the earlier quarrel over the Kentucky Insurance Company, and Clay's real sympathy lay with the creditors. Not only was he actively suing debtors for the BUS in this period, but he genuinely believed that recovery would come faster if property rights were respected and courts continued to enforce the sanctity of private contracts.

But Henry Clay was not content to be a bill collector forever. He returned to Congress in 1823 and reclaimed his old post as Speaker of the House while his mind turned to the looming presidential election of 1824. President James Monroe was approaching the end of his second term, and there was no obvious candidate from the Revolutionary generation to succeed him. Instead, a number of ambitious junior leaders were angling for the office of president, each with his own secure base in a different section of the country.

With the Federalist Party now extinct, all the leading contenders were nominally Republicans, but party designations had lost much of their meaning in the Era of Good Feelings. William H. Crawford of Georgia, formerly secretary of war but now in charge of Treasury, had a strong following among strict constructionists from the South and those Republicans who still believed that a caucus of congressional members should nominate the Republican candidate for president and present him to the country for popular ratification. Secretary of State John Quincy Adams of Massachusetts opposed this procedure and looked to his own base of support in New England. Secretary of War John C. Calhoun vied briefly for the honor but eventually settled for the vice presidency instead. Henry Clay thought it was high time a westerner was elected and saw no reason why the man should not be himself. There were also whispers that General Andrew Jackson desired the honor, but Clay dismissed such rumors. Though he had warned against the possible rise of a "military chieftain" in his speech on the First Seminole War, he did not take his own warning seriously enough.

ROUND ONE: 1824

It is instructive to compare how Henry Clay and Andrew Jackson went about seeking the presidency in 1824. In the days of fierce rivalry between Federalists and Republicans, the Republicans had used a special meeting, or caucus, of congressional Republicans to choose a presidential candidate and to impose party discipline. Those who still believed that a strong party organization was essential to good government (New York senator Martin Van Buren, for example) favored a continued reliance on the caucus, but Clay and Jackson both realized that the days of the caucus were over. Not only did they each lack support among caucus organizers, but they also realized that the custom smacked of intrigues and manipulation. Unlike Jackson, however, Clay assumed that established leaders in the most influential states would choose the president. Where electoral votes were awarded by a popular election, the voters would naturally follow the directions of their leading men. Where electoral votes were still determined by state legislatures, senior regional statesmen would make the decision directly. In either case, the candidate's job was to round up a circle of loyal followers at the top of each state's political hierarchy (Clay always called them his "friends") and let them do the rest.

In contrast to Clay, Jackson lacked standing among the powerful men who were equally comfortable in Washington and the leading state houses. By this time, Jackson himself was a wealthy gentleman farmer whose own efforts for the common man had mostly been limited to conquering more territory from the Indians. His best friends were also men who had struggled up from humble origins to become the rulers of frontier Tennessee. Despite his wealth and powerful friends, Jackson still identified with ordinary settlers and regarded his work in Florida as a struggle to shield "the poor and humble from the Tyranny of wealth and power."[48] His quarrels with Congress and the War Department had convinced him that leading national circles were rife with corruption and selfish ambition and that virtue resided only among the people at large. Like Jackson, these voters had come to doubt the worth of established elites and had come to see exploits like Jackson's as signs that the general possessed the sterling personal character that was even more important than civilian experience as a qualification for high office. Jackson's presidential campaign therefore relied on popular rallies and "spontaneous" bursts of public approval in remote and obscure places rather than on caucus decisions or the favor of notable gentlemen.

Clay took the opposite approach, corresponding extensively with well-connected men in various states whose friendship he had gained in Congress. His optimistic letters to them dealt expansively with the imagined movement of state-level power blocs rather than public opinion in the modern sense. "If during her next legislature, New York comes out in

---

[48]Quoted in Robert V. Remini, *Andrew Jackson and the Course of American Freedom, 1822–1832* (New York: Harper & Row, 1981), 34.

my favor . . . ," Clay predicted to a friend from that state, "the immediate and inevitable consequence . . . would be the relinquishment of Mr. Crawford by his southern friends; the confinement of the contest to Mr. Adams and me; and I should obtain the support, probably without exception of all [states] South & West of New York."[49]

Clay also worked hard to put together policy positions that would appeal to state leaders and conform to his own vision of what would be best for the country. The panic and the Missouri crisis had worried him considerably, and he forcefully advocated programs that he hoped would restore prosperity and bind the Union together in a firm network of what he called "certain great national interests."[50] For Clay, "interests" were not sordid distractions from sound statesmanship but the enduring foundations of national greatness, the material building blocks of prosperity and union. Properly understood, the nation's leading economic interests were not in conflict with one another but mutually supportive. The right federal policies could benefit them all and knit the nation together by making rival sections dependent on each other.

Federal aid to internal improvements was an important part of Clay's plans for the adjustment of interests, but his favorite policy was the federal protective tariff, and he outlined his hopes for it in a prominent two-day speech of March 1824. (See Document 6.) A modest level of protection already existed, but Clay wanted more. He began by invoking the legacy of the recent panic. "In casting our eyes around us, the most prominent circumstance which fixes our attention, and challenges our deepest regret, is the general distress which pervades the whole country," he declared. Clay explained the persisting depression on the overproduction of American crops. The coming of peace had returned European harvests to normal, so America's agricultural surplus could no longer find a foreign market, and farm prices suffered accordingly.

In making the case for tariff protection, Clay described the cardinal institution of the Market Revolution as the cornerstone of civilization itself. "The greatest want of civilized society," he proclaimed, "is a market for the sale and exchange of the surplus of the labor of its members." With adequate protection, he predicted, the United States could create such a market at home because Americans could produce their own manufactures when European products were excluded by the tariff. Unsuccessful farmers could then take jobs in manufacturing, and the

---

[49]Henry Clay to Peter B. Porter, June 15, 1823, in James F. Hopkins, et al., eds., *The Papers of Henry Clay,* 11 vols. (Lexington: University Press of Kentucky, 1959–1992), 3:434, hereinafter abbreviated as *Clay Papers.*

[50]Ibid., 433.

remaining cultivators could make good profits by selling them food and raw materials. Critics objected that protection was unfair to the South because higher prices for manufactures would cost the planters money, while the prevalence of slavery would prevent them from resorting to factories of their own. Clay rejected this criticism. Obviously reasoning from his experience back in Lexington, he predicted that slaves could work in factories as readily as fields and that planters who did not become manufacturers could follow the example of Kentucky hemp growers and sell their products to a protected American textile industry. According to his stirring conclusion, protection would not divide the sections but would bind the nation together in a magnificent and interdependent Union.

While Henry Clay was writing letters and making speeches to an audience of middle- and upper-level politicians in the most influential states, Andrew Jackson remained at the Hermitage and watched the reaction of public gatherings around the country. Tennessee's legislature had launched Jackson's candidacy almost inadvertently, as part of a maneuver by the general's friends to upstage their local factional rivals. Much to everyone's surprise, the idea caught on around the country, as militia musters and similar gatherings came forward with avowals of support. Jackson no doubt took special pleasure from a report from a talented but poorly educated supporter in Pittsburgh whose friends had used his own candidacy for a militia generalship as a surrogate test of Jackson's popularity. (See Document 7.) According to Edward Patchell, "The names of the several candidates ware put on nomination, and . . . ware severally hissed by nine tenths of the multitude; Untill my name was reached on the list, when shouts of Old Hickory resounded from all parts of the house, nine cheers for Old Hickory, was the word, 'when the crowd burst in upon me . . .' and bore me out on their shoulders into the public square; I assure you General I felt more proud of your nickname 'than I now feel of the Generalship.'" Summing up the election's meaning, Patchell regretted his own lack of polish but rejoiced in Jackson's prospects. "And altho I well knew that my talents were unadiquate to the task, yed I depended not only on my personal courage alone, but I trusted in my God, and your God, whome hath raised you up for to be a Saviour and a deliverance to his people." Henry Clay was always popular among his friends, but only Jackson inspired comparisons to the Messiah.

After his nomination by the Tennessee legislature, strangers from around the country approached Jackson and asked his permission to launch a campaign in their own states or regions. Jackson responded with a studied dignity that could only endear him further to voters who had grown disgusted with the maneuvers of insiders. In a typical answer to Henry Baldwin of Pennsylvania (whom he later appointed to the U.S. Supreme Court), Jackson declared that "the course ever pursued by me and which I have allways thought congenial with the republican principles of my country, was on no occasion to solicit for office, but at the same [time] not to decline any public demand made upon my services."[51] The answer was disingenuous, for Jackson was seeking the presidency very assiduously in his own disguised fashion, but he probably believed his own rhetoric. Over and over he stressed that the president must be chosen by the people and not by the corrupt and self-interested actions of their leaders. "I have great reliance upon the good sense and virtue of the people, and I hope with yourself that coalition intrigue and management will never place a citizen in the highest office in the gift of the people to bestow."[52] The two greatest intriguers, Jackson made clear, were his long-standing enemies and rivals, Henry Clay and William H. Crawford.

As Jackson's campaign gathered support, the Tennessee legislature boosted his visibility by electing him to the U.S. Senate in 1823. Once in Washington, Jackson had to confront the policy issues raised by Clay, and he adopted positions that were surprisingly temperate, considering his later opposition to similar measures. In a widely republished letter, he expressed support for a "judicious" tariff, but unlike Clay, he justified it by citing the need to stimulate production of defense materials. (See Document 8.) He also cited the need for tariff revenues to reduce the national debt. He even acknowledged the value of drawing off workers from agriculture to industry, but significantly, he drew the line at creating what he called a "moneyed aristocracy" based on banking and public credit. Just as personal indebtedness put an individual under the control of his creditors, so a borrowing nation would be governed by its bondholders, men who lived off the interest from their loans and contributed nothing useful to society. Rejecting the famous advice of Alexander Hamilton, Jackson declared, "I am one of those who do not believe that a national debt is a national blessing, but rather a curse to a republic; inasmuch as it is calculated to raise around the administration a moneyed aristocracy dangerous to the liberties of the country." When the protectionist tariff of 1824 came to the floor of the Senate, Jackson voted in favor of it. In other words, Jackson made concessions to the demands for

[51]Andrew Jackson to Henry Baldwin, January 23, 1823, in John Spencer Bassett, ed., *The Correspondence of Andrew Jackson*, 7 vols. (Washington: Carnegie Institute of Washington, 1926–1935), 3:184, hereinafter abbreviated as *Jackson Correspondence.*
[52]Andrew Jackson to John C. Calhoun, August 1823, *Jackson Correspondence*, 3:203.

tariff protection, but he did so in terms that evoked the values of an older, simpler society.

Based on their private papers and campaign positions in 1824, it appears that Andrew Jackson and Henry Clay had already settled into the intellectual and political positions that would dominate the rest of their careers. Both claimed loyalty to the republican values of the founders, but Jackson put his faith in the ordinary voter while Henry Clay relied on the guidance of established leaders. Both men claimed support for national prosperity, but Henry Clay embraced government policies to stimulate economic development. Jackson regarded such policies with caution and worried about their impact on the "liberties of the country." Both men would refine and deepen their positions in the future, but their fundamental preferences were already in place in the emerging debate over development and democracy.

In the end, neither Clay nor Jackson won the election of 1824. Jackson gained the most popular and electoral votes, and Clay won the least, but none of the four leading candidates captured a majority. In such cases, the Constitution directs the House of Representatives to choose a winner from the three highest vote getters, so Clay was eliminated and Jackson, Adams, and Crawford faced each other in a runoff. As Speaker and as leader of the principal bloc of undecided House members, Clay held great influence over the final outcome. The Kentucky legislature had instructed Kentucky congressmen to support Jackson, the western favorite, but Clay did not feel bound by their instructions. From the beginning, he favored Adams and told his friends so. Despite differences in their personal styles, Clay easily realized that he and Adams shared similar goals for the country, while he saw little of value in the policies of Jackson and Crawford. Crawford, moreover, lay deathly ill and could not perform the duties of the presidency. Clay made no promises to Adams, however, at least until a private meeting just before the vote. About the same time, however, Jacksonians began to charge that Clay would support Adams in exchange for the office of secretary of state. It was just the sort of "coalition intrigue and management" that Andrew Jackson had warned about, but no solid proof of the charge has ever come to light.

Whatever the merit of the accusations, events seemed to prove them true. Clay and his friends did support Adams in the House, the House did choose Adams as president over Jackson and Crawford, and Adams did give the State Department to Henry Clay. Because most of the previous presidents had been secretaries of state in the administrations of their predecessors, this decision put Clay in line to succeed Adams as the next chief executive. Andrew Jackson, who had won the most popular votes (though less than a majority), had been spurned by the power brokers.

Jacksonians everywhere were outraged. They directed most of their fury at Clay, who seemed to have sold the election, rather than at Adams, who seemed to have bought it. The general himself set the tone by pronouncing that "the *Judas* of the West has closed the contract and will receive the thirty pieces of silver. his end will be the same."[53] Baffled at the furor, Clay struggled to explain himself in a personal letter that was widely reprinted in the national press. (See Document 9.) His vote for Adams was a matter of "conscience," he said, not sale. He could not vote for Crawford because the Georgian was too ill. As for Jackson, Clay dismissed his claims in terms that the general and his followers could only find highly offensive. "As a friend of liberty, & to the permanence of our institutions," Clay wrote, " I cannot . . . contribut[e] to the election of a military chieftain, [and thus] . . . give the strongest guaranty that this republic will march in the fatal road which has conducted every other republic to ruin."

Clay's rejection of Jackson as a man who could destroy the republic did nothing to calm the storm. Newspaper columns teemed with angry denunciations of the "corrupt bargain" or the "bargain and sale" of the nation's highest office. They denounced Clay for violating his instructions and for scorning the "will of the people." Above all, the press denounced the election as a violation of majority rule. An editorial in the pro-Jackson Washington *Gazette* struck a typical note. (See Document 10.) "If the People thought Gen. Jackson worthy, is it for Henry Clay to pronounce him unworthy? Is it for him to say to his fellow-citizens, 'You shall not have the man you wish, but the man I will?' " Answering his own question, the editor articulated a new interpretation of republican principles. Though the Constitution clearly allows the House to choose any of the three final candidates, the editor denounced all constitutional intermediaries between government decisions and the people's will:

> No. — Henry Clay himself has inflicted the deepest wound on the fundamental principle of our government. *He* has insulted and struck down the majesty of the People: *He* has impugned their sovereignty: *He* has interposed between the current of their sentiments and the object of their choice; and seeks to justify himself by stale electioneering excuses. A thousand "military chieftains" could not have done so much harm to our constitutional principles.

Equally bold claims for the superior authority of direct democracy or the immediate rule of the people themselves became typical of the Jackson movement.

[53]Andrew Jackson to Major William B. Lewis, February 14, 1825, *Jackson Correspondence*, 3:276.

Politically speaking, Clay and Adams had evidently miscalculated badly. They had shared the assumption of the Constitution's Framers that the presidency could and should be conferred by the nation's senior officials, acting after solemn deliberation in the Electoral College and, if necessary, in the House of Representatives. A generation of practice with more popular forms of election had convinced many voters, however, that nothing should interfere "between the current of their sentiments and the object of their choice." The Framers, however, had reasoned that men of wealth and wisdom would be most likely to possess the independence and public virtue necessary to discern the common good and act on it. Jacksonians countered that if all men were truly equal, elites were just as likely to be corrupt and self-interested as anyone else. Only the "great body of the people," as they often put it, could be trusted to act virtuously for the common good because only the people as a whole could have no incentive to injure themselves. Unperceived by Clay and Adams, convictions like these had taken hold among a large portion of the citizenry, and the "corrupt bargain" seemed to confirm their worst suspicions. The new president and secretary of state took office under a serious cloud of mistrust.

John Quincy Adams did little to improve things while president. His first State of the Union message called for an elaborate program of federally sponsored internal improvements and educational and scientific initiatives that confirmed the worst fears of those who worried that the son of a Federalist president could not resist the lure of big government projects that would drain the treasury and stretch the Constitution. To make matters worse, Adams knew that his ideas would be unpopular, so he deliberately asked Congress to ignore the voters' opinions. "Were we to slumber in indolence or fold up our arms and proclaim to the world that we are palsied by the will of our constituents," he asked, "would it not be to cast away the bounties of Providence and doom ourselves to perpetual inferiority?"[54] Congress was especially scandalized by this seemingly contemptuous suggestion, and left Adams's proposals to gather dust. Reception of the administration's foreign policy was equally disappointing. Secretary of State Clay had a strong interest in the success and vitality of the newly independent South American republics, but suspicious congressmen frustrated his efforts to establish Pan-American solidarity. Clay was also unsuccessful in negotiations with Britain over the boundary with Canada and trade with the Caribbean Islands. After a dispiriting four years in office, neither man could have faced the prospect of a reelection campaign with much optimism.

[54]Richardson, *Messages and Papers*, 2:316.

ROUND TWO: 1828

Jackson's supporters had spent the four years of the Adams administration planning for a rematch in 1828. (See Figures 5 and 6.) The crowd of contenders from 1824 had given way to a field of two as all the opponents of Adams and Clay coalesced behind Old Hickory. The former leader of the Crawford forces was a crucial recruit, for Senator Martin Van Buren of New York brought to the Jackson camp a firm conviction that strong party organization was not only the way to win elections but also the only way to defend the integrity of American republicanism. To elect Jackson in 1828, Van Buren proposed to revive the party strife of the early republic, casting the general as the champion of the Democratic-Republicans and thrusting Adams and Clay into the hated role of Federalists. Applying the lessons he had learned in Jeffersonian New York, Van Buren believed that politics without strong party lines would degenerate into a corrupt and unseemly scramble of personal rivalries (as in 1824) or a deadly sectional contest between the slave states and the free, as in the Missouri crisis. As he wrote to Virginia editor Thomas Ritchie, "political combinations between the inhabitants of the different states are unavoidable & the most natural & beneficial to the country is that between the planters of the South and the plain Republicans of the North." Without strict party divisions and a North-South alliance in the old Democratic-Republican Party, Van Buren declared, "Geographical divisions founded on local interests or, what is worse prejudices between free & slave holding states will inevitably take their places."[55]

Van Buren used his persuasive talents to bring the remainder of the old Crawford faction into the Jackson camp, while a central committee in Nashville kept up an active correspondence with Jacksonian politicians throughout the country. Led by the *United States Telegraph* of Washington, D.C., a strong corps of party newspapers spread enthusiasm for the cause of "Jackson and the People." To stress their ties to Jefferson's old party, the Jacksonians embraced the label "Democratic-Republicans" and later shortened it to "Democrats."

Van Buren's partisan strategy meshed smoothly with the ideological message of the Jackson candidacy. Supported by the general's own firm convictions that he and the people had both been robbed in 1825, political activists used the "corrupt bargain" charge and Adams's unfortunate disparagement of "the will of our constituents" to cast the election as a referendum on democracy and majority rule. In the words of Jackson's chief newspaper, the *United States Telegraph,* the mission of the Democratic-Republican Party and its candidate was "The great cause of

[55]Martin Van Buren to Thomas Ritchie, January 13, 1827, in Martin Van Buren Papers, Library of Congress Manuscripts Division, Washington, D.C.

JACKSON TICKET

Honor and gratitude to the man who has filled
the measure of his country's glory—*Jefferson*

FOR THE ASSEMBLY
GEORGE H. STEUART,
JOHN V. L. McMAHON.

Figure 5.   The Jackson Ticket
Figure 6 *(opposite).*   The Coffin Handbill
The election of 1828 was a clear-cut contest between the incumbent, John
Quincy Adams, and the challenger, Andrew Jackson. The two sides worked
hard to capture the imagination of ordinary voters and created sharply con-
trasting images of Jackson in the process. On the left, Pennsylvania Jacksonians portrayed Old Hickory as a statesman like George Washington or Thomas
Jefferson and linked his name to ambitious local politicians. On the right, Adams
forces produced the "Coffin Handbill," portraying Jackson as a bloodthirsty vil-
lain who executed innocent soldiers under his command and slaughtered anyone who defied him.

Jacob Wells   David Morrow   John Harris   Henry Lewis   David Hunt   Edward Lindsey the many against the few, of equal rights against privileged orders, of democracy against aristocracy."[56]

Jacksonians did not limit themselves to purely symbolic efforts on Old Hickory's behalf. The general would need support in New York, Pennsylvania, and other mid-Atlantic states where the protective tariff was very popular. As a military man, Jackson had long supported a protective tariff to encourage the manufacture of articles necessary for national defense, and his New York and Pennsylvania supporters made sure voters there knew all about the general's endorsement of a "judicious tariff." Going further, congressional Jacksonians from the middle states pressed successfully for sizable tariff increases in 1828, overwhelming the strenuous protests of southerners who called their bill the "Tariff of Abominations." Jackson himself kept silent about specific tariff levels, and his more opportunistic supporters called him a low-tariff man in the South and a protectionist in the North.

Friends of the administration tried to distinguish themselves as the "National Republicans" but never matched the level of party organization and popular enthusiasm of their rivals. Indeed, many National Republican journals devoted long columns to denouncing the folly and corruption of all forms of party organization and tried to counter Jackson's appeal with earnest sermons about the need for tariffs and internal improvements. When administration supporters did adopt a less sober approach to the campaign, they resorted to gutter attacks on Jackson's character and ancestry that were just as likely to backfire. Charles Hammond of the Cincinnati *Gazette* spread the story of General Jackson's irregular marriage and asked, "Ought a convicted adultress and her paramour husband to be placed in the highest offices of this free and christian land?" Stooping even further, Hammond announced in his paper that "General Jackson's mother was a COMMON PROSTITUTE, brought to this country by the British soldiers! She afterwards married a MULATTO MAN, with whom she had several children, of which number General JACKSON IS ONE!!!"[57] Another widely circulated handbill featured pictures of six coffins for the six militiamen executed for mutiny in the Creek War and promised readers "Some Account of some of the Bloody Deeds of General Jackson." Replying in the same vein, the Jackson press called Adams a Federalist, a monarchist, and even a pimp who had pro-

---

[56] *United States Telegraph,* September 11, 1828, reprinted in Arthur M. Schlesinger, Jr. and Fred L. Israel, eds., *History of American Presidential Elections, 1789–1968,* 4 vols. (New York: Chelsea House, 1971), 1:482.

[57] Quoted in Robert V. Remini, *The Election of Andrew Jackson* (Philadelphia: Lippincott, 1963), 151–55.

cured an American virgin for the lust of the Russian czar. The Adams papers struggled valiantly to refute such nonsense, while portraying Jackson as a duelist, a gambler, a cockfighter, a Sabbath breaker, and an all-round frontier savage who was no more civilized than the Indians he persecuted.

It was no use. All states but South Carolina and Delaware allowed their electoral votes to be determined by popular ballot, and Jackson won 56 percent of the total. Adams's strength was mostly isolated in New England, while Jackson carried New York, Pennsylvania, and virtually every state from the South and West, even Clay's native Kentucky. The National Republicans' account of Jackson's personal habits and character convinced many orderly and decorous voters that the general was morally unfit to be president, but they had not turned the tide, and they only deepened Jackson's hatred of his enemies. When Rachel Jackson suddenly died after discovering what the newspapers were saying about her, Jackson was devastated by grief and pinned the blame on Clay, branding the Kentuckian "the bases[t], meanest, scoundrel that ever disgraced the image of his god."[58] Jackson's brand of democracy had seemingly triumphed over Adams's and Clay's support for development, but the victory had brought more bitterness than exultation to Old Hickory.

THE HERO BECOMES A PRESIDENT

Andrew Jackson's presidential inauguration has become a classic fable of American political folklore. The crowds in Washington were immense on the morning of March 4, 1829, as thousands of ordinary citizens joined the expected crowd of Washington dignitaries at the east portico of the Capitol. The new president was still crushed with grief by the death of his wife and impressed everyone, friends and enemies alike, with the dignity of his bearing and the simple republican sentiments of his brief inaugural address.

When the ceremony concluded, the presidential party made its way to the White House, followed by a throng of spectators, described by one witness as "country men, farmers, gentlemen, mounted and dismounted, boys, women and children, black and white." Arriving at the White House, the people followed Jackson inside and began to help themselves to the refreshments that had been prepared for a much smaller party.

The most vivid account of this gathering was left in a letter from Mrs. Margaret Bayard Smith. (See Document 11.) Mrs. Smith's husband was

---

[58] Andrew Jackson to Sam Houston, December 15, 1826, *Jackson Correspondence,* 3:325.

the president of the Washington branch of the Bank of the United States; she herself was a leading hostess in Washington's high society and a great friend of the Clays. The Smiths thus had no particular fondness for Andrew Jackson's policies or his democratic methods, but Mrs. Smith respected the general's personal demeanor and character. So long as they were well behaved, according to her notions, she also had respect for the American people, as her account of the inaugural ceremony reveals. But when the people lost their sense of order and respect for proper ranks in society, Mrs. Smith was appalled, and she left a horrified description of the democratic melee inside the White House.

Mrs. Smith described how masses of ordinary citizens abandoned their subordinate positions and pushed into the president's reception. "Cut glass and china to the amount of several thousand dollars had been broken in the struggle to get to the refreshments. . . . Ladies fainted, men were seen with bloody noses and such a scene of confusion took place as is impossible to describe." The scene inevitably reminded Mrs. Smith of the worst excesses of the French Revolution, and she allowed herself to wonder whether democracy might lead to the destruction of civilization itself. Given Mrs. Smith's social and political values, we may doubt whether the scene was quite as deplorable as she remembered, but her letter is a clear example of how the leveling practices of the Jackson movement were seriously frightening to at least some elements in the highest ranks of American society.

The new administration unfolded in a complex interplay of personal and policy disputes. Underestimating the general's taste for command, many of his followers assumed that Jackson would remain for only a single term, and plotting for the succession began immediately. Vice President John C. Calhoun of South Carolina had high hopes of becoming the next president, but careful political observers quickly noted that Martin Van Buren, the new secretary of state, seemed closer to the president's confidence. Their relationship grew even closer when Jackson became convinced that Calhoun had encouraged his wife to ostracize Peggy Eaton, wife of the secretary of war, on the grounds of alleged sexual improprieties. Convinced of Mrs. Eaton's innocence and mindful of his own wife's persecution, Jackson suspected Calhoun of whipping up a scandal to disrupt the administration and force him to follow Calhoun's orders in the selection of his cabinet members. As a widower, Van Buren could lavish polite attention on the Eatons without fear of domestic reproaches, and his friendship with the president flourished while Calhoun's deteriorated. The vice president's souring relationship with Jackson would soon have major policy repercussions when South Carolina forced a confrontation over the rising level of the federal tariff.

Jackson's eight years in the White House were intense and controversial. Many of the debates that swirled around presidential policies grew directly out of the larger debate over economic development and democracy—that is, equality for white men, majority rule, and the establishment of an egalitarian culture. Other topics raised separate but related questions, particularly those touching on slavery or racial inequality. While the president and his opponents fiercely debated the first set of questions, they preferred to avoid the second.

There were approximately two million slaves in the United States when Andrew Jackson became president, most of them in the states south of Washington, D.C. African Americans bitterly resented their enslavement, and they let their owners know it. In 1831, halfway through Andrew Jackson's first term, a Virginia slave named Nat Turner led a bloody uprising that took the lives of almost sixty whites. Other forms of slave resistance included running away, breaking tools, avoiding work, and occasional acts of personal violence. Most of the time, most white southerners told themselves that slaves were safe and passive, but African American resistance to slavery fanned southern whites' pervasive anxiety that public criticisms of slavery might incite the slaves to violent rebellion.[59]

Jackson's presidency also saw the rise of a militant antislavery movement in the North. A small number of white and black abolitionists denounced human bondage as a sin against God and a violation of republican principles. The majority of white northerners disliked slavery, but they disliked the abolitionists even more. Convinced of black inferiority, they had no sympathy for a movement that might lead to demands for racial equality. Most political leaders likewise preferred to keep the slavery question out of public life. In the South, public criticism of slavery was condemned as insurrectionary. In the North, criticism of slavery could alienate a national politician's southern friends, while defense of slavery might offend some voters back home. In both sections, politicians worried that discussion of slavery might provoke another Missouri crisis and bring about disunion. Most of the time, the less said about slavery, the better.

Despite the pressure for silence, the slavery question entered politics

---

[59]John Ashworth, *Slavery, Capitalism, and Politics in the Antebellum Republic,* vol. 1, *Commerce and Compromise, 1820–1850* (Cambridge: Cambridge University Press, 1995), 1–10.

in several ways. Abolitionists wanted to use the public mails to send their message to the South, but southern mobs interfered and destroyed their literature. Although faced with a clear violation of freedom of speech, the Jackson administration sided with the mob and refused to deliver "incendiary" publications to southern addresses. Abolitionists also wanted to petition Congress for various antislavery causes, which would allow antislavery congressmen to support their petitions on the floor and force the matter into public discussion. Bowing to southern demands, Jacksonian Democrats upheld a gag rule to ban reception of such petitions. After Jackson left office, the demand for territorial expansion also raised the question of the spread of slavery. In other words, the conflict between slavery and freedom was so blatant and so severe that the issue kept entering public discussion despite political efforts to keep it out. Ultimately, the slavery question would take over politics entirely and bring on the Civil War. For most of the Jackson administration, however, both parties agreed that slavery should be avoided in favor of safer controversies.

The question of Indian policy was a partial exception, for whites often justified the inferior positions of African Americans and Native Americans by the same arguments of racial inferiority. Indian fighting had been central to President Jackson's public career, and he entered the White House determined to continue his campaign for their lands. In his first annual message to Congress, Jackson demanded legislation that would permit him to offer permanent reservations in the West in exchange for the lands of all Indian tribes living east of the Mississippi River. (See Document 12.) The effect would be to open vast new tracts of eastern land for white settlement.

The biggest concentrations of eastern Indians were in the southern states of Georgia, Florida, Alabama, and Mississippi, where the Cherokees, Creeks, Choctaws, Chickasaws, and Seminoles still retained extensive domains for their traditional ways of life. As a legal matter, Jackson thought the existence of semi-independent Indian nations inside the boundaries of American states was constitutionally absurd. Paradoxically, Jackson's message acknowledged that the so-called Five Civilized Tribes had "made some progress in the arts of civilized life" but also said that they must move west for their own protection. More fundamentally, he thought that "savages" simply had no permanent right to land that was wanted by a "higher" civilization. He also knew that his own supporters in the affected states wanted the land very badly and that they would turn against any administration that failed to support their desires.

According to Jackson's policy, Indians who refused to move were free to remain where they were, but they would lose title to most of their lands, as well as the right to govern themselves as tribes. They would also be subject to state laws that refused them equal rights, like the right to testify against whites in court. Most observers recognized that these laws would leave the Indians with no protection against white thievery and harassment.

Most of the eastern Indians bitterly protested this proposal, but Jackson gave them little room to maneuver, as he refused to protect them from hostile frontiersmen and their state governments and offered generous bribes to chiefs who would sign treaties committing their people to the move. National Republicans put up vocal resistance to the plan, but Henry Clay was no longer in Congress and could not join them. In his place, Senator Theodore Frelinghuysen of New Jersey led the fight against Indian removal with an eloquent speech in Congress. (See Document 13.) Frelinghuysen would later become Henry Clay's running mate when he ran for president in 1844.

The opposition's eloquence was almost successful, for the key votes in Congress were quite close. In the end, however, the Indian Removal Act of 1830 became Andrew Jackson's first major legislative success. The southwestern tribes continued to resist removal for most of the 1830s, but most of them finally accepted defeat and took up new lands in what is now Oklahoma. Almost one out every four Cherokees died on the "Trail of Tears" that finally took the tribe west, but Jackson always viewed Indian removal as one of his proudest achievements.

In addition to Indian affairs, four special areas of policy debate in the Jackson administration stand out as important aspects of the larger contemporary conflict between democracy and development—rotation in office, internal improvements, federal tariffs, and banking policy. Not surprisingly, these were all areas of sharp dispute between Andrew Jackson and Henry Clay. Jackson favored a regular turnover in federal offices in order to democratize the operations of the federal government, and he became very hostile to prodevelopmental policies in regard to internal improvements, tariffs, and banks. Clay denounced what he saw as Jackson's attempts to politicize the bureaucracy and continued to favor the developmental policies he had always supported. As the two men clashed repeatedly, their respective supporters carried the dispute into a political party system that dominated American politics for most of the remainder of the antebellum period.

Even before his election, Jackson had suspected that corrupt federal bureaucrats had feared the prospect of his presidency and had used their power to support Adams and Clay. Once he took office, the suspicion hardened into certainty as audits of various departments uncovered numerous financial and political abuses. The general determined to clean house and announced his intention to remove federal officeholders who were dishonest, incompetent, or improperly active in federal elections. Supporters of Clay and Adams correctly assumed that this meant that Jackson intended to replace National Republicans on the public payroll with good, sound Jackson men, but the president made no apologies. In his first annual address, he denied that officeholders had any permanent right to their jobs and suggested that long tenure in office made federal workers insensitive to public needs. "The duties of all public officers are, or at least admit of being made, so plain and simple that men of intelligence may readily qualify themselves for their performance; and I cannot but believe that more is lost by the long continuance of men in office than is generally to be gained by their experience."[60]

In actuality, Jackson's policy of "rotation in office" led to relatively few dismissals. In the fall of 1830, the Washington *Globe* reported that 919 federal officers out of 10,093, or 9.1 percent, had lost their jobs since the administration took office. A recent study of the Post Office is much more critical of Jackson's dismissal policy but concludes that the administration discharged about 973 postmasters, or 13 percent of the total number, during its eight years in office.[61] The worst aspect of Jackson's policy of rotation in office was not its immediate effect on government administration but in the opening it created for a "spoils system." Before the institution of a merit system in the federal civil service in the late nineteenth century, even the humblest government positions were regularly filled by the campaign workers for the party in power, and incumbent bureaucrats were routinely fired to make room for new political appointees whenever the government changed hands. Jackson did not create this system, but his successors did by building on the precedents he established.

Spotting a political opportunity, Henry Clay was quick to denounce Jackson's removal policy, ignoring the widespread belief that his own appointment as secretary of state had also come about as a political payoff. Describing the removals as a policy of punishing elderly public servants for their sincere political convictions, Clay called the practice an "intolerable oppression" of individuals that could also undermine free gov-

[60]Andrew Jackson, First Annual Message, in Richardson, *Messages and Papers*, 2:449.
[61]Leonard D. White, *The Jacksonians: A Study in Administrative History, 1829–1861* (New York: Macmillan, 1954), 307–08; Richard R. John, *Spreading the News: The American Postal System from Franklin to Morse* (Cambridge, Mass.: Harvard University Press, 1995), 223.

ernment.[62] His efforts were unavailing. State governments had already used the spoils system, and Jackson's egalitarian defense of rotation in office had irresistible appeal. When Clay's party finally replaced the Jacksonians, they protected and rewarded themselves with the same system they had previously denounced.

Jackson's initial policy on internal improvements bore a close resemblance to his ideas about tariffs. While he was a member of the Senate and a candidate for president in 1824, he voted for protective tariffs and internal improvement bills, explaining to a correspondent "as regards internal improvements, Congress can constitutionally apply their funds to such objects as may be deemed National."[63] The line between national and purely local improvements was fuzzy, of course, and over the course of his presidency, Jackson became convinced that the internal improvement policies favored by his enemies were a species of corruption and an outrageous drain on the treasury. Invariably claiming national economic benefits for purely local schemes, log-rolling politicians would get subsidies for their pet projects by trading votes with fellow legislators to gain majority support for a hodgepodge of measures that could never win approval individually. Not coincidentally, the resulting high level of federal expenditures would provide an excuse for keeping the tariff high in order to pay for them. Beneficial in intent, indiscriminate federal aid to internal improvements seemed to lead ineluctably to corruption, and Jackson decided to oppose it.

The occasion arose when Congress agreed to purchase stock in the Maysville, Washington, Paris, and Lexington Turnpike Company, a private corporation that intended to build a highway across Kentucky to the western terminus of the National Road, on the banks of the Ohio River. The new turnpike would lie wholly inside a single state, but proponents called it a national measure because it would extend the reach of the National Road, linking the Midwest to the Chesapeake basin. Jackson had been looking for a way to reassure southerners of his support for strict construction, however, and he had no desire to deliver federal favors into Henry Clay's backyard. When the bill reached his desk, he had already decided to veto it.

Jackson's Maysville Road veto began with support for the goals of internal improvement but shifted immediately to constitutional objections. (See Document 14.) Like his contemporaries, Jackson envisioned two ways in which the federal government might undertake such measures.

---

[62]Quoted in Remini, *Henry Clay,* 349.
[63]Andrew Jackson to James Lanier, May 15 (?), 1824, *Jackson Correspondence,* 3:253.

First, it could perform the work directly and maintain jurisdiction over the facilities thereafter. Jackson rejected this approach out of hand because he did not think the Constitution permitted such a direct trespass on the sovereignty of the states. Second, the Congress could grant the states money for internal improvements or purchase stock in state-chartered transportation corporations, leaving construction and ultimate jurisdiction with the state authorities. This was the formula that Jackson had voted for in the past and that backers proposed for the Maysville Road. This time, however, Jackson reminded Congress that the formula could apply only to specific projects with national rather than local benefits, and the Maysville Road could not pass this test.

The president did not stop there. Even if the Maysville Road were a national measure, Jackson said he would still veto it because the treasury was now exhausted and the road could not be built without an increase in the national debt. In his view, reducing and repaying that debt were far more important than an immediate rush to improve transportation. Why? Here he invoked the power of republican principles. Jackson still believed that the existence of a national debt gave inordinate power to the nation's creditors. As long as the debt existed, the equality of citizens and security of the republic were uncertain. Jackson agreed that prosperity was good, but one thing was more important—"The preservation and success of the republican principle." If the United States could extinguish its debt and reduce its taxes, republican principles would be vindicated throughout the world and be even safer in America itself. No tawdry and short-term economic benefit, Jackson implied, could possibly compensate for the loss of this magnificent result.

Pounding the message home, the president beat a clear but unacknowledged retreat from the constitutional interpretation he had embraced in 1824. Despite his earlier statements and votes, he now claimed to doubt the constitutionality of the established procedure for appropriating federal money to state-sponsored projects of internal improvement. To clear up the confusion, Jackson called for a constitutional amendment spelling out the exact conditions under which the federal government could undertake these expenditures. To allow expediency and custom to override this procedural nicety would be courting disaster, he claimed, for it would prove that Americans could not follow their own rules or practice self-restraint and would thereby demonstrate "the degrading truth that man is unfit for self-government." Faced with what he saw as a conflict between republican principles and economic development, Andrew Jackson came down firmly for principles.

The recent election had sent Henry Clay back to private life, so he had no forum for a conspicuous reply to the Maysville veto. His own support for internal improvements was well known, however, and the public knew that Clay did not see the conflict between principle and prosperity that worried President Jackson. For him, the power to promote prosperity was one of the greatest advantages of republican government, and Clay rejoiced to his friends that the president had handed him a superb political issue. Even western Jacksonians worried that the new policy would injure their popularity, but Jackson knew better. The president realized that voters would listen when he warned against official corruption and constitutional decay. The previous controversies over banking and relief legislation had demonstrated that Clay's own constituents were worried about the dangerous implications of economic change. "Where it has lost me one, it has gained me five friends," Jackson boasted. Even "in Kentucky [it] has done no harm."[64]

The principles Jackson invoked in the Maysville veto became even more significant in his policy on banking and currency. Ever since his disastrous entanglement with David Allison, Jackson had been suspicious of paper credit, and he had long shared the popular suspicion of banks that had fueled the attack on the Kentucky Insurance Company. As he endlessly repeated, debt was a threat to independence, for an indebted individual or nation would always be ruled by its creditors. Were those creditors linked together by a charter of incorporation (as in the case of a bank), they would operate like a conspiracy and assume more power over the government than any group of ordinary individuals ever could, no matter how wealthy. They would become, in other words, a "moneyed aristocracy," operating contrary to the will of the people, and Jackson loathed the very idea. "Every one that knows me, does know," he later confided to James K. Polk, "that I have been always opposed to the U. States Bank, nay all Banks."[65]

Jackson's concerns may sound far-fetched in a world where banking is taken for granted, but they had solid roots in the world of the early

[64] Andrew Jackson to William B. Lewis, June 28, 1830, *Jackson Correspondence*, 4:157.

[65] Andrew Jackson to James K. Polk, December 23, 1833, *Jackson Correspondence*, 5:236. Like his claims to have never sought public office, Jackson's claim that he had always opposed all banks was a bit disingenuous. While he may have opposed banks in principle, as a practical matter he certainly used their services. He kept his money in banks, he sometimes borrowed from banks, and in 1815 he even purchased a few shares in the Bank of Nashville, the first bank in Tennessee. When Jackson withdrew the federal deposits from the Bank of the United States, he had them deposited in selected state banks, despite his opposition to banks in general. Presumably he saw no practical alternative at that time, but his successor President Martin Van Buren withdrew government funds from all banks and lodged them in an "independent treasury," with Jackson's approval.

republic. There had been no banks at all in colonial and revolutionary America, the scene of Jackson's boyhood. Alexander Hamilton, architect of the first Bank of the United States, had candidly admitted that he did not think that the nation could survive without the support of its creditors—a "moneyed aristocracy," in effect—and his policies on banking and currency were specifically designed with the interests of creditors in mind. As banks took root and spread across the American landscape in the generation after Hamilton's career, their paper currency and their lending practices were at the center of the Market Revolution. Rural merchants typically used bank loans to obtain the cash to purchase farmers' surpluses and repaid the loans when they sold the crops in more distant markets. More bank loans financed their purchases of consumer goods to supply their country customers. Bank notes and bills of exchange were the medium that connected commercial farmers to distant consumers and manufacturers, and it was often a bank that took possession when financial panic finished off a struggling business. As Jackson suspected, banks and bank officers readily made financial contributions to influence the outcome of elections, and banks were at the center of a process of economic change that was creating new and unfamiliar forms of hierarchy and inequality in American society. Men who feared or resented these changes found the banks a tempting and logical target.

For most supporters of the Market Revolution, the advantages of the BUS counterbalanced its imagined shortcomings. The United States was a young country with tremendous potential but starved for capital to finance expansion. Capital could come from credit, but lenders would not provide it without reassurance that their loans would be secure. When foreigners and wealthy Americans bought stock in the BUS, the Bank used the money to make loans to country banks, the country banks made loans to country merchants, the merchants bought the farmers' produce, and everybody benefited. Without a healthy BUS, this chain of credit would be broken. By the same token, when farmers spent the notes of country banks, the notes circulated freely until someone used them to make a payment or a deposit at the Bank of the United States. The BUS returned these notes to their banks of origin and demanded specie, in order to make sure the local banks were not issuing more notes than they could redeem. The process was intended to keep local banks honest, and most of the time it worked, helping to assure Americans that the bank notes they passed from hand to hand were really worth the money they claimed to be.

The Bank of the United States also made direct loans to private customers at very attractive interest rates. Paper from its branches circulated throughout the country at the lowest possible discount. The existence of the Bank made it possible for the government to collect taxes in one place and spend money in another with the least possible cost or delay in transferring funds. The Bank made it easier to make payments on the national debt or to arrange new loans in case of emergency. Above all, the Bank was a symbol that the United States government knew how businesses worked and knew how to arrange its policies with businessmen's needs in mind. To the men whose lives were entwined with the success of the Market Revolution, its advantages were obvious and overwhelming.

In 1831, Henry Clay returned to Washington as the new senator from Kentucky and took command of the anti-Jackson forces in the Congress. His political skill, personal popularity, and rhetorical brilliance soon made him the logical candidate to oppose Jackson's reelection bid in 1832. Gathering under the banner of the National Republican Party, Clay's friends nominated him for president in December 1831, and the fate of the second BUS soon became joined to Clay's own. The Bank's charter was due to expire in 1836, but nervous supporters hoped to obtain a new charter long before the expiration of the old one, and Clay anticipated that the question of the Bank could help him win the election. If Congress passed a new charter, Jackson might decide that the Bank was too popular to disturb in an election year. If Jackson chose to veto the recharter, Clay could use the issue against him in the campaign.

Even nominally Jacksonian politicians and editors often liked the Bank, in part because it freely distributed loans and favors to its more powerful friends. Even more important, top political leaders usually came from the social strata where the Bank's advantages were well understood and where the benefits of economic development were felt directly. Congress readily passed a new charter in July 1832, but Jackson returned it a week later with a thundering veto message that became the central document of his entire career. (See Document 15.)

Working from voluminous notes supplied by Jackson himself, presidential advisers Amos Kendall and Roger Taney had composed the veto message with great care. They treated the Bank's charter as a licensed monopoly privilege for its stockholders and not as an institution designed to benefit the whole nation. The message began by denouncing the favoritism showered on these stockholders, many of them foreigners, and "a few hundred of our own citizens, chiefly of the richest class." Reasserting the spread-eagle nationalism he had long used against the British, Jackson warned of the danger of allowing foreigners to control a key national asset and then attacked the Bank on constitutional grounds. Though Chief Justice John Marshall had ruled in favor of the Bank in the famous cases of *McCulloch v. Maryland*[66] and *Osborn v. Bank of the United States*,[67] Jackson brushed aside the arguments of the Supreme Court and declared that as an equal branch of the government, the president must enforce the Constitution "as he understands it, and not as it is understood by others." Using strict constructionist arguments, Jackson found the Bank both unnecessary and improper and therefore in violation of the Constitution's mandate.

The veto message concluded by returning to the theme of special privilege and delivered a crushing condemnation of government-sponsored inequality.

> It is to be regretted that the rich and powerful too often bend the acts of government to their selfish purposes. Distinctions in society will always exist under every just government. Equality of talents, of education, or of wealth can not be produced by human institutions. In the full enjoyment of the gifts of Heaven and fruits of superior industry, economy, and virtue, every man is equally entitled to protection by law; but when the laws undertake to add to these natural and just advantages artificial distinctions, to grant titles, gratuities, and exclusive privileges, to make the rich richer and the potent more powerful, the humble members of society—the farmers, mechanics, and laborers—who have neither the time nor the means of securing like favors to themselves, have a right to complain of the injustice of their Government.

Though Jackson acknowledged that some measure of inequality was inevitable, the inequality that Jackson saw growing up around him came from private individuals who had gained more from government than they should. Unlike modern liberals, who favor government assistance to help the weak, Jackson wanted to protect equality by withdrawing government assistance from the strong. If the government would stop creating inequality by giving artificial stimulation to the engines of the Market Revolution, he implied, men would be left in a state of modest but natural inequality, with no more to divide them than the different gifts they had all been born with.

Unequal treatment of the citizens was more than simply unfair, Jackson explained. If wealthy men could grow wealthier by political favoritism, then rival groups of greedy factions would soon be competing for government favor. In the ensuing scramble to control the government, enrich themselves, and deprive their competitors, tensions would arise that would undermine the Union and, with it, republican government itself.

[66] 4 Wheaton 316 (1819).
[67] 9 Wheaton 738 (1824).

The safety of the American experiment in self-government demanded the destruction of the Bank and all its kindred.

Clay, Webster, and the Bank's president, Nicholas Biddle of Philadelphia, reacted to the veto message with a mixture of glee and outrage. "As to the veto message, I am delighted with it," Biddle exulted in a letter to Clay. "It has all the fury of a chained panther biting the bars of his cage. It is really a manifesto of anarchy," he claimed, comparable to the radical propaganda of the French Revolution.[68] The banker was so convinced that the veto made Jackson look reckless and irresponsible that he printed thousands of copies at the Bank's expense and distributed it as anti-Jackson campaign material in the upcoming election.

In fact, the veto was a splendid popular success. Voters applauded the president's defense of public equality, even if they did not follow the subtle economic arguments in favor of central banking. Jacksonian newspapers throughout the country sang the veto's praises, and hostility to banking in general (and the BUS in particular) emerged as a central theme of the Jackson movement.

Still attuned to the voice of elite opinion, Henry Clay joined Biddle and Webster in dismissing the veto's importance. In Congress, he branded it as another sign of the "military chieftain's" dictatorial ambitions. More fundamentally, Clay incorporated the cause of the Bank into an interlocking system of proposals for the nation's future that he thought would have infinitely greater appeal than the cheap patriotism, rank class resentments, and sterile view of public liberty represented by Jackson's veto.

Clay called his program "the American System." Besides the national bank, it would consist of a high tariff to protect the nation's manufacturers and a plan to distribute the revenue from the public lands to the states, in order to finance a nationwide system of internal improvements and other reforms. If enacted, Clay's proposal would mean a wholehearted embrace of economic development by the federal government and a planned effort to promote the Market Revolution systematically across the country. Much of the plan had been implicit in Clay's earlier proposals, but the golden-tongued senator gave the program its fullest explanation in a series of speeches to Congress that were understood to be his campaign platform for the election of 1832.

Clay began with a three-day speech on the tariff in February 1832. (See Document 16.) With support from key Jacksonians, tariff levels had gone up in 1828, the last year of the Adams administration. In the meantime,

[68]Nicholas Biddle to Henry Clay, August 1, 1832, *Clay Papers,* 7:556.

southern protests against this so-called Tariff of Abominations had grown so loud that many representatives had agreed that its rates should come down, and Clay's job was to keep them as high as possible. He did so by recalling the nation's condition seven years earlier. In 1824, he reminded the Senate, Clay had offered a higher tariff to a nation in the grip of economic ruin. (See Document 6.) Now he claimed the country matched his lyrical image of the ideal state of society:

> [W]e behold cultivation extended, the arts flourishing, the face of the country improved, and our people fully and profitably employed, and the public countenance exhibiting tranquillity, contentment, and happiness. And if we descend into particulars, we have the agreeable contemplation of a people out of debt; land rising slowly in value, but in a secure and salutary degree; a ready though not extravagant market for all the surplus productions of our industry; innumerable flocks and herds browsing and gamboling on ten thousand hills and plains, covered with rich and verdant grasses; our cities expanded, and whole villages springing up, as it were, by enchantment; our exports and imports increased and increasing; our tonnage, foreign and coastwise, swelling and fully occupied; the rivers of our interior animated by the perpetual thunder and lightning of countless steamboats; the currency sound and abundant; the public debt of two wars nearly redeemed; and, to crown all, the public treasury overflowing, embarrassing Congress, not to find subjects of taxation, but to select the objects which shall be liberated from the impost.

Proudly, Clay attributed the country's prosperity to the success of the tariff and boasted that none of the evil effects predicted by the southern opponents of high tariffs had come true. Warming to his subject, Clay declared that the constitutionality of the tariff was "not debatable" and taunted Vice President John C. Calhoun, who presided over the Senate and now rejected protection on constitutional grounds, for having supported the Tariff of 1816. He denounced the notion of "free trade" and declared that since other nations would always discriminate against American products, excessive reduction of the tariff would only subordinate America to its foreign rivals, especially to the neocolonial ambitions of Great Britain. Clay also went to great lengths to prove that the tariff was not injurious to its southern opponents, but as always, his closing arguments did not rest on simple calculations of profit and loss. He insisted that protection was just as important to manufacturing states as free trade was to South Carolina and appealed to common principles of union and compromise to protect the great interests of both, holding out the promise that tariff revenues could be lessened when the national debt was finally repaid.

Like Clay, Jackson had supported the general principle of tariff protection and had used a portion of the Maysville veto to reiterate his position. Jackson was more sensitive to the needs of tariff opponents, however, and his spokesmen in Congress worked hard for compromise rates midway between the high levels demanded by Clay and the extreme cuts sought by South Carolinians. Bending to presidential pressure, Congress complied by reducing the existing tariff while leaving its basic protectionist features intact. Pleased by the reductions, Jackson signed the measure on July 14, 1832, four days after issuing his Bank veto.

A second major feature of the American System, as Clay presented it, was a special policy for the sale of the public lands. The nation had acquired vast acreage from the purchases of Louisiana and Florida, and its established policy was to privatize the public domain by selling individual tracts to private buyers. Led by Senator Thomas Hart Benton of Missouri, some politicians were concerned that land prices were too high. At current prices, only wealthy planters and speculators could afford to buy. Snapping up the choicest sections, they left large portions of "refuse" land unsold and beyond the reach of the poor farmer who would be happy to purchase a lesser-quality tract for a lower price. To preserve equal opportunity for the landless yeoman and to hasten the settlement of the western states, Senator Benton proposed to "graduate" the prices of public lands by reducing the cost of unsold tracts to fit the pocketbooks of the poorest purchasers. Clay was deeply opposed to such a policy and advanced an alternative as a companion proposition to his campaign for a high tariff.

In a report from his Committee on Manufactures (and in a subsequent speech to the Senate), Clay advanced a policy he called "distribution." Instead of cutting the price of public land to giveaway levels, Clay asked that prices remain high. For him, rapid settlement of the West or securing a farm to everyone who wanted one was less important than making sure that public resources were not wasted. Instead of using revenue from land sales for ordinary expenses, however, Clay asked that it be distributed to the states in proportion to their "federal population" (that is, all the free people and three-fifths of the slaves). The states could then use the money for a variety of worthy purposes, including "education, internal improvement, or colonization [of free blacks]."[69]

As Clay presented it in the spring and summer preceding the election of 1832, the American System consisted of three interlocking parts—a

---

[69]"Report on the Public Lands," *Register of Debates in Congress*, 22nd Cong., 1st sess., Appendix, 117.

high protective tariff to promote industrialization, distribution of the proceeds of the sale of public lands to finance internal improvements, and a strong national bank to supervise the financial system and to control the nation's credit system. In the eyes of Jacksonians, the program was an anathema. Southerners despised the tariff, and Jackson himself had sought reductions in the Tariff of 1832. In the Maysville veto, Jackson had hinted that something like distribution might be acceptable to him, but Jacksonians now retreated from the proposal. As they saw it, Clay's policy of distribution would lead to an expensive program of internal improvements (not to mention risky experiments with free blacks), financed on the broken backs of American yeomen who desperately needed to reestablish themselves on cheap public lands. As for the Bank of the United States, Jackson's veto had said all there was to say on that subject forever.

The election of 1832 thus took shape as a clash between Clay's and Jackson's rival views of democracy and public policy. The simplest and most visible issue was the Bank veto, and Jacksonians played it for all it was worth. As one administration paper put it, "The Jackson cause is the cause of democracy and the people, against a corrupt and abandoned aristocracy," and thousands of Jackson voters accepted this analysis at face value.[70] Though the National Republicans took advantage of the new device of a national political convention to nominate Clay, they were still averse to the most popular forms of campaign activity and did not pull together as a well-coordinated political party. Clay himself pursued the presidency much as he had in 1824, writing letters to his friends and counting on the support of leading citizens. Jacksonians responded with parades, rallies, barbecues, and exuberant public entertainment. In the end, Clay reduced Jackson's share of the popular vote by 1.5 percentage points below the results in 1828, but Jackson still won the election by a landslide, with 219 electoral votes to 49 for Clay, 41 for William Wirt, and 11 for John Floyd.

Despite his landslide, Jackson's reelection did not fully settle the outstanding public issues before the country. The Bank was still in existence, and Congress might make another effort to recharter it. South Carolina, moreover, was outraged by Congress's failure to significantly lower the tariff. In his Bank veto, Jackson had warned that special favors to regional interests could undermine the Union. Soon after the election, that prediction began to come true, as South Carolina began to take steps to overthrow the tariff policy so beloved by Henry Clay.

---

[70]Quoted in Schlesinger and Israel, *American Presidential Elections*, 1:509.

Carolina leaders like Vice President John C. Calhoun explained to southern audiences that a protective tariff reduced America's purchases of foreign goods and thus automatically reduced foreigners' ability to purchase American products like cotton. In their view, protection inevitably benefited manufacturing states at the expense of agricultural and exporting states, and since they felt that justice required that all states be treated equally, they concluded that the protective tariff was inherently unfair. Going further, they argued that the Constitution permitted taxes only to fund the government and not to steer the economy or to favor some states at the expense of others. Revenue tariffs were therefore permissible, they admitted, but the protective tariff was blatantly unconstitutional.

South Carolinians were particularly worried about the tariff because generations of settlement had already depleted the fertility of their lands, and emigrants were already streaming out of the state in search of richer soils to the west. Together with the lingering effects of the Panic of 1819, emigration eroded the land values of those who remained and contributed to a general appearance of economic decline throughout the Southeast. The prospect of encroaching poverty was especially frightening to the aristocrats of South Carolina, who lived surrounded by large African American majorities and were not accustomed to frustration or contradiction. If their plantation economy went bankrupt, who would control the black population? Obsessively, even at times hysterically, South Carolina extremists began to argue that the federal tariff was worse than unconstitutional: it was a threat to slavery and to white supremacy. As South Carolina Governor James Hamilton, Jr. put it to a public meeting in Columbia, "The same doctrines *'of the general welfare'* which enable the general government to tax our industry, for the benefit of the industry of other sections of this Union, and to appropriate the common treasure to make roads and canals for them, would authorize the federal government to erect the *peaceful* standard of servile revolt, by establishing colonization offices in our State, to give their bounties for emancipation here, and transportation to Liberia afterwards." Surrender on the question of internal improvements and the tariff would automatically lead to federal interference with slavery, the governor predicted: "The last question follows our giving up the battle on the other two, as inevitably as light flows from the sun."[71] The crisis was so severe, some South Carolinians argued, that the very principle of majority rule should be discarded. Congressman

---

[71] Gov. James Hamilton, Jr., to John Taylor et al., September 14, 1830, *Charleston Mercury,* September 29, 1830, reprinted in William W. Freehling, ed., *The Nullification Era: A Documentary Record* (New York: Harper & Row, 1967), 100–01.

George McDuffie gave vent to this outraged conclusion in a speech that the newspapers reported with all his accompanying sound effects:

> Sir, South Carolina is oppressed [a thump]. A tyrant majority sucks her life blood from her [a dreadful thump]. Yes, sir [a pause], yes, sir, a tyrant [a thump] majority unappeased [arms aloft], unappeasable [horrid scream], has persecuted and persecutes us [a stamp on the floor]. We appeal to them [low and quick] but we appeal to them in vain [loud and quick]. . . . We work with them; we fight with them; we vote with them; we petition with them [common voice and manner]; but the tyrant majority has no ears, no eyes, no form [quick], deaf [long pause], sightless [pause], inexorable [slow, slow]. Despairing [a thump], we resort to the rights [a pause] which God [a pause] and nature has given us [thump, thump, thump]. . . .[72]

Ultimately, it was this rejection of majority rule by the antitariff extremists that would most alarm Andrew Jackson and lead him to uncompromising hostility to their cause.

Vice President John C. Calhoun was the intellectual leader of the South Carolina protesters. Rigid, brilliant, and obsessed by the logic of constitutional reasoning, Calhoun had once been a fervent nationalist and War Hawk who had supported measures like tariff protection and internal improvements for the sake of national defense and national unity. With the passage of the Tariff of Abominations, however, he became convinced that northerners would push the principle of protection so far that slaveholding interests could be destroyed. He also feared that his fellow South Carolinians would throw him over for a more radical leader if he did not keep pace with their escalating outrage, so in 1828 he had polished some ideas already circulating in his state and presented them in an anonymously published essay called "The South Carolina Exposition."

South Carolinians called the plan "nullification" or "state interposition," and Calhoun saw it as a constitutional response that one oppressed state could make to the unconstitutional behavior of a federal majority. He argued that the Union was a compact of states and insisted that the states alone had final authority to decide whether the terms of the compact were being observed. If an aggrieved state could get no relief through regular channels, it could call a special state convention comparable to the state conventions that had ratified the U.S. Constitution,

---

[72] *Columbia Telescope*, April 16, 1833, quoted in William W. Freehling, *Prelude to Civil War: The Nullification Crisis in South Carolina, 1816–1836* (New York: Harper & Row, 1965), 147.

proclaim an obnoxious federal law unconstitutional, and therefore find it null, void, and unenforceable within its borders. The state's obstruction of federal law would obviously provoke a test case in the courts, but it would also force the other states to respond to the minority's complaints. They could resolve the problem by calling another federal convention to clarify the Constitution's language, but if they refused to make an adjustment, the minority state or states could secede from the Union.

Initially, Calhoun and his fellow South Carolinians had taken heart from Jackson's successful election in 1828. They clearly hoped that Jackson would press for repeal of the oppressive Tariff of Abominations, but Calhoun's rising personal conflicts with Jackson were not encouraging. First came Jackson's belief that Calhoun had encouraged his wife to ostracize Peggy Eaton, the wife of the secretary of war, and then Van Buren's friends revealed to Jackson that Calhoun, while secretary of war under President Monroe, had favored Jackson's censure in the crisis over the First Seminole War. Calhoun had always led Jackson to believe that he had been a loyal supporter in that supersensitive controversy, and the truth destroyed all Jackson's trust in his vice president. When the election of 1832 arrived, it would be Martin Van Buren, not Calhoun, who held the second spot on the administration's ticket.

When the new tariff bill provided only modest relief in 1832, Calhoun faced up to his hopeless position in Washington. He resigned as vice president and accepted a seat in the U.S. Senate to carry South Carolina's battle to the floor of Congress. Following his constitutional tutelage, South Carolina called a special state convention that solemnly proclaimed the Tariffs of 1828 and 1832 to be null and void in South Carolina, beginning on February 1, 1833. To give teeth to its actions, the convention authorized the legislature to pass laws punishing federal officials who tried to collect the tariff in South Carolina and required all state officials, including judges and jurors, to swear an oath to support the ordinance of nullification. If a case involving the tariff came before the courts, a verdict for the nullifiers would thus be a foregone conclusion. South Carolina's actions naturally provoked a furious confrontation with the federal government.

Clay and Jackson each played pivotal roles in the nullification controversy, but each acted somewhat differently from what might have been expected. Everything about Clay's record predisposed the Kentuckian to fight the nullification movement tooth and nail, except his preference for the compromise of clashing interests for the sake of the Union and his tendency to regard all the enemies of Andrew Jackson as potential friends. In this case, Jackson too had endorsed the tariff, but mostly for the sake of the national defense and the national debt and not for Clay's long-term purpose of transforming the American economy. Like Calhoun, Jackson was a cotton planter whose traditional constituents thought protective tariffs were unreasonable and oppressive; normally he might be tempted to sympathize with the South Carolinians.

But nullification was not a normal procedure, and as usual with Jackson, personal factors intersected with larger matters of policy. In the first place, nullification was Calhoun's darling, and Jackson had come to hate Calhoun as an ambitious conspirator whose main object was to disgrace Jackson and make himself president instead. Second, Jackson viewed South Carolina's attempt at tariff nullification as an assault on democracy, the Union, and majority rule. In his view, the federal Constitution and the government it established were not a compact of states but the creation of the whole American people. Defiance of the federal government's legitimate authority was defiance of the people's will, and Jackson would not stand for that. Because he was the elected president, and even more, because of a deep emotional identification that predated his election, Jackson saw himself as the personal representative and defender of the American people. As such, he would not be bullied by anybody, even by the leaders of his native state.

While not committing himself to any particular level of tariff protection, Jackson responded to nullification by insisting on the supremacy of federal law. In his fourth annual message, submitted to Congress in December 1832, he began by acknowledging that the national debt was almost repaid, so the existing tariff rates might well be lowered again. Applying the language of republicanism and the lessons he had recently drawn in the Bank veto, he pointed out that federal legislation for special interests was dangerous, not only because it could "beget . . . a spirit of discontent and jealousy dangerous to the stability of the Union" but also because it could "concentrate wealth into a few hands, and . . . [create] those germs of dependence and vice . . . so destructive of liberty and the general good." Even while Jackson recognized the legitimacy of South Carolina's grievances, however, he gently warned that the existing tariff was still a legitimate federal law and he would insist on its uniform enforcement.[73]

When Jackson asked Congress for a lower tariff, his manner was so soothing that many observers thought he had caved in. The following week, however, Jackson addressed a different message to South Carolina itself and his tone changed completely. On December 10, 1832, he issued

---

[73]Fourth Annual Message, December 4, 1832, Richardson, *Messages and Papers,* 3:599.

a "Proclamation" that was intended as a reasoned reply to the arguments of the nullifiers. (See Document 17.)

Drawing on the drafting skills of his adviser Edward Livingston, Jackson's Proclamation used simple, forceful language to argue that nullification was illogical and absurd and implied that South Carolina intended to secede from the Union. While Jackson admitted that some unnamed future outrage might morally justify a revolution against the U.S. government, he rejected the idea of a peaceful and voluntary rupture of the Union. Using language that anticipated Abraham Lincoln's response to the secession crisis in the next generation, Jackson declared that "the Constitution of the United States, then, forms a *government,* not a league" and that "disunion by armed force is *treason.*" Evoking a host of patriotic images of national unity and Revolutionary pride, he called on South Carolinians to rejoin their fellow citizens. If they did not, Andrew Jackson left no doubt that he would use armed force to preserve the Union and enforce the law.

For many loyal Democrats who opposed nullification, especially Jackson's fellow southerners, it was a frightening message that exceeded conventional wisdom about the perpetuity and supremacy of the federal government. Jackson immediately backed it with a request to Congress for a "Force Bill" authorizing him to raise troops and use them to execute the revenue laws. To avoid such a necessity, however, he also asked permission to collect federal tariffs on government ships stationed outside the ports of entry, which would make it impossible for South Carolina officials to interfere. To show that he was still open to compromise, moreover, Jackson supported a proposal by Representative Gulian C. Verplanck of New York that would lower tariff rates. He obviously hoped that the fear of bloodshed and the prospect of tariff relief would combine to bring South Carolina to its senses. Defending his state in the Senate, Calhoun actually hoped for a compromise that would lower the tariff, avoid war, and leave South Carolina within the Union. Compromise would not be easy, however, since crucial material interests seemed to hang in the balance. To complicate matters further, most of the major players in this drama were proud men with big egos who could take their differences to the dueling grounds (or the battlefield, if it came to that) before submitting to a loss of face.

There were also the sincere protectionists to think about. Daniel Webster, the towering champion of New England's interests, leaped to embrace the president's constitutional doctrines but vowed to block any effort to reduce the tariff. Of all the members of the Senate, Henry Clay was the only one with the will, the tact, and the prestige to negotiate a compromise, but he had built his entire career around the cause of tariff protection. Would he dismantle a key provision of his American System to avoid the threat of civil war?

The Verplanck bill would cut the tariff right away but maintain a modest level of protection thereafter. With Calhoun's support, Clay proposed instead to lower the tariff very gradually for nine more years and then reduce it quickly and more steeply, until the tariff levels in 1842 would be fixed at 20 percent, the level the government needed for ordinary revenue. In other words, Clay proposed to give the manufacturers almost one more decade of protection to put themselves on a fully competitive footing and then to withdraw the privilege altogether. Calhoun preferred this solution, believing that it offered the South a better deal in the long run than Verplanck's policy of continued moderate protection.

As usual, Clay made a powerful speech on behalf of his ideas and stressed the compatibility of the nation's different interests and the horrors of civil war. (See Document 18.) In Charleston, the nullifiers agreed to extend their deadline to give compromise a chance to pass, and after weeks of negotiating, cajoling, and arm twisting, the House and Senate passed Clay's Compromise Tariff in February 1833. Jackson signed it into law on March 2, 1833, two days before his second inauguration. For good measure, Congress also passed his bill for the distribution of the proceeds of the public lands before adjourning, but Jackson killed the measure with the nation's first pocket veto. To everyone's relief, South Carolina accepted the compromise and rescinded its ordinance of nullification in mid-March, and the crisis was over.

FOUR MORE YEARS

Andrew Jackson began his second term soon afterward, on March 4, 1833. The Union had been saved, and the most extreme proponents of states' rights and the protective tariff had both retreated for the sake of compromise. Clay received most of the credit, however, and resentments lingered over Jackson's earlier policies, including the Bank veto, the Force Bill, and the pocket veto of distribution. Most especially, the continuing problem of the Bank of the United States undermined any hopes for peace and harmony during Jackson's second term.

Jackson's veto had killed the Bank's new charter, but the old charter had not expired yet, so the BUS remained in business. Its friends still hoped that a second attempt at recharter might pass by a veto-proof majority, and they hoped for a favorable set of returns from the next congressional elections. For his part, Andrew Jackson began to fear that the existing Bank might use its immense funds to bribe representatives and manipulate elections in order to produce a pliable Congress. "The hydra of corruption is only *scotched, not dead*," he warned intimates, and moved to finish the job the veto had only begun.[74]

The U.S. government was the biggest depositor in the Bank of the United States. By its charter, the Bank was entitled to the government's deposits unless the secretary of the treasury (*not* the president) ruled otherwise. If he removed the deposits, the secretary was required to report his reasons to Congress. Louis McLane, the incumbent secretary of the treasury, opposed the idea of removal, but he would soon be moving to the State Department. Despite the law governing the deposits, Jackson came to believe that he had the authority as president to order their removal and that if he did so, the Bank would have insufficient funds to corrupt Congress. With no federal deposits, the Bank would therefore die for certain, and the effect of the veto would be safe. Though Congress had recently pronounced the Bank a safe repository, Jackson decided in the spring of 1833 that the government deposits must be removed and assumed without much reflection that the new secretary of the treasury, William J. Duane, would do as he was told.

The president developed his new policy slowly, first sending his trusted political operative Amos Kendall on a national tour to identify alternative banks where the government's money would be safe. By autumn, he was ready to direct the secretary of the treasury to begin the process of transfer but found to his intense irritation that Secretary Duane refused to act. Duane opposed recharter of the BUS, but he worried about the wisdom of entrusting the government's money to the state banks. Above all, he insisted that he was not simply a tool of the president but an independent official with responsibility to Congress. After weeks of patient negotiation over the summer of 1833, Duane refused to withdraw the deposits and also refused to resign.

To explain his position definitely, Jackson prepared a paper that he had read to the cabinet on September 18, 1833. Most other members of the cabinet joined Duane in his doubts as to the wisdom or legality of deposit removal, and Jackson pointed out to them once more that he had long opposed the Bank, that the Bank had sought recharter in 1832 in order to swing the presidential election, and that the Bank had expanded its loans, especially to pliable newspaper editors, "to bring as large a portion of the people as possible under its influence." Despite these menacing

---

[74]Andrew Jackson to James K. Polk, December 16, 1832, *Jackson Correspondence*, 4:501.

steps, the president had issued his veto and appealed the case to the voters. They had sustained him. Still influenced by a deferential view of politics, in which voters submitted to the wisdom of their leaders, the cabinet was dismayed to hear Jackson claim that the election of 1832 had not simply been a personal choice of leaders but a plebiscite on the Bank. "On that ground the case was argued to the people; and now the people have sustained the President, notwithstanding the array of influence and power which was brought to bear on him, it is too late . . . to say that the question has not been decided." Because the Bank would soon cease to exist, it was only prudent to seek a new depository for the government's money.[75]

Stubbornly, Duane still refused to comply, so Jackson decided he had no choice but to fire him and bring in someone more cooperative. Attorney General Roger B. Taney became the new secretary of the treasury, and he went to work right away because the Senate was not in session and his confirmation could wait. Beginning on October 1, 1833, the United States began to make all its normal withdrawals from its accounts in the Bank of the United States but placed its new deposits of revenue in five regional banks (soon dubbed "pets" by the furious opposition), continuing the process until its accounts in the BUS were exhausted.

The veto had been controversial, but nothing Andrew Jackson ever did was so widely condemned as deposit removal. The action seemed to many observers a direct violation of the Bank's charter rights and a virtual assertion that the president was above the law. Critics howled that Congress, not the president, should hold ultimate control of the nation's money and that Jackson's action was a gross usurpation of power. Congressmen, editors, and public meetings warned that the president's seizure of "the purse and the sword" was the logical precursor of a dictatorship and that the establishment of pet banks was a far greater source of corruption than the behavior of the BUS. Even within the Democratic Party, many senior leaders questioned the wisdom of deposit removal, but those who wished to remain in Old Hickory's good graces knew better than to voice their criticisms publicly.

Protests only escalated as Nicholas Biddle began to respond to the shift in policy. Without government deposits, the Bank could not make as many loans, but Biddle determined to reduce his lending to the utmost in order to put public pressure on the president. Businessmen who needed credit in order to conduct their affairs would suffer losses, lay off

---

[75]"Removal of the Public Deposits," September 18, 1833, Richardson, *Messages and Papers*, 3:1224–38.

employees, and petition Congress for relief. The pressure of hard times would thus knock some sense into the demagogic politicians who dared to tamper with the Bank of the United States. "Nothing but the evidence of suffering abroad will produce any effect in Congress," he confided to a trusted correspondent. "All the other Banks and all the merchants may break, but the Bank of the United States shall not break," he told another.[76]

Protesting businessmen soon bombarded Washington with petitions and delegations. Jackson received his angry visitors with as much patience as he could, but he firmly believed that the complainers were merely the dupes or corrupted tools of the Bank's ambition. "Go to Nicholas Biddle!" he roared at one party of supplicants. "We have no money, here, gentlemen. Biddle has all the money. He has millions of specie in his vaults, at this moment, lying idle, and yet you come to *me* to save you from breaking. I tell you, gentlemen, it's all politics."[77]

Deposit removal galvanized the president's enemies and encouraged silent dissenters to come out in vocal opposition. Many who would not defend the Bank itself, or who had acquiesced in the veto in hopes of passing another charter later, drew the line at Jackson's attempt to defy the law, override Congress, bully the secretary of the treasury, and seize personal control of the government's money. As Senator Willie P. Mangum of North Carolina put it, "The question is not, nor ever was, 'bank or no bank.' The question was emphatically, 'law or no law — constitution or no constitution.' "[78] Like many of the new critics, Mangum was a nominal Jacksonian who had long been uneasy about the president's claims of centralized power. Nullification had been so unpopular in North Carolina that Mangum had not dared to break with the president over that issue, but he welcomed deposit removal as a credible public excuse to renounce an administration he had privately rejected much earlier.

Seeing his opportunity, Henry Clay stepped quickly to lead the opposition and to articulate their outrage in terms that could unify the Bank's old friends among the National Republicans with new critics from among the president's former supporters. His celebrated speech on deposit removal, launched on the day after Christmas 1833, stressed the lawless

[76]Nicholas Biddle to William Appleton, January 27, 1834; Nicholas Biddle to J. G. Watmough, February 8, 1834, quoted in Arthur M. Schlesinger, Jr., *The Age of Jackson* (Boston: Little, Brown, 1945), 103.

[77]Quoted in James Parton, *Life of Andrew Jackson,* 3 vols. (New York: Mason Brothers, 1861), 3:549–50.

[78]*Register of Debates,* 23rd Cong., 1st sess., 272.

and dictatorial dimensions of the president's actions and not their harmful effects on the Bank itself. (See Document 19.)

Clay began by introducing a pair of resolutions condemning deposit removal. The first declared that Jackson's dismissal of Secretary Duane was "the exercise of a power over the treasury of the United States not granted to him by the Constitution and laws, and dangerous to the liberties of the people." The second criticized the reasons for removal given by the new secretary, Roger B. Taney, as "unsatisfactory and insufficient." The senator made clear, however, that his biggest complaint was not the treatment of the Bank but Jackson's efforts to enlarge the powers of the presidency. "We are in the midst of a revolution," he cried, "hitherto bloodless, but rapidly tending toward a total change of the pure republican character of the government, and to the concentration of power in the hands of one man." He continued, "In a term of eight years . . . , the government will have been changed into an elective monarchy—the worst of all forms of government."

Clay's argument for the first resolution rested on the idea that the secretary of the treasury was legally accountable to the Congress and not to the president. While the president appointed the secretary, the Senate confirmed him, and he made his reports directly to the Congress. Clay concluded that the law thus gave Congress ultimate control over the Treasury Department and that Jackson had no right to fire one secretary and install another in order to find a subordinate who would do his bidding. This portion of the speech was a direct reply to the argument Jackson had made in the paper he had read to the cabinet, asserting that the president had final authority over the executive departments and that the results of the 1832 election were a binding popular mandate against the conduct of the Bank. Jackson's position paper had declared that he had acted in order "to preserve the morals of the people, the freedom of the press, and the purity of the elective franchise," but Clay only snorted with disgust. "Morals of the people! What part of the Constitution has given to the president any power over 'the morals of the people'? None. . . . No, sir, it gives him no such power." Would the president next claim power over "the religion of the people"?

On the second day of his philippic, Clay dissected in great detail the official reasons given by Secretary Taney for deposit removal. One by one he rejected them all, from the claim that the coming expiration of the charter demanded some action, to the claim of a public mandate from the last election, to various claims that the Bank had acted illegally or corruptly. But Clay's conclusion did not depend on technical details. His fundamental argument was that the direct election of the president did not give Jackson broad power to act in the name of the people but that he was bound instead by existing laws and interpretations of the Constitution to act in cooperation with the other senior leaders of the country. The alternative was not democracy, in Clay's opinion, but dictatorship. It was not Jackson but his opponents, Clay insisted, who were the true defenders of the country's republican traditions. He warned in conclusion, "The premonitory symptoms of despotism are upon us; and if Congress do not apply an instantaneous and effective remedy, the fatal collapse will soon come on, and we shall die—ignobly die! base, mean, and abject slaves—the scorn and contempt of mankind—unpitied, unwept, unmourned!"

The House of Representatives was firmly in Jacksonian hands, but Clay's resolutions of censure became the central preoccupation of the Senate in the so-called Panic session in the winter of 1833 to 1834. Because the resolutions condemned Jackson for an abuse of power and a violation of the Constitution, the president and his supporters called them an unwarranted attempt at impeachment—a responsibility of the House, not the Senate. Undeterred by this legalistic objection, one senator after another rose throughout the winter to condemn or defend Jackson's actions. It was not long before the president's critics reached back into history and began to call themselves "Whigs," after the party in British politics (and the American Revolution) that had always resisted the expansion of the powers of the Crown. To complete the analogy, Whig editors and cartoonists began to call the president "King Andrew the First." (See Figure 7.) The name "Whig" then appeared as a popular party label in the New York City municipal elections that spring, and by the fall Whigs were contesting local elections in many parts of the country as an organized opposition party. Over the next couple of years, the Whig coalition emerged nationwide, even in places where the National Republicans had never been viable, and a stable, two-party political system began to dominate American elections as never before.

A modified version of Clay's resolution finally passed in March 1834, and Jackson quickly defended himself in an official "Protest" against the Senate resolutions. (See Document 20.) Describing the charge of constitutional violation as an impeachable offense, Jackson denied the power of the Senate to impeach him and protested that he had been condemned without trial. He reiterated once more the reasons for his order to the secretary of the treasury: The Bank was corrupt; it attempted to manipulate the electoral process; it purchased editors and violated its charter; and it generally conducted itself in contempt of public and lawful authority. Under the circumstances, it was the president's undoubted right and

Figure 7. King Andrew the First

Clay and his supporters viewed Jackson's war on the Bank of the United States as "executive usurpation" and an abuse of power. Counterattacking, they tried to associate Jackson with the ambitions of a monarch and called themselves "Whigs" after the party in British politics that traditionally resisted the prerogatives of the Crown. Copyright © Collection of the New York Historical Society.

duty to remove the secretary and replace him with someone who would bring the Bank to heel. In other words, Jackson utterly rejected Clay's argument that he lacked the power to remove his cabinet officers at will. As he put it, "The whole executive power being vested in the President, who is responsible for its exercise, it is a necessary consequence that he should have a right to employ agents of his own choice to aid him in the performance of his duties, and to discharge them when he is no longer willing to be responsible for their acts." For a man who had always claimed to believe in limited government, it was a sweeping assertion of authority.

Jackson went even further. "The President is the direct representative of the American people," he boldly declared, "but the Secretaries are not." If the president had no power over the public purse, the people had none either, and that supposition was intolerable in a democracy. Because the president was the only officer directly elected by the whole people, he alone had the power and authority to give order and direction to the national government. Without the overriding power of the president to subject all departments of the executive branch to the mandate of the popular will, the Union and republican government itself would collapse into unbearable confusion. "At length," he worried, "some form of aristocratic power would be established on the ruins of the Constitution or the States be broken into separate communities."

Jackson thus rested his case as Clay did, claiming that his version of the case was the only salvation of the nation's republican traditions. His argument in favor of a strong presidency, morally and legally justified by an appeal to the democratic will of the whole people, broke new constitutional ground in defining the office of the president. It slowly became accepted as the prevailing view of the president's powers, but contemporary Whigs remained horrified. If the president were "the direct representative of the American people," where did that leave Congress and the courts? If a popular majority could reach over the heads of locally elected leaders and dictate national policy through a single elected despot, how could the lives and property of the minority ever be safe? If democracy meant that the president was all powerful when he acted in the name of the people, what would happen to liberty under law?

Backing down a little, Jackson later issued a statement confirming that the powers of the president must be exercised only according to the law and recognizing Congress's legitimate right to designate the place of deposit for the public money. He continued to imply, however, that the existing law was sufficiently ambiguous to allow him to do what he had done. The concession did not mollify the Whigs, who continued to brand Jackson a usurper who claimed virtually unlimited power as "the direct representative of the American people." Pointing to the elaborate system of indirect selection of the president by the Electoral College, Daniel Webster fumed that "the Constitution nowhere calls him the representative of the American people; still less their direct representative."[79] Clay himself drew on his long-standing criticism of Jackson as an untrustworthy "military chieftain" to decry the novel doctrine that all government officers were responsible to the president and subject to his orders. He called it "altogether a military idea . . . wholly incompatible with free government." Instead, he insisted, "all are responsible to the law only, or not responsible at all."[80]

Andrew Jackson's alleged abuses of power quickly emerged as the most vulnerable political target of the new Whig Party. Supporters of the tariff, the bank, and internal improvements all found there was broader opposition to Jackson's seemingly arbitrary methods than to the specific substance of his policies. Even southern nullifiers, who recoiled from the provisions of the American System, could agree that the doctrines of Jackson's Proclamation against South Carolina were shockingly "consolidationist" and justified a coalition with the Whigs. Some, like John C. Calhoun, soon broke from the coalition on the grounds that Whigs were just as undependable as Jacksonians on sectional issues, but others remained to become staunch leaders of the southern Whig Party. In preparation for the 1836 elections, local Whig organizations took shape, held meetings, nominated candidates for office, and passed resolutions against the tendencies of Andrew Jackson's presidency. The common theme throughout was that Jackson's claim to rule in the name of the people had led to arbitrary abuse of power by the man at the top and to corrupt and grotesque efforts to manipulate public opinion at the grassroots. The "Address" of the New York State Whig convention of 1836 provided a typical bill of particulars that pointed to the terrifying implications of cardinal Jacksonian doctrines like rotation in office, free use of the veto power, deposit removal, "pet" banking, and the practice of party discipline:

> The rapid advance of organized corruption; the effrontery of the minions of power grown bold by success; the unblushing avowal of detestable principles of action; the prostitution of public duty to individual interest; the perversion of offices into the means of corrupt influence and sordid profit; the preparations for the next fatal step in the downfall of free institutions, open bribery with money; thirty millions of the public funds distributed throughout the Union in irresponsible hands for party purposes; an utter and intolerable proscription, dis-

---

[79]Daniel Webster, "The Presidential Protest," May 7, 1834, in J. W. McIntyre, ed., *The Writings and Speeches of Daniel Webster*, 18 vols. (Boston: Little, Brown, 1903), 7:144.
[80]*Register of Debates*, 23rd Cong., 1st sess., 1575–81; Remini, *Henry Clay*, 465, 467.

carding from office the honest and capable, and leaving all things in the hands of those who disregard the public good in scrambling for the spoils of victory; — are not these indications, which leave no room for doubt or time for delay? Do they not exhibit a fearful rapidity of transformation in the lineaments of our free institutions?[81]

The Whigs did not attack popular democracy directly or seek a retreat from universal white male suffrage. They did deplore the Jacksonians' efforts to reach those new voters by what they regarded as illegitimate means — stirring up class resentments, constructing political machines, and bypassing the established leadership of local communities in favor of direct appeals to a mass electorate. Nor did Whig politicians forget the specific measures of economic development that Clay had assembled together in the American System. When they got the chance, they pushed those measures in state governments and later at the federal level as well. For the rest of the 1830s, however, they found that protests against "executive usurpation" worked better at the polls than demands for government aid for economic change.

While the Whigs publicly shied away from issues that might be construed as overt appeals to economic class, Jackson became ever more explicit in blaming the nation's political conflicts on the competing interests of social classes. Even before the actual removal crisis, Jackson had become convinced that a sinister elite of bankers, merchants, and "moneyed aristocrats" had laid siege to the government and had taken possession of significant portions of Congress and the press. By the summer of 1833, he had outgrown the idea that these schemers were simply the tools of one corrupt institution, the Bank of the United States, and blamed instead a whole layer of society, whom he described as "the selfish, interested classes" and "the predatory portion of the community." (See Document 21.) In a personal letter to Tilghman A. Howard, a Democratic activist from Indiana, Jackson made it plain that the men he was talking about were not just those who owned more property than others but those who formed the vanguard of the Market Revolution. By themselves, he said, the rich were not dangerous. "It is only when they can identify themselves with privileged joint stock Companies, with the Stockholders in a national Bank or the log rolling system of Internal Improvements, Squandering the taxes raised on the whole people, in benefitting particular classes and maintaining a personal influence by partial legislation in congress," Jackson observed, "that these men have the power to be mischievous." Nor did Jackson point to a single oppressed class, like Karl Marx's industrial pro-

---

[81]New York State Whig Convention of 1836, "Address to the People of New York," reprinted in Arthur M. Schlesinger, Jr., ed., *History of U.S. Political Parties,* 4 vols. (New York: Chelsea House, 1973), 1:390–96.

letariat, who were the special victims of exploitation by the "aristocracy." He focused instead on "the whole people" or the "great body of the people," who evidently included all the hardworking and enfranchised Americans who did not seek special favors from the government. Since they were inevitably the majority, these good citizens could always keep the scoundrel minority at bay, if only they would work and vote together.

How could this be done? Here General Jackson fell back on his military experience. He remembered that "the *trained Band*" would always triumph over the "undisciplined classes of the community," just as regular troops would always triumph over a militia, unless the citizen-soldiers were as rigorously trained and disciplined as his Tennesseans had been at New Orleans. Like militiamen, the masses must be drilled and disciplined in order to protect their liberties. He commended to Tilghman A. Howard the system practiced by Pennsylvania (and also by Van Buren's New York) of holding regular political party conventions and using them to require all good Democrats to support the policies and the nominees of the party. In practice, this meant that if a local Democratic faction disliked a party nominee for a certain position, they must never run an alternative candidate who might split the Democratic vote and allow the Whigs to win. Any Democrat who did such a thing must be read out of the party, just as a mutinous militiaman might be shot by his own commander. As one Van Buren lieutenant had told his followers during New York's campaigns of the 1820s, "They are safe if they face the enemy, but . . . the first man we see *step to the rear*, we *cut down*. . . . They *must* not falter, or they perish."[82] Only by suppressing private preferences and submitting to the wisdom of the party majority could the people's political army stay in office and enforce what Jackson called "the great radical principle of freedom—equality among the people in the rights conferred by the Government."

Later on in his administration, Jackson became even more specific and laid out his support for strict party discipline even more thoroughly in an 1835 letter to Joseph Conn Guild of Tennessee. (See Document 22.) Even in Jackson's home state, Whig opponents had emerged to challenge Democratic control of Jackson's succession by nominating for president a former Jacksonian, Judge Hugh Lawson White, who claimed to be more faithful to Jackson's original principles than the party nominee, Vice President Martin Van Buren. Jackson wrote to Guild to express his opposition to Judge White's apostasy and to insist on the importance of a strong party movement to link the president and the people:

---

[82]Silas Wright, quoted in Richard Hofstadter, *The Idea of a Party System: The Rise of Legitimate Opposition in the United States, 1780–1840* (Berkeley: University of California Press, 1972), 244.

No one can carry on this Govt. without support, and the Head of it must rely for support on the party by whose suffrages he is elected, or, he must betray the expectations of those who invest him with power to obtain support from their adversaries. . . .

. . . I have long believed, that it was only by preserving the identity of the Republican party as embodied and characterized by the principles introduced by Mr. Jefferson that the original rights of the states and the people could be maintained as contemplated by the Constitution. I have labored to reconstruct this great Party and bring the popular power to bear with full influence upon the Government, by securing its permanent ascendancy.

Contemporaries were right, therefore, when they charged that the Democrats were more ruthless and dedicated in party organization than the Whigs. For the Democrats, following Jackson himself, strict party discipline was essential to the preservation of democracy, and this conviction flowed directly from their class analysis of the nation's circumstances. Without apology, they plunged into the culture of public rallies, torchlight parades, and committees of vigilance to bring every Democratic voter to the polls. (See Figure 8.) They energetically organized county, state, and national conventions to choose their nominees to public office, and they firmly insisted that good Democrats must support the party's nominees or be expelled from party fellowship. The Whigs, by contrast, turned to party mechanisms as a form of self-defense and never felt entirely comfortable with populist hoopla or the subordination of private judgment to collective decisions. From time to time, especially in the raucous presidential election of 1840, when the symbol of the log cabin and the lavish consumption of hard cider became tests of party spirit, the Whigs could put on as grand a spectacle as anyone, but they mostly preferred to think of themselves as dedicated to principle over what they regarded as mindless fanaticism.

The Democrats were hardly devoid of principle themselves, however, and the doctrines they carried into state and national government evolved directly from the epic battles of Jackson's presidency. More thoroughly and convincingly than the Whigs, they upheld the values of popular democracy and majority rule, championing broader suffrage for white men and the power of voters to control their representatives with binding instructions. They were much more receptive than Whigs to the influx of European immigrants to America and quickly welcomed the newcomers to the privileges of citizenship, but they strictly drew the color line against the claims of nonwhite Americans. Whigs were far more tolerant of voting rights for racial minorities than the Jacksonian Democrats. Partly as a consequence, the white immigrants of the 1830s, especially the large numbers of German and Irish Catholics, streamed into Democratic party

Figure 8. *The County Election, 1851–1852,* **by George Caleb Bingham**
The formation of the Whig and Democratic Parties led to a dramatic expansion
of voter turnout in presidential and local elections, as voters got an opportunity
to participate in clear-cut contests that linked national debates with local issues
like banking and internal improvements. Notice how the artist shows the wide
range of popular involvement in the election, from the sober conversation of the
farmers on the right, to the anxious courtesy of the office seeker tipping his hat,
to the stupor of the drunken voter on the left.

ranks, but the few African American men who enjoyed the right to vote
in Jacksonian America almost invariably cast their ballots for the Whigs.

In Congress and most of the state legislatures, Democrats also opposed
the grant of charters to business corporations as well as subsidies for internal improvement or other government assistance to the forces of economic
development. They favored limited government and states' rights, adopting as a party slogan "the best government is that which governs least."
Never seriously considering the argument advanced by twentieth-century

Democrats that strong government could protect the "common man" from excessively powerful private interests, Jacksonian Democrats consistently opposed government interventions in the marketplace because they were convinced that such actions would benefit only the "moneyed aristocracy." They did not favor weak government in order to give private interests free rein; they supported weak government in order to starve and undermine the corporate interests they feared would attack republicanism. While Democrats cheered as President Jackson did his best to strengthen the institution of the presidency, most did so because they knew he wanted to use his power to prevent economic and social change or even to reverse it. As Henry Clay put it bitterly in a speech against Jackson's "Protest" message, "Except an enormous fabric of Executive power for himself, the President has built up nothing, constructed nothing, and will leave no enduring monument of his administration. He goes for destruction, universal destruction; and it seems to be his greatest ambition to efface and obliterate every trace of the wisdom of his predecessors."[83]

In the years after 1834, Whigs continued to fume over Jackson's policies, and Democrats continued to glorify their champion, but the great ideological currents of the Jackson administration had crested in the deposit removal crisis. The federal deposits did not return to the BUS, and the Bank's federal charter expired on schedule in 1836. The Bank won a reprieve, however, in the form of a charter from the state of Pennsylvania and continued to function as a large state bank for several years thereafter. The minipanic caused by Nicholas Biddle's contraction of credit quickly passed as the "pet" banks used the federal deposits as the basis for new loans to take the place of those denied by the BUS, and many charged that credit became even easier under the new system than the old.

Businesses certainly prospered in 1835 and 1836, and speculation in the public lands surged once more, igniting new fears that the banking industry as a whole could be just as corrupting as a single "monster" bank had been. In fact, the new boom was fueled by generous British credit, a rising demand for cotton in Europe, and changes in the world bullion market that were little known or understood in American political circles.[84] Still struggling to understand the complex operation of a modern market economy, American leaders understandably preferred to explain contemporary events as part of the recent drama of the Bank war and in terms that seemed meaningful to their own constituents, rather than turning to seemingly extraneous factors from abroad.

---

[83]*Register of Debates*, 23rd Cong., 1st sess., 1559, 1564, 1575–81.
[84]Peter Temin, *The Jacksonian Economy* (New York: Norton, 1969), 113–47.

In any event, President Jackson decided that the only circulating medium contemplated by the Constitution was a currency of gold and silver coins. The government should withdraw its approval of paper money by refusing to accept it as payment for public lands and by calling for the retirement of all paper bills with a face value lower than twenty dollars. He hoped these symbolic displays of the government's lack of confidence in paper money would lead people to shun it in favor of precious metals, but it was no use. Paper money banking was too popular, and speculation continued until shortly after Jackson left office. The crash came in the spring of 1837, with a sudden drop in the European price of cotton, the failure of several large cotton brokerage houses, and a rapid suspension of specie payments by American banks. The result was like 1819 all over again, with a sharp contraction in the availability of credit, widespread unemployment in the cities, numerous bankruptcies, collapsing land values, and mounting numbers of foreclosures and forced sales. After a feeble recovery, panic conditions returned in 1839 and a serious depression gripped the American economy until the mid- to late 1840s. Whigs blamed the Democrats for their reckless experiments with the currency; Democrats blamed Whigs for "over-trading and speculations," and each party grew more deeply convinced of the truth and righteousness of its own ideological analysis of the political economy of the 1830s.

In the years following the showdown over deposit removal, Jackson's Democrats continued their organizing efforts, and Jackson gave his blessing to Martin Van Buren as his chosen successor. Having spent so much energy in denouncing the Democrats for nominating candidates in "despotic" party conventions, the Whigs found it impossible to assemble a convention of their own and thus entered the 1836 election with three presidential candidates. Henry Clay was not among them, for "Prince Hal" carried too many scars from the party brawls of the last eight years. Instead, General William Henry Harrison hoisted the Whig banner in the West and the mid-Atlantic states, and Hugh Lawson White stood forth in the South, while Daniel Webster tried his luck in Massachusetts. Van Buren beat them all. He even avoided a runoff in the House of Representatives, allaying fears of another "corrupt bargain," as in 1825.

As he prepared to transmit his legacy to the triumphant Van Buren, Jackson turned his mind to history and the lessons of his presidency. Following the example of George Washington, he decided to issue a Farewell Address and asked Roger Taney, whom he had since appointed Chief Justice of the Supreme Court, to help him draft a message to the people. (See Document 23.) Jackson used the Farewell Address to sum up the great issues of his presidency, to draw some general conclusions about the lessons of the last eight years, and to offer some cautionary advice for the future. The president never delivered the "Address" in the form of a speech, but it appeared in pamphlet form on the day he left office in 1837. Though it lacked some of the rhetorical fireworks and immediate political consequences of the Bank veto, the Nullification Proclamation, or the papers related to deposit removal, the Farewell Address is the most mature and reflective statement of Jackson's political principles.

Old Hickory began by thanking the American people for their favor and confidence and congratulated them on the approaching fiftieth anniversary of the signing of the Constitution. He mentioned several important episodes of his administration that gave him special pride, including Indian removal and his successes in foreign affairs. His main thrust, however, concerned the future of liberty in America. His first premise was that the Constitution and the federal Union were essential to the preservation of American liberty and must remain permanent. The fervent and sincere nationalism that marked his earliest public statements thus reappeared in his last. "At every hazard and by every sacrifice," he solemnly declared, "this Union must be preserved."

The greatest threat to the Union, Jackson recognized, was the tension between North and South that had been so prominent in the Missouri controversy and the nullification crisis. Southern Whigs had roused it even more recently by falsely accusing Martin Van Buren of abolitionist leanings. Jackson deplored this tendency to agitate sectional questions and invoked the wisdom of George Washington to denounce it. Even more significantly, he voiced an argument that Abraham Lincoln would later express more sketchily but nevertheless memorably in the Gettysburg Address. Lincoln would point to the American founding principle of equality and call the war for the Union an effort to determine "whether that nation or any nation, so conceived and so dedicated, can long endure." Jackson made a similar point by saying that the preservation of the American Union was essential to the preservation of republicanism. Why? Because a single rupture in the Union would inevitably be followed by others, with civil war and anarchy between the remaining fragments, until the people turned to a dictator who would restore order at the price of their liberties.

For Jackson, democracy for white men was the first key to preserving the Union, and he elevated the direct voice of the majority to a nearly divine status. "Never for a moment believe," he admonished, "that the great body of the citizens of any State or States can ever deliberately intend to do wrong." The reason was simple: Wrongdoing would inevitably injure the people themselves, so "their own interest requires them to be just to others, as they hope to receive justice at their hands." For majority rule to work, however, the will of the majority must have teeth. Unjust or unconstitutional laws could be repealed by Congress or voided by the courts, but until then even bad laws represented the voice of the majority and must be obeyed by the minority. There could be no revival of nullification if the Union were to last.

Jackson did acknowledge that some future act of unspecified oppression might justify a revolution by the minority against the majority. Whether he would have regarded the election of an antislavery president like Abraham Lincoln as an oppressive act by a nonslaveholding majority against a slaveholding minority is obviously impossible to determine. Certainly many of his southern followers later saw Lincoln's election in exactly that light and seceded from the Union in 1860–61 with the firm belief that their actions were consistent with Jackson's legacy.

Whatever Old Hickory might have thought about the crisis of 1860–61, he was certainly dead set against abolitionism and moved directly from the theoretical discussion of revolution to a stern rebuke of antislavery agitation. The Union depended on fraternal harmony as much as laws, he observed, and urged his fellow citizens not to damage it by criticizing the local practices of other states. "All efforts on the part of people of other States to cast odium upon their institutions, and all measures calculated to disturb their rights of property or to put in jeopardy their peace and internal tranquillity, are in direct opposition to the spirit in which the Union was formed, and must endanger its safety." Though he stood with Lincoln for an indissoluble Union, in other words, Jackson believed in a Union where the doctrines of abolitionism would be unmentionable and slavery remained sacrosanct.

Predictably, Jackson's greatest emphasis was on economic affairs, and here too, he worried about the safety of liberty and the Union. The nullification crisis had taught him that the power of special interests to enact legislation like the tariff, which operated unequally to benefit some and burden others, was the greatest threat to the stability of the government. As long as the government operated in this unequal way, jealousies and resentments would arise that could once more lead to sectional conflict. The need to pay off the debt from two wars, the Revolution and the War of 1812, was the only possible excuse for such a policy, and that excuse had ended when Jackson, for the first and only time in U.S. history, completely paid off the national debt. With a surplus now accumulating in the federal treasury, the tariff should go even lower. The advocates of economic development would undoubtedly clamor for protective tariffs and then spend the surplus on internal improvements. Jackson thus denounced the leading principle of Clay's American System as unconstitutional and socially unjust. "The surplus revenue will be drawn from the pockets of the people," he predicted, " — from the farmer, the mechanic, and the laboring classes of society," but it would only be spent for pork barrel projects to benefit the friends of state politicians.

Having disposed of a high tariff, distribution, and internal improvements, Jackson moved on to banking policy. He insisted that the Constitution had intended a currency of gold and silver but that chartered banks had driven out this medium with unreliable paper bills that overstimulated the business cycle and led to ruinous financial panics. Cycles of boom and bust not only inflicted direct material losses, but even worse, degraded public life because they "engender a spirit of speculation injurious to the habits and character of the people." Jackson thus directed his heaviest condemnation at the market practices that had actually created his own private fortune and that motivated the thousands of hopeful and ambitious plungers in the Market Revolution. It is doubtful he was conscious of the irony, for Jackson was never prone to self-doubt or self-criticism, and he undoubtedly saw his own rise as the just reward of hard work, frugality, and careful management. He was certain, however, that what he called "this eager desire to amass wealth without labor" was undermining civic virtue and that thinkers and moralists had always known that virtue was fundamental to a republic.

Banks, of course, were the sources of this corrupting paper currency, and Jackson longed to see them eliminated. The Bank of the United States had been crushed, but the true enemy now was not the BUS or Nicholas Biddle but all those who favored a credit-based economy, those whom Jackson variously called "the moneyed power" and "the great moneyed corporations." The real danger came from a whole class of Americans who were anxious for economic change and institutional growth—the merchants, managers, stockholders, lawyers, clerks, customers, politicians, editors, depositors, borrowers, and all the rest who hoped to gain by the expansion of credit and the Market Revolution. Jackson had seen these men's influence in the numerous petitions and delegations that descended on Washington in the deposit removal crisis. No matter how numerous, however, he did not believe that bank dependents could never become "the great body of the people of the United States," whose ranks were filled by more virtuous citizens—"[t]he planter, the farmer, the mechanic, and the laborer," as he called them.

Approaching his conclusion, Jackson solemnly conjured "the bone and sinew of the country" to be watchful. "Eternal vigilance by the people is the price of liberty," he reminded them, and the majority must continue the effort to root out the paper money system once and for all. The great danger was that the people might not be morally equal to the task. Foreign enemies were no longer significant; the real danger came from the possible weakness of the people themselves. "It is from within, among yourselves—from cupidity, from corruption, from disappointed ambition and inordinate thirst for power—that factions will be formed and liberty endangered." In closing, Jackson could only hope and pray that the people would be strong enough to prevail.

The Whigs made no audible reply to the Farewell Address, but they certainly did not share its mood of mournful pessimism. The institutions Jackson had identified as subversive of liberty and virtue—banks, tariffs, and internal improvements—were those they counted on to improve and uplift America. How could a nation be free or virtuous when crippled by poverty? How could poverty be cured without growth, development, expansion, and change? For Whigs like Henry Clay, the answer seemed self-evident, and Jackson's moralizing did nothing but obscure the ways his presidency had destroyed the achievements of a rising people and glorified the ascendancy of an ignorant and frightened mob. Indeed, many Whigs prided themselves with the thought that it was their party that did the most for the country's morals, since Whigs were more likely to acknowledge the country's imperfections and demand improvements and reforms of all kinds, from new economic institutions to efforts for the promotion of temperance, literacy, evangelism, and even abolition and women's rights.

AFTERMATH

The years ahead brought no easy resolution of the debate between Democrats and Whigs, though changes in fortune and circumstance naturally came to all the leading debaters. Jackson himself retired to the Hermitage to nurse his numerous wounds and illnesses and to enjoy the assorted nieces, nephews, and their offspring who served him as surrogate children and grandchildren. He continued to advise Democratic leaders, especially his protégé Martin Van Buren, but reduced his active role in national politics. He lived long enough to see Tennessee Democrat James K. Polk win the White House in 1844 over Clay and to savor the American acquisition of Texas, just before his death on June 8, 1845, at the age of seventy-eight.

Van Buren relished the presidency Jackson had bequeathed him, but the disastrous Panic of 1837 struck the country just after he assumed office. Van Buren's response was an effort to continue Jackson's campaign against the banking industry by indirect means, asking Congress for an "Independent Treasury" that would keep the government's money without depositing it in any bank whatsoever. Democrats hoped that this tangible demonstration of the government's lack of confidence in the banks would deal the whole industry a mortal blow, while Whigs and businessmen naturally opposed the idea. They wanted sound state banks (formerly smeared as the "pets") to be able to keep using the government's deposits as the Bank of the United States had, to make loans to deserving borrowers so as to continue to stimulate the economy, and incidentally, to generate interest revenue for the banks. The Independent Treasury finally passed after prolonged congressional squabbling, but it never succeeded in eliminating paper money banking as its proponents had hoped. Van Buren did not make himself personally as popular as Jackson, and the persistence of hard times throughout his administration gave him an almost insuperable hurdle to clear when he faced the prospect of a reelection campaign in 1840.

Henry Clay spent the Van Buren years as leader of the Senate opposition, doing his best to frustrate the Democrats' wrong-headed efforts, as he saw them, to further destabilize the economy. When 1840 approached, Clay naturally hoped for the Whig nomination, but party managers were unwilling to take chances on a man who was as much despised by his enemies as loved by his friends. The nomination went instead to General William Henry Harrison of Ohio. Like Jackson, Harrison was a hero of the Indian wars, having defeated the famed Shawnee chief Tecumseh at the Battle of Tippecanoe in 1811 and a combined force of British and Indians at the Battle of the Thames in 1813. He had proven his vote-getting ability in the election of 1836, while he also refrained from making enemies and avoided controversial positions on policy issues. In campaign literature, Van Buren's reputed tastes for personal luxury prompted damaging Whig contrasts between White House opulence and the sufferings of voters still reeling from the effects of the panic. A chance insult by a Democratic newspaperman even inspired the Whigs to champion Harrison as a simple man who lived in a log cabin and whose favorite beverage was homemade cider. In their most tumultuous and successful presidential campaign, the Whigs swept Van Buren from office in 1840 and rejoiced at the victory of "Old Tippecanoe."

Clay saw Harrison's victory as a superb opportunity. In a reaction to Jackson's own peremptory leadership, Whig party doctrine stressed the importance of consensus leadership and congressional domination of policy making, so Clay had plenty of reason to think that he, as the outstanding senior Whig in the Senate, would actually guide the nation. In short order he put together new plans for another national bank, a "revenue" tariff with "incidental" protection for American products, and a distribution to the states of the proceeds from the sale of public lands, confidently anticipating a second chance for the American System. Clay's Senate speeches in favor of these proposals compared well with his earlier efforts but added little intellectually to the positions he staked out in the Jackson years.

Despite Clay's high hopes, a cruel accident blasted his plans. President Harrison died of pneumonia only one month after taking office, passing the presidency to Vice President John Tyler of Virginia. Unfortunately for Clay, Tyler was not an orthodox Whig but a states'-rights Virginian who had joined the party in a fearful response to Jackson's menacing posture toward South Carolina. Unlike his fellow Whigs, Tyler wanted to fight the abuse of power by restricting the government's share of it, so as quickly as the Whig Congress approved elements of Clay's American System, Tyler struck them down with his veto. Henry Clay's vision for America faltered once more.

Clay got one more serious chance to lead the country in 1844. This time he won the Whig nomination for president, and his Democratic rival was the undistinguished former governor of Tennessee, James K. Polk. Ever the optimist, Clay thought victory was assured and once more thrilled his supporters with bright promises about the beneficial effects of a coordinated and centrally directed plan for American economic improvement. The Whig party platform of 1844 reflected this confidence in the tried and true doctrines of the past. (See Document 24.)

Unperceived by Clay, however, the mood of the country had shifted. A handful of northern voters had become deeply concerned about the slavery issue and steadily pressed the Whigs to take a stronger and stronger stance against the menace they called "the slave power." A much larger number of southerners reacted with intense anger to agitation of the slavery issue and demanded federal policies that would demonstrate the value and permanence of human bondage. Year by year, it became ever harder for a moderate politician like Clay to satisfy both groups by acknowledging the evils of slavery on the one hand, the impossibility of doing anything about it on the other, and the importance of harmony and union above everything else.

One way to mollify southerners and unite them with broader nationalistic currents was to clamor for territorial expansion, with the implied promise that new southwestern territories would be open for the expansion of slavery. James K. Polk and the Democrats accordingly called for the "re-annexation of Texas and the re-occupation of Oregon," territories they claimed had slipped away from America's grasp by the fumbling of previous administrations. Clay dismissed the idea of geographic growth as less important than economic growth inside the territory America already had, and he worried that new acquisitions would not only lead to a war with Mexico but also generate a sectional rift in Congress. He was right on both counts, but the voters were in no mood to listen. Clay found himself scrambling to "explain" his position on Texas, trying to sound cautious enough to satisfy his antislavery constituency in the North while also trying to hang on to expansionist and proslavery supporters in the South. The voters, however, were not convinced, and elected James K. Polk by the margin of 1.5 percent of the popular vote. It was the closest Henry Clay ever came to winning the presidency.

In 1848, Henry Clay expressed his hopes for another chance at the White House, but party managers had to refuse him. At seventy-one, the Whigs' senior statesman had become too old and too shopworn for serious consideration. Ironically, the party chose instead another "military chieftain," General Zachary Taylor, a hero of the Mexican War. In yet another sign that Clay's favorite issues were becoming obsolete, Taylor won the nomination and the presidency without ever committing himself to most of the public questions that Clay and Jackson had disputed so fiercely.

Prince Hal was not ready for complete retirement yet, however. His best-remembered political service came at the end of his life, when the dire consequences he had predicted from territorial expansion had come true. The annexation of Texas in 1845 did lead to the Mexican War (1846–48), and the victorious President Polk had demanded the surrender of all Mexico's remaining territory between Texas and the Pacific. Almost instantly, northern and southern leaders of both parties fell to quarreling over whether the new territory should be slave or free. By 1849, Congress had ground to a standstill over a proposal by Representative David Wilmot of Pennsylvania to ban slavery from all the new territories. Northerners favored the idea, but once again, enraged southerners began to threaten a breakup of the Union if they were not granted equal rights with northerners to carry their legal and legitimate property into every part of the lands taken from Mexico.

In the midst of overwhelming sectional bitterness, the seventy-three-year-old Clay accepted reelection to the Senate in 1849 and stepped forward to save the Union. He cobbled together an eight-point program designed to settle the controversy by another compromise, drawing on his profound conviction that all the great interests of the United States were essentially compatible. As in 1820 and 1833, what was good for the North would be good for the South and vice versa. Slavery was a regrettable problem, but the federal government could not interfere with it, and time alone could be the source of a solution. Above all, he believed the Union was more important than the future of slavery or anything else, so Clay begged and wheedled and lectured his colleagues on the value of the Union. (See Document 25.)

Ironically, Clay's speech in support of the Compromise of 1850 began by blaming the crisis on the political party system that Clay himself had helped to create and begged his colleagues to put aside "the violence and rage of party." (See Figure 9.) In the desperate scramble for enough votes to gain a popular majority, each party had searched for charges to bring against its rival, for accusations that might shave off a few adherents from the competition. This feverish competition had given unwarranted power to small but zealous minorities who held the balance of power between the two major parties. Clay cited the example of abolitionists in the North, but he and his audience were also thinking of the fanatical band of proslavery extremists in the South. In an effort to win the votes of these key minorities, the two parties in each section had advocated measures that assaulted the legitimate interests of Americans in the other section. For the sake of the Union, Clay pleaded, this mindless search for petty local advantage must cease, and all Americans must once more make compromises for the sake of Union.

Clay did not ask for sacrifices of principle. In a painstaking and exhausting speech of two long days, he went over his eight resolutions, explaining one by one why each one might go against the grain of sectional preference without requiring the loss of any important principle or interest. He asked southerners to give up protection for slavery in New Mexico, for example, but only because nature had made slavery impractical there already. He likewise asked northerners to accept a stronger fugitive slave act, but the surrender of fugitives was already required by the Constitution.

In conclusion, Clay characteristically asked the Senate, "Was there ever a nation upon which the sun of heaven has shone that has exhibited so much of prosperity?" Why should any purely symbolic quarrel over slavery justify disturbing its overwhelming material achievements? He reminded his colleagues that northern policies had predominated during the Federalist era, while southern ones had controlled the era of the unnamed Andrew Jackson. Who could justly complain that his own section had been mistreated? Finally, he drew on his deeply felt love of the Union, not to mention his undimmed oratorical powers, to beg Americans to put away all talk of disunion and civil war:

> Sir, I implore gentlemen, I adjure them, whether from the South or the North, by all that they hold dear in this world—by their love of liberty—by all their veneration for their ancestors—by all their regard for posterity—by all their gratitude to Him who has bestowed on them such unnumbered and countless blessings—by all the duties which they owe to mankind—and by all the duties which they owe to themselves, to pause, solemnly to pause at the edge of the precipice, before

Figure 9.   Clay on the Floor of the U.S. Senate, 1850
Henry Clay won his greatest fame as an orator in the U.S. Congress. Many of his
speeches went on for several days. In this popular engraving, Clay addresses a
spellbound Senate in support of the Compromise of 1850. Other national leaders
in the picture include Senators John C. Calhoun, Daniel Webster, Thomas Hart
Benton, William Seward, and Vice President Millard Fillmore.

> the fearful and dangerous leap be taken into the yawning abyss below,
> from which none who ever take it shall return in safety.

Clay fought for his compromise for most of the long, dispiriting summer
of 1850. Ultimately he collapsed from exhaustion, and it was left to others to shepherd his measures through a suspicious and divided Congress.
In the final analysis, however, everyone recognized the settlement as the
work of Henry Clay.

The Compromise of 1850 was not only Clay's last prominent service: It was the turning point for his entire political generation. Jackson had died five years earlier. Calhoun prepared his last great speech urging the defeat of the Compromise, but he was too sick to deliver it himself. A junior colleague read it for him, and the old nullifier died only four weeks later. Clay himself lingered on in crippled health until June 1852, finally succumbing at the age of seventy-five. Daniel Webster followed him four months later. Together, Clay, Calhoun, and Webster had been known as the Great Triumvirate. As much as anything else, their passing marked the end of Jackson-era political leadership and the turn to a new generation of leaders whose supreme challenge would be the crises of Civil War and Reconstruction.

Andrew Jackson and Henry Clay, along with their respective colleagues, had framed an important national debate over democracy and economic development. The debate had spread far beyond their own personal quarrels and engaged voters and politicians throughout the country. The controversy between democracy and development had this appeal not simply because Jackson and Clay were both brilliant and charismatic personalities but because it grew out of the tangible experiences of enfranchised Americans and their intense aspirations for liberty, equality, and material prosperity. Seeking to bolster their rival visions of the American future, supporters of both men had done more than cheer their respective champions; they created enduring political parties that shaped electoral contests in almost every state in the Union for a period of at least two decades.

In the course of the debate, Andrew Jackson had increasingly broadened his conception of democracy. Beginning with an inchoate faith in "the great body of the people," he came to see himself and his office as the direct embodiment of their voice. His 1824 defeat led him to articulate a powerful assertion of the superior rights of the popular majority. Once in office, moreover, he expanded his concept of majority rights beyond the simple question of political power and into the realm of social and economic justice. While he never sought to use the government like a New Deal liberal, to uplift or protect the weakest members of society, he did strengthen the office of the presidency in order to restrain the most powerful. Along the way, he created a rhetorical link between the preservation of liberty and equality and the perpetuity of the American Union that would be fundamental to the Union victory in the Civil War. Even more significantly, he laid a basis for the belief that the American government had an obligation to do more than defend simple political equality among the citizens: It also was bound to advance some version of social and economic equality. Repeatedly transformed, that belief has under-pinned social and political movements from the Populism of the 1890s to the New Deal of the 1930s, to the civil rights movement of the 1960s. Iron-ically, Andrew Jackson himself would probably not have expended much sympathy on many of the specific goals of these movements, and his emphasis on white manhood, military strength, limited government, and states' rights has made an equally important contribution to the endur-ing conservative tradition in America.

Henry Clay articulated a comparably powerful vision of a prosperous and progressive America, guided by a wise and active government in a path of continuing improvement. Unlike Jackson, he did not worry that the infant institutions of corporate America might someday stifle the lib-erty and equality of the ordinary citizen. Even if a few received more ben-efits than the many, Clay was satisfied that his plans for progress would penalize no one. Like Jackson, he championed the preservation of the American Union, but his conception of the Union was more a harmonious network of distinct but interdependent economic interests than a homo-geneous body of like-minded farmers, planters, and artisans.

In the fierce contest between Whigs and Democrats, Henry Clay's spe-cific vision fell victim to a Jacksonian majority: the BUS collapsed, and the American System was never fully enacted. Clay's hopes for a politi-cally sponsored transition from a subsistence republic to a commercial and industrial empire, however, were not entirely dependent on federal approval. Especially in states where Whigs predominated, state and local governments poured aid into railroads and canals and fostered the state banks that partly compensated for the death of the BUS itself. After the Civil War, federal grants of public lands were crucial to the financing of a nationwide railroad network. These investments by an activist govern-ment played a vital role in accelerating industrial expansion, strength-ening the American economy, and eventually elevating the United States to the status of world industrial power. Though Henry Clay lost virtually every particular battle he ever fought with Andrew Jackson, the United States today has more in common with his dreams for its future than it does with the simple agrarian republic of Old Hickory.

Historian Michael Holt has commented on the irony that it was the very divisiveness of the Jacksonian party system that actually preserved the Union in the decades between the Missouri crisis of 1820 and the bit-ter sectionalism of the 1850s.[85] So long as the Whigs of Alabama, for exam-ple, felt more in common with their fellow Whigs of New York than with

---

[85]Michael F. Holt, *The Political Crisis of the 1850s* (New York: Wiley, 1978), 11–16.

Democrats in their own state and region, and their party rivals the Democrats felt likewise, a complete sectional breakdown was impossible. Important as it was intrinsically, the prolonged national controversy over economic development thus served to distract attention from the even more divisive issues of slavery and free labor. Despite the power of economic issues to deflect the slavery controversy, however, the repeated confrontations that Clay and Jackson both experienced over sectional matters demonstrated the fragility of the party system they helped to create.

In the end, the American electorate was determined to have both democracy and development, and the enduring tension between the two has colored U.S. politics ever since. This was the type of decision that Americans could not make on the subject of freedom and slavery, however. On that matter, they were forced to choose one or the other.

PART TWO

The Documents

1

ANDREW JACKSON

Division Orders
to the Tennessee Militia

March 7, 1812

Shortly before the beginning of the War of 1812, Congress asked for 50,000 volunteer troops to join the armed forces of the United States. Major General Andrew Jackson issued the following "division order" to his troops in the Tennessee state militia, urging them to respond to Congress's invitation.

What does this document tell you about Jackson's character and personality? About his intended audience? Jackson asks his readers, "Who are we? and for what are we going to fight?" Why were these questions so important in 1812? How effectively does Jackson answer them? Why do you think the average soldier was apparently so sensitive to the difference between republican and monarchical government?

Volunteers to Arms!

Citizens! Your government has at last yielded to the impulse of the nation. Your impatience is no longer restrained. The hour of national vengeance is now at hand. The eternal enemies of american prosperity are again to be taught to respect your rights, after having been compelled to feel, once more, the power of your arms. War is on the point of breaking out between the united States and the King of great Britain! and the martial hosts of america are summoned to the Tented Fields!

Citizens! An honourable confidence in your courage and your patriotism has been displayed by the general government. To raise a force for the protection of your rights she has not deemed it necessary to recur to the common mode of filling the ranks of an army. No drafts or compulsory levies are now to be made.

A simple invitation is given to the young men of the country to arm for their own and their countries rights. On this invitation 50,000 volunteers, full of martial ardor, indignant at their countries wrongs and burning with

John Spencer Bassett, ed., *The Correspondence of Andrew Jackson,* 7 vols. (Washington, D.C.: Carnegie Institution of Washington, 1926–1935), 1: 220–23.

impatience to illustrate their names by some signal exploit, are expected to repair to the national standard.

Could it be otherwise? Could the general government deem it necessary to force *us* to take the field? We, who for so many years have demanded a war with such clamorous importunity — who, in so many resolutions of town meetings and legislative assemblies, have offerred our lives and fortunes for the defence of our country — who, so often and so publickly, have charged this verry government with a pusillanimous deference to foreign nations, because she had resolved to exhaust the arts of negociation before she made her last appeal to the power of arms. No under such circumstances it was impossible for the government to conceive that compulsion would be wanting to bring us into the field. And shall we now disappoint the expectations which we ourselves have excited? Shall we give the lie to the professions which we have so often and so publickly made? Shall we, who have clamoured for war, now skulk into a corner the moment war is about to be declared? Shall we, who for so many years have been tendering our lives and fortunes to the general government, now come out with evasions and pitifull excuses the moment tender is accepted?

But another and a nobler feeling should impell us to action. *Who are we? and for what are we going to fight?* are we the titled Slaves of George the third? the military conscripts of Napolon the great? or the frozen peasants of the Rusian Czar? No — we are the free born sons of america; the citizens of the only republick now existing in the world; and the only people on earth who possess rights, liberties, and property which the[y] dare call their own.

For what are we going to fight? To satisfy the revenge or ambition of a corrupt and infatuated ministry? to place another and another diadem on the head of an apostate republican general?[1] to settle the ballance of power among an assasin tribe of Kings and emperors? "or to preserve to the prince of Blood, and the grand dignitaries of the empire" their overgrown wealth and exclusive privileges? No. Such splendid atchievements as these can form no part of the objects of an american war. But we are going to fight for the reestablishment of our national charector, misunderstood and vilified at home and abroad; for the protection of our maritime citizens, impressed on board British ships of war and compelled to fight the battles of our enemies against ourselves; to vindicate our right to a free trade, and open a market for the productions of our soil, now perishing on our hands because the *mistress of the ocean* has forbid us to carry them to any foreign nation; in fine, to seek some indemnity for past

[1]The apostate republican general is French Emperor Napoléon Bonaparte.

injuries, some security against future aggressions, by the conquest of all the British dominions upon the continent of north america.

Here then is the true and noble principle on which the energies of the nation should be brought into action: *a free people compelled to reclaim by the power of their arms the right which god has bestowed upon them, and which an infatuated King has said they shall not enjoy.*

In such a contest will the people shrink from the support of their government; or rather will the[y] shrink from the support of themselves? Will the[y] abandon their great unprescriptible rights, and tamely surrender that illustrious national charector which was purchased with so much blood in the war of the Revolution? No. Such infamy shall not fall upon us. The advocates of Kingly power shall not enjoy the triumph of seeing a free people desert themselves, and crouch before the slaves of a foreign tyrant. The patriotic tender of voluntary service of the invincible grays Capt. F. Stumps independant company and a correspondent display of patriotism by the voluntary tender of service from the counties of Davidson Sumner Smith and Rutherford, is a sure pledge that the free sons of the west will never *submit to such degradation. . . .*

To view the stupendous works of nature, exemplified in the falls of Niagara and the cataract of Montmorenci; to tread the consecrated spot on which Wolf and Montgomery fell, would of themselves repay the young soldier for a march across the continent. But why should these inducements be held out to the young men of america? They need them not. Animated as they are by an ambition to rival the exploits of Rome, they will never prefer an inglorious sloth, a supine inactivity to the honorable toil of carrying the republican standard to the heights of abraham.[2]

In consideration of all which and to carry into effect the object of the general government in demanding a voluntary force, to give to the valiant young men of the second military Division of the state of Tennessee an

---

[2]In this paragraph, Jackson seeks to inspire his troops by references to natural and historical landmarks associated with Anglo-American incursions into Canada. In Jackson's day, Niagara Falls on the United States–Canadian border were widely regarded as the most spectacular natural phenomenon in North America. The "cataract of Montmorenci" is a 275-foot waterfall on a tributary of the St. Lawrence River, not far from the city of Québec. Nearby, British Major General James Wolfe commanded British and American troops at the decisive battle of the British conquest of Canada from the French in the Seven Years War, also called the French and Indian War (1757–63). In 1759, under cover of darkness, Wolfe's troops scaled the cliffs known as the Heights of Abraham and defeated a French army the next day on the Plains of Abraham, atop the Heights. Though British troops triumphed, General Wolfe lost his life in this battle. In 1775, at the beginning of the American Revolution, an American Army commanded by Brigadier General Richard Montgomery also invaded Canada and attacked Québec. Like Wolfe, Montgomery died in the battle, but his invasion did not succeed.

opportunity to evince their devoted affection to the service of the republick; the Major General of the said division has thereupon ordered

1. That the militia of the second military division of the state of Tennessee be forthwith mustered by the proper officers.
2. That the act of congress for raising a volunteer corps of 50,000 men be read at the head of each company.
3. That all persons willing to volunteer under the said act be immediately *enrolled* formed into companies, officered, and reported to the Major Genl.
4. The Generals of Brigade, attached to the second division are charged with the prompt execution of these orders.

2

"The Hunters of Kentucky"
Jacksonian Campaign Song
1822

This poem was written by Samuel Woodworth and set to a popular tune by the actor Noah Ludlow, who performed it in New Orleans in 1822. The audience was filled with rough-hewn boatmen and frontiersmen who came down the Mississippi on rafts and keelboats and poled them back again. In his memoirs, Ludlow remembers that they greeted the song with "loud applause of hands and feet, and a prolonged whoop, or howl, such as Indians give when they are especially pleased." The song was so popular among the men who called themselves "half-horse and half-alligator" that Ludlow had to sing it three times before they were satisfied. In the next several years, the popularity of the song spread across the country, and Jackson supporters reworked it into a favorite campaign song for the presidential election of 1828.

What do you think made this song popular in the 1820s? Compare its message to Jackson's Division Orders of 1812 (see Document 1). What kinds of voters would respond favorably to this campaign song? Would anyone be likely to respond unfavorably?

John William Ward, *Andrew Jackson: Symbol for an Age* (New York: Oxford University Press, 1955), 217–18.

1. Ye gentlemen and ladies fair,
    Who grace this famous city,
   Just listen if you've time to spare,
    While I rehearse a ditty;
   And for the opportunity
    Conceive yourselves quite lucky,
   For 'tis not often that you see
    A hunter from Kentucky
   O Kentucky, the hunters of Kentucky!
   O Kentucky, the hunters of Kentucky!

2. We are a hardy, free-born race,
    Each man to fear a stranger;
   Whate'er the game we join in chase,
    Despising toil and danger,
   And if a daring foe annoys,
    Whate'er his strength and forces,
   We'll show him that Kentucky boys
    Are alligator horses.
          Oh Kentucky, &c.

3. I s'pose you've read it in the prints,
    How Packenham[1] attempted
   To make old Hickory Jackson wince,
    But soon his scheme repented;
   For we with rifles ready cock'd,
    Thought such occasion lucky,
   And soon around the gen'ral flock'd
    The Hunters of Kentucky.
          Oh Kentucky, &c.

4. You've heard, I s'pose how New-Orleans
    Is fam'd for wealth and beauty,
   There's girls of ev'ry hue it seems,
    From snowy white to sooty.
   So Packenham he made his brags,
    If he in fight was lucky,
   He'd have their girls and cotton bags,

---

[1]Major General Sir Edward M. Packenham commanded British forces at the Battle of New Orleans, in which he died.

In spite of old Kentucky.
Oh Kentucky, &c.

5. But Jackson he was wide awake,
And was not scar'd at trifles,
For well he knew what aim we take
With our Kentucky rifles.
So he led us down to Cypress swamp,
The ground was low and mucky,
There stood John Bull in martial pomp
And here was old Kentucky.
Oh Kentucky, &c.

6. A bank was rais'd to hide our breasts,
Not that we thought of dying,
But that we always like to rest,
Unless the game is flying.
Behind it stood our little force,
None wished it to be greater,
For ev'ry man was half a horse,
And half an alligator.
Oh Kentucky, &c.

7. They did not let our patience tire,
Before they showed their faces;
We did not choose to waste our fire,
So snugly kept our places.
But when so near we saw them wink,
We thought it time to stop 'em,
And 'twould have done you good I think,
To see Kentuckians drop 'em.
Oh Kentucky, &c.

8. They found, at last, 'twas vain to fight,
Where *lead* was all the *booty,*
And so they wisely took to flight,
And left *us* all our *beauty.*
And now if danger e'er annoys,
Remember what our trade is,
Just send for us Kentucky boys,

And we'll protect ye, ladies.
Oh Kentucky, &c.

3

SCAEVOLA [HENRY CLAY]

"To the Electors of Fayette County"
April 16, 1798

Henry Clay reached adulthood during the presidency of Thomas Jefferson, in a period when many states were experimenting to find the ideal governing structure for a society based on liberty and equality for white men. Soon after he moved to Kentucky, Clay threw himself into this effort and, less than a week after his twenty-first birthday, wrote the following letter in support of a state constitutional convention.

Clay begins his letter to the Lexington Kentucky Gazette *with a vigorous defense of the very idea of a constitutional convention. Why would a convention be controversial? Do you agree with Clay's idea that "the will of the enlightened representatives of a free people should not be checked by any power upon earth, except it be the people themselves"?*

Clay here demands the abolition of Kentucky's state senate and wants to give the state legislature the authority to end slavery in Kentucky. Why did he choose these particular reforms? Would they appeal to a preference for direct self-government? For humanitarianism? For economic development? What would Andrew Jackson have thought about Clay's proposals?

Following contemporary custom, Clay signs his letter with a pseudonym taken from ancient Rome: "Scaevola." His proposals were not adopted in 1798, though he continued to press for some plan of gradual and compensated emancipation of the slaves for the rest of his life.

Fellow Citizens:

The time approaching at which you are to decide, in pursuance of the invitation of your *immediate* representatives upon the all-important ques-

James F. Hopkins et al., eds., *The Papers of Henry Clay,* 11 vols. (Lexington: University Press of Kentucky, 1959–1992), 1: 3–8.

tion with respect to a convention, it becomes the duty of every man to form an impartial and candid judgment; it is not only his duty to quiet his own mind, but to contribute, as far as he can, towards placing the question in a fair and dispassionate point of view, before the public. In attempting this, suffer me to state to you the reasons which have been offered against summoning a convention, and the defects which, it is conceived, make an alteration in our constitution necessary.

That there exist defects in the constitution is not denied by the most violent opposers of a convention. But it is said, that, if we attempt an alteration of it now, we shall expose it to the attacks of the wicked and designing, and that, by endeavouring to expunge the defective parts, we hazard a loss of the perfect. An appeal too is made to the tranquility of the state, and it is asked, with exultation, if every one is not happy under the present form of government; whether the weight of oppression bows down the neck of any one. A grave refutation of these arguments is only necessary, from the respectability of the persons who urge them, and from the influence they have acquired.

How do we endanger the good parts of the constitution, by a convention? Those who urge this objection seem to suppose that, instead of an assemblage of the most wise and enlightened citizens of the state, canvassing the constitution and availing themselves of the lessons of experience, and the dictates of reason, we are to expect a convention of the most wicked and ignorant, shaking government and attacking property. They pay but a poor compliment to the discernment and integrity of the people. They appear to have forgotten that the members of the convention will be chosen by the voluntary suffrages of a free people. That the persons thus chosen, elevated by the dignity of their station, assemble together for the discussion of subjects, in which they are equally interested with their constituents. That they will have no motive for abusing the confidence of the public. And they seem unaware of the extent of their argument, it striking at all representative government, since if we cannot trust our delegates in establishing fundamental or elementary principles, they are equally unfit for the purpose of ordinary legislation. Has it ever been known that the cause of truth was hurt by enquiry and investigation? If not, why are we to apprehend that the sound parts of our constitution will be endangered by a convention? But it is said that it is yet too young to be touched. Its infancy is a powerful reason for amending it at the present time. It has not yet acquired that strength, that maturity, which will enable it to resist the efforts of reformation.

The first dawn of disease is the moment for remedy. The longer it continues, the more difficult is cure. The longer a government operates, the greater is the difficulty of change. Habit, the creation of new offices, their influence, a thousand relations and tyes combine to oppose a reform of abuses in an old government. We have innumerable examples of the truth of this idea. . . .

But, compelled to abandon this ground of opposition as untenable, the enemies to a convention assume a bolder aspect upon the other, the supposed happiness of the people. It may not be improper here to remark that arguments of this kind, if founded in fact, prove nothing. Because we find that it is a principle of our nature to endeavour to be contented with present situation. The inhabitant of the most dismal dungeon, the parent who has lost the most affectionate and promising child, after the first paroxisms of grief, cease their unavailing complaints. The subjects of the most despotic prince, the African who has the most ruthless and inexorable master, seem contented and happy, and rarely heave a sigh of misery. The true question with the philosopher and statesman should be, not whether men are contented, for there is a tranquility of the mind, which has the countenance of happiness, but can the present sum of human happiness, by the reform of corrupt institutions, or the change of licentious manners, be increased.

It is not however true that the people of Kentucky are contented and happy under the present government. The vote of so large a number, in favor of a convention, at the last election, and the present stir in the country, prove the contrary. Can any humane man be happy and contented when he sees near thirty thousand of his fellow beings around him, deprived of all the rights which make life desirable, transferred like cattle from the possession of one to another; when he sees the trembling slave, under the hammer, surrounded by a number of eager purchasers, and feeling all the emotions which arise when one is uncertain into whose tyrannic hands he must next fall; when he beholds the anguish and hears the piercing cries of husbands separated from wives and children from parents; when in a word, all the tender and endearing ties of nature are broken asunder and disregarded; and when he reflects that no gradual mode of emancipation is adopted either for these slaves or their posterity, doubling their number every twenty-five years. To suppose the people of Kentucky, enthusiasts as they are in the cause of liberty, could be contented and happy under circumstances like these, would be insulting their good sense.

Having thus obviated the objections against a convention, permit me to hint at some of the alterations which appear to me to be necessary to our constitution.

In addition to other misrepresentation, to which the enemies to a convention, despairing of success by a fair mode of reasoning, have had recourse, they have addressed themselves insidiously to the fears of the slaveholders, and held out as the object of the friends to a convention, an immediate and unqualified liberation of slaves. However just such a measure might be, it certainly never has been the intention of any one to attempt it; and the only motive in ascribing it to them has been to awaken the prejudices, and mislead the judgment of the public. But it is the wish of some of them, that a gradual plan of emancipation should be adopted. All America acknowledges the existence of slavery to be an evil, which while it deprives the slave of the best gift of heaven, in the end injures the master too, by laying waste his lands, enabling him to live indolently, and thus contracting all the vices generated by a state of idleness. If it be this enormous evil, the sooner we attempt its destruction the better. It is a subject which has been so generally canvassed by the public, that it is unnecessary to repeat all the reasons which urge to a conventional interference. It is sufficient that we are satisfied of this much, that the article prohibiting the legislature from making any provision for it, should be expunged, and another introduced either applying the remedy itself, or authorising the legislature at any subsequent period to do it. There can be no danger in vesting this power in them. They can have no motive but public good to actuate them, and there will be always a number of them who will themselves hold slaves. The legislature of Virginia possess this power without abusing it. The next objection which I shall mention to the present constitution, is the senate, a body which to me seems adverse to republican principles, and to be without use. I am aware that I shall be opposed by the examples of all nations, who enjoy any portion of liberty. Fortunately however the present enlightened age is not to be seduced into an opinion by precedent alone: reason must be addressed and satisfied before any is embraced. The division of the legislature into two chambers, has been founded upon the principle of two classes of men, whose interests were distinct, living under the same government. It was necessary that the rights of the nobility and commonalty should be guarded and protected by a body of legislators, representing each. These distinctions not existing in America, the use of the senate has ceased. What is the object of a representative legislature? It is to collect the will of the people, and to assemble the intelligence of the state, for the purpose of legislation. It is not necessary to this end that there should be two separate bodies of delegates. But if it be, as the object certainly is, the assemblage of wisdom, and as there is a greater chance of wise men being in a large assembly than in a small one, each chamber should be composed of an equal number of members. If the will of the people is to be the governing principle of decision, certainly that will is better expressed by the lower house, since the members of that are more numerous and come more immediately from the body of the people. . . .

With respect to the check which the senate is supposed to impose upon the impetuosity and precipitancy of the lower house, this scarcely deserves an audience. To it I answer first, the will of the enlightened representatives of a free people should not be checked by any power upon earth, except it be the people themselves. And secondly, that it is not true that the senate is composed in general of men less impetuous and more wise than the other house. . . . The objection, then conducts us to the aristocratic plan of managing the people by a few. . . . I cannot conceive how the lower house, depending upon the people for an annual election, and responsible to them, can be induced to pass laws detrimental to the public, since they are a part of that public, and since the laws equally affect them. . . .

Having attempted to shew, and I think succeeded in manifesting, in the preceding observations, that there exists no good reason why a convention should not be summoned; that there ought to be a gradual mode of emancipation established, or, at least, that the legislature should be invested with the power of forming one, when the situation of the country should render it necessary; and that the senate should be abolished or at least reformed. I shall conclude by observing to you fellow citizens, that the present is the moment for coming forward, and that it is impossible to foresee the consequences of inactivity.

4

HENRY CLAY

On the Proposed Repeal
of the Non-Intercourse Act

February 22, 1810

In February 1810, Henry Clay joined the U.S. Senate to serve the unexpired term of a previous member and quickly joined the "War Hawk" faction of the Republican Party. The United States was struggling with the efforts of European powers to regulate its trade during the Napoleonic wars, and Clay voiced his impatience at the ineffectiveness of economic sanctions in protecting the nation's independence. Over the next two years, voices like Clay's were very important in pushing the United States toward a declaration of war against Great Britain.

Closely examine Clay's thoughts about military achievement. Why does he feel the need for "a new race of heroes"? What are his concerns about military leadership in a republic? How would you compare the sentiments in this speech with Andrew Jackson's appeal for military enlistments in 1812 (see Document 1)?

Mr. President—At all times embarrassed when I have ventured to address you, it is with peculiar diffidence I rise on this occasion. The profound respect I have been taught to entertain for this body—my conscious inadequacy to discuss as it deserves the question before you— the magnitude of that question—and the recent seat I have taken in this house, are too well calculated to appal, and would impel me to silence, if any other member would assume the task I propose attempting. But, sir, when the regular troops of this house, disciplined as they are in the great affairs of this nation, are inactive at their posts, it becomes the duty of its raw militia, however lately enlisted, to step forth in defence of the honor and independence of the country. . . .

Sir, have we not been for years contending against the tyranny of the ocean? Has not congress solemnly pledged itself to the world not to surrender our rights? Has not the nation, at large, in all its capacities of meet-

James F. Hopkins et al., eds., *The Papers of Henry Clay,* 11 vols. (Lexington: University Press of Kentucky, 1959–1992), 1: 448–52.

ings of the people, state and general governments, resolved to maintain, at all hazards our maritime independence? Your whole circle of commercial restrictions, including the non-importation, embargo and non-intercourse acts, had in view an opposition to the offensive measures of the belligerents, so justly complained of by us. They presented *resistance*—the *peaceful* resistance of the law. When this is abandoned, without effect, I am for resistance by the *sword*.

No man in the nation desires peace more than I. But I prefer the troubled ocean of war, demanded by the honor and independence of the country, with all its calamities, and desolations, to the tranquil, putrescent pool of ignominious peace. If we can accommodate our differences with one of the belligerents only, I should prefer that one to be Great-Britain. But if with neither, and we are forced into a selection of our enemy, then am I for war with Britain; because I believe her prior in aggression, and her injuries and insults to us were atrocious in character. . . . Britain stands preeminent, in her outrage on us, by her violation of the sacred personal rights of American freemen, in the arbitrary and lawless impressment of our seamen—the attack on the *Chesapeake*[1]—the murder, Sir, I will not dwell on the long catalogue of our wrongs & disgraces, which has been repeated until the sensibility of the nation is benumbed by the dishonorable detail.

But we are asked for the means of carrying on War; and those who oppose it triumphantly appeal to the vacant vaults of the treasury. With the unimpaired credit of the government, invigorated by a faithful observance of public engagements, and a rapid extinction of the debt of the revolution; with the boundless territories in the west, presenting a safe pledge for reimbursement of loans to any extent—is it not astonishing that despondency itself should disparage the resources of this country? . . . And are we to regard as nothing the patriotic offer so often made by the states to spend their last cent, and risk their last drop of blood in the preservation of our neutral priviledges? Or, are we to be governed by the low, groveling parsimony of the counting room, and to cast up the actual pence in the drawer before we assert our inestimable rights? It is said, however, that no object is attainable by war with Britain. In its fortunes we are to estimate not only the benefit to be derived to ourselves, but the injury to be done the enemy. The conquest of Canada is in your power. I trust I shall not be deemed presumptuous when I state, what I verily believe, that the militia of Kentucky are alone competent to place Montreal and Upper Canada at your

---

[1] In 1807, the British warship *Leopard* fired on the U.S.S. *Chesapeake* off the coast of Virginia, killing three Americans, wounding eighteen, and impressing four seamen into the British Navy.

feet. Is it nothing to the British nation—is it nothing to the pride of her monarch to have the last of the immense North American possessions held by him in the commencement of his reign, wrested from his dominion? Is it nothing to us to extinguish the torch that lights up savage warfare? Is it nothing to acquire the entire fur trade connected with that country, and to destroy the temptation and the opportunity of violating your revenue and other laws?

War with Britain will deprive her of those supplies of raw materials and provisions, which she now obtains from this country. . . . The pressure upon her, contemplated by your restrictive laws, will then be completely realised. She will not have the game, as she will if you pass this bill without an efficient substitute, entirely in her own hands. The enterprize and valor of our maritime brethren will participate in the spoils of capture.

Another effect of war will be the re-production and cherishing of a martial spirit amongst us. Is there not danger that we shall become enervated by the spirit of avarice unfortunately so predominant? I do not wish to see that diffusive military character which, pervading the whole nation, might possibly eventuate in the aggrandizement of some ambitious chief, by prostrating the liberties of the country. But a certain portion of military ardor (and this is what I desire) is essential to the protection of the country. The withered arm, and wrinkled brow of the illustrious founders of our freedom, are melancholy indications that they will shortly be removed from us. Their deeds of glory and renown will then be felt only through the cold medium of the historic page. We shall want the presence and living example of a new race of heroes to supply their place, and to animate us to preserve unviolated what they achieved. . . .—If we surrender without a struggle to maintain our rights, we forfeit the respect of the world, and what is infinitely worse, of ourselves.

We are often reminded that the British navy constitutes the only barrier between us and universal dominion; and warned that resistance to Britain is submission to France. . . . I cannot subscribe to British slavery upon the water, that we may escape French subjugation upon land. I should feel myself debased and humbled as an American citizen, if we had to depend upon any foreign power to uphold our independence. And I am persuaded that our own resources, properly directed, are fully adequate to our defence. I am therefore for resisting oppression, by whomsoever attempted against us, whether maritime or territorial.

Considering then that the bill, as amended in this house, in furnishing no substitute for the law of non-intercourse which it repeals nor the propositions of the other house intended to take its place, is a total dereliction of all opposition to the edicts of the belligerents, I cannot vote for it in its present form. I move a recommitment of the bill to supply this defect. What ought to be the substitute I confess I have not satisfied myself, not expecting that it would fall to my lot to make you this motion. The committee however can deliberate upon the subject and propose one.—I would suggest two for consideration.—Either a total non-importation, which our laws can doubtless enforce; or to arm our merchantmen and authorize convoys. . . . On our part a war thus produced, will be a war of defence.

But Mr. President if after all our deliberation it shall be deemed unwise to adopt either of these expedients, perhaps some other unexceptionable course may occur. I insist that you do not return the bill to the other branch of the legislature in its present form. They have sent you a measure I acknowledge weak. It is however not submission. It professes to oppose in form at least the injustice of foreign governments. What are you about to do? To breathe vigor and energy into the bill? No sir, you have eradicated all its vitality and are about to transmit back again the lifeless skeleton. I entreat the Senate to recollect the high ground they occupy with the nation. I call upon the members of this house to maintain its character for vigor. I beseech them not to forfeit the esteem of the country. . . .

5

HENRY CLAY

On the Seminole War

January 20, 1819

In 1817, Major General Andrew Jackson took command of American troops fighting the First Seminole War. The following year, when the Seminoles retreated from Georgia into Spanish Florida, Jackson pursued them and did not stop until he had captured the provincial capital of Pensacola and hanged several Indians and two Englishmen whom he blamed for instigating the war. Jackson's conduct outraged Britain and Spain, but the general justified himself on the grounds that he had secret orders from President

James F. Hopkins et al., eds., *The Papers of Henry Clay,* 11 vols. (Lexington: University Press of Kentucky, 1959–1992), 2: 636–60.

James Monroe and that it was no crime to invade Spain's colony if the Span-
ish could not control the Indians themselves.

Henry Clay had begun his congressional career as a "War Hawk,"
demanding both swift military retaliation against Great Britain and even
the invasion of Canada (see Document 4). By the time of the First Semi-
nole War, however, he had become more cautious, showing greater sympa-
thy for peaceful measures and firmly insisting on the supremacy of law. Jack-
son's apparent defiance of lawful authority led Clay and other congressmen
to demand that he be censured for misconduct. Their efforts failed, but Clay
used this speech to spell out many rhetorical themes that he would continue
to use against Andrew Jackson.

He begins by blaming the Seminole War on the harsh terms of the Treaty
of Fort Jackson imposed on the Indians by General Jackson himself in 1814.
How do humanitarian concerns continue to be present in this speech? Clay
also insists that Jackson's conduct raises questions about the supremacy of
law in a republic. Why was this important to Clay? What factors or experi-
ences might have led some contemporaries to share his concern?

Mr. Clay, *(Speaker)* rose. In rising to address you, sir, said he, on the very
interesting subject which now engages the attention of Congress, I must
be allowed to say, that all inferences, drawn from the course which it will
be my painful duty to take in this discussion, of unfriendliness to either
the Chief Magistrate of the country, or to the illustrious military chieftain,
whose operations are under investigation, will be wholly unfounded. . . . I
have no interest, other than that of seeing the concerns of my country well
and happily administered. It is infinitely more gratifying to behold the prosperity of my country advancing, by the wisdom of the measures adopted
to promote it, than it would be to expose the errors which may be committed, if there be any, in the conduct of its affairs. Mr. C. said . . . he would,
with the utmost sincerity, assure the committee, that he had formed no
resolution, come under no engagements, and that he never would form
any resolution, or contract any engagement, for systematic opposition to
his administration, or to that of any other Chief Magistrate. . . .

In noticing the painful incidents of this war, it was impossible not to
inquire into its origin. He feared that would be found to be the famous
treaty of Fort Jackson, concluded in August, 1814. . . . He had never
perused this instrument until within a few days past, and he had read it
with the deepest mortification and regret. A more dictatorial spirit he had
never seen displayed in any instrument. He would challenge an exami-

nation of all the records of diplomacy, not excepting even those in the most haughty period of imperious Rome, when she was carrying her arms into the barbarian nations that surrounded her; and he did not believe a solitary instance could be found of such an inexorable spirit of domination pervading a compact purporting to be a treaty of PEACE. It consisted of the most severe and humiliating demands—of the surrender of large territory—of the privilege of making roads through even what was retained—of the right of establishing trading-houses—of the obligation of delivering into our hands their prophets. And all this, of a wretched people, reduced to the last extremity of distress, whose miserable existence we had to preserve by a voluntary stipulation to furnish them with bread! When even did conquering and desolating Rome fail to respect the altars and the gods of those whom she subjugated! Let me not be told that these prophets were imposters, who deceived the Indians. They were *their* prophets—the Indians believed and venerated them, and it is not for us to dictate a religious belief to them. It does not belong to the holy character of the religion which we profess, to carry its precepts, by force of the bayonet, into the bosoms of other people. Mild and gentle persuasion was the great instrument employed by the meek founder of our religion. We leave to the humane and benevolent efforts of the reverend professors of Christianity to convert from barbarism those unhappy nations yet immersed in its gloom. But, sir, spare them their prophets! Spare their delusions! Spare their prejudices and superstitions! Spare them even their religion, such as it is! from open and cruel violence. When, sir, was that treaty concluded? On the very day, after the protocol was signed, of the first conference between the American and British Commissioners, treating of peace, at Ghent. . . . What a contrast is exhibited between the cotemporaneous scenes of Ghent and of Fort Jackson: What a powerful voucher would the British Commissioners have been furnished with, if they could have got hold of that treaty! The United States *demand.* The United States *demand,* is repeated five or six times. And what did the preamble itself disclose? That two thirds of the Creek nation had been hostile, and one third only friendly to us. Now, he had heard (he could not vouch for the truth of the statement) that not one hostile chief signed the treaty. He had also heard that perhaps one or two of them had. If the treaty really were made by a minority of the nation, it was not obligatory upon the whole nation. It was void, considered in the light of a national compact. And, if void, the Indians were entitled to the benefit of the provision of the ninth article of the Treaty of Ghent, by which we bound ourselves to make peace with any tribes with whom we might be at war, on the ratification of the treaty, and to restore to them their lands as they held them in 1811. Mr. C. said he did not know how the honorable Senate, that body for which he held so high a respect, could have given their sanction to the treaty of Fort Jackson, so utterly irreconcileable as it is with those noble principles of generosity and magnanimity which he hoped to see his country always exhibit, and particularly towards the miserable remnant of the aborigines. . . . That treaty, Mr. C. said, he feared, had been the main cause of the recent war. And if it had been, it only added another melancholy proof to those with which history already abounds, that hard and unconscionable terms, extorted by the power of the sword and the right of conquest, served but to whet and stimulate revenge, and to give to old hostilities, smothered, not extinguished, by the pretended peace, greater exasperation and more ferocity. A truce thus patched up with an unfortunate people, without the means of existence, without bread, is no real peace. The instant there is the slighest prospect of relief, from such harsh and severe conditions, the conquered party will fly to arms, and spend the last drop of blood rather than live in such degraded bondage. Even if you again reduce him to submission, the expenses incurred by this second war, to say nothing of the human lives that are sacrificed, will be greater than what it would have cost you to have granted him liberal conditions in the first instance. This treaty, he repeated it, was, he apprehended, the cause of the war. . . .

I should be very unwilling, Mr. C. said, to assert, in regard to this war, that the fault was on our side; but he feared it was. . . . Mr. C. said that he was far from attributing to Gen. Jackson any other than the very slight degree of blame which attached to him as the negociator of the treaty of Fort Jackson, and which would be shared by those who subsequently ratified and sanctioned that treaty. . . . He knew, he said, that, when Gen. Jackson was summoned to the field, it was too late to hesitate—the fatal blow had been struck in the destruction of Fowl Town, and the dreadful massacre of Lieut. Scott and his detachment;[1] and the only duty which remained to him was to terminate this unhappy contest.

The first circumstance which, in the course of his performing that duty, fixed our attention, had, Mr. C. said, filled him with regret. It was the execution of the Indian chiefs. How, he asked, did they come into our pos-

---

[1]Fowl Town was a Seminole village in south Georgia just north of the Florida border, located on lands which the Creeks ceded to the United States in 1814 in the Treaty of Fort Jackson. When the Seminoles refused to evacuate, American troops attacked and burned the town in November 1817. In retaliation, the Seminoles ambushed a boat commanded by Lieutenant Richard W. Scott on the nearby Apalachicola River. Scott and most of his party of forty American soldiers and eleven women and children were killed. These two incidents marked the beginning of the First Seminole War.

session? Was it in the course of fair, and open, and honorable war? No; but by means of deception—by hoisting foreign colors on the staff from which the stars and stripes should alone have floated. Thus ensnared, the Indians were taken on shore, and without ceremony, and without delay, were hung. Hang an Indian! We, sir, who are civilized, and can comprehend and feel the effect of moral causes and considerations, attach ignominy to that mode of death. . . . But, Mr. C. said, he regarded the occurrence with grief for other and higher considerations. It was the first instance that he knew of, in the annals of our country, in which retaliation, by executing Indian captives, had ever been deliberately practised. There may have been exceptions, but if there were, they met with contemporaneous condemnation, and have been reprehended by the just pen of impartial history. The gentleman from Massachusetts[2] may tell me, if he pleases, what he pleases about the tomahawk and scalping knife—about Indian enormities, and foreign miscreants and incendiaries. I, too, hate them; from my very soul I abominate them. But, I love my country, and its constitution; I love liberty and safety, and fear military despotism more even than I hate these monsters. . . .

However guilty these men were, they should not have been condemned or executed, without the authority of the law. He would not dwell, at this time, on the effect of these precedents in foreign countries, but he would not pass unnoticed their dangerous influence in our own country. Bad examples are generally set in the cases of bad men, and often remote from the central government. . . . The influence of a bad example would often be felt when its authors and all the circumstances connected with it were no longer remembered. . . . In conclusion of this part of the subject, Mr. C. said, that he most cheerfully and entirely acquitted general Jackson of any intention to violate the laws of the country, or the obligations of humanity. He was persuaded, from all that he had heard that he thought himself equally respecting and observing both. With respect to the purity of his intentions, therefore, he was disposed to allow it in the most extensive degree. Of his *acts,* said Mr. C. it is my duty to speak with the freedom which belongs to my station. . . .

Of all the powers conferred by the constitution of the United States, not one is more expressly and exclusively granted than that is to congress of declaring war. The immortal convention who framed that instrument

---

[2]The gentleman from Massachusetts refers to Representative John Holmes, who had previously spoken in Jackson's defense.

had abundant reason for confiding this tremendous power to the deliberate judgment of the representatives of the people, drawn from every page of history. It was there seen that nations are often precipitated into ruinous war from folly, from pride, from ambition, and from the desire of military fame. . . . It was to guard our country against precisely that species of rashness, which has been manifested in Florida, that the constitution was so framed. If then this power, thus cautiously and clearly bestowed upon Congress, has been assumed and exercised by any other functionary of the government, it is cause of serious alarm, and it became that body to vindicate and maintain its authority by all the means in its power, and yet there are some gentlemen, who would have us not merely to yield a tame and silent acquiescence in the encroachment, but to pass even a vote of thanks to the author. . . .

The honorable gentleman from Massachusetts had endeavored to derive some authority to General Jackson from the message of the President, and the letter of the Secretary of War to Governor Bibb.[3] The message declares that the Spanish authorities are to be respected wherever maintained. What the President means by their being maintained, is explained in the orders themselves, by the extreme case being put of the enemy seeking shelter under a Spanish fort. If even in that case he was not to attack, certainly he was not to attack in any case of less strength. The letter to Governor Bibb admits of a similar explanation. When the Secretary says, in that letter, that Gen. Jackson is fully empowered to bring the Seminole war to a conclusion, he means that he is so empowered by his orders, which, being now before us, must speak for themselves. . . . He was instructed . . . to consider himself at liberty to . . . pursue the enemy; but, *if he took refuge under a Spanish fortress, the fact was to be reported to the Department of War.* These orders were transmitted to Gen. Jackson, and constituted, or ought to have constituted, his guide. There was then no justification for the occupation of Pensacola, and the attack on the Barancas, in the message of the President, the letter to Gov. Bibb, or in the orders themselves. . . . If it were right in him to seize the place, it is impossible that it should have been right in the President immediately to surrender it. We, sir, are the supporters of the President. We regret that we cannot support Gen. Jackson also. The gentleman's liberality is more comprehensive than ours. I approved, with all my heart, of the restoration of Pensacola. I think St. Marks ought, perhaps, to have

[3]William W. Bibb, territorial governor of Alabama and first governor of the state of Alabama, 1816–1820.

been also restored; but I say this with doubt and diffidence. That the President thought the seizure of the Spanish posts was an act of war, is manifest from his opening message, in which he says, that to have retained them, would have changed our relations with Spain, to do which the power of the Executive was incompetent, Congress alone possessing it. The President has, in this instance, deserved well of his country. He has taken the only course which he could have pursued, consistent with the constitution of the land. . . . The Spanish posts were not in the possession of the enemy. One old Indian only was found in the Barrancas, none in Pensacola, none in St. Marks. There was not even the color of a threat of Indian occupation as it regards Pensacola and the Barrancas. . . . Mr. C. said he rejoiced to have seen the President manifesting, by the restoration of Pensacola, his devotedness to the constitution. When the whole country was ringing with plaudits for its capture, he said, and he said alone, in the limited circle in which he moved, that the President must surrender it; that he could not hold it. . . .

. . . Recal to your recollection, said he, the free nations which have gone before us. Where are they now, and how have they lost their liberties? If we could transport ourselves back to the ages when Greece and Rome flourished in their greatest prosperity, and, mingling in the throng ask a Grecian if he did not fear some daring military chieftain, covered with glory, some Philip or Alexander, would one day overthrow his liberties? No! no! the confident and indignant Grecian would exclaim, we have nothing to fear from our heroes; our liberties will be eternal. If a Roman citizen had been asked, if he did not fear the conqueror of Gaul might establish a throne upon the ruins of the public liberty, he would have instantly repelled the unjust insinuation. Yet Greece had fallen, Caesar had passed the Rubicon, and the patriotic arm even of Brutus could not preserve the liberties of his country! The celebrated Madame de Stael, in her last and perhaps best work, has said, that in the very year, almost the very month, when the President of the Directory declared that monarchy would never more show its frightful head in France, Bonaparte, with his grenadiers, entered the palace of St. Cloud, and, dispersing, with the bayonet the deputies of the people, deliberating on the affairs of the state, laid the foundations of that vast fabric of despotism which overshadowed all Europe. He hoped not to be misunderstood; he was far from intimating that Gen. Jackson cherished any designs inimical to the liberties of the country. He believed his intentions pure and patriotic. He thanked God that he would not, but he thanked him still more that he could not, if he would, overturn the liberties of the Republic. But precedents, if bad, were fraught with the most dangerous consequences. Man has been described, by some of those who have treated of his nature, as a bundle of habits. The definition was much truer when applied to governments. Precedents were their habits. There was one important difference between the formation of habits by an individual and by governments. He contracts it only after frequent repetition. A single instance fixes the habit and determines the direction of governments. Against the alarming doctrine of unlimited discretion in our military commanders, when applied even to prisoners of war, he must enter his protest. It began upon them; it would end on us. He hoped that our happy form of government was destined to be perpetual. But if it were to be preserved, it must be by the practice of virtue, by justice, by moderation, by magnanimity, by greatness of soul, by keeping a watchful and steady eye on the Executive; and, above all, by holding to a strict accountability the military branch of the public force.

We are fighting, said Mr. C. a great moral battle for the benefit, not only of our country, but of all mankind. The eyes of the whole world are in fixed attention upon us. . . . Every where the black cloud of legitimacy is suspended over the world, save only one bright spot, which breaks out from the political hemisphere of the West, to brighten, and animate, and gladden the human heart. Obscure that, by the downfall of liberty here, and all mankind are enshrouded in one universal darkness. . . . When the minions of despotism heard, in Europe, of the seizure of Pensacola, how did they chuckle, and chide the admirers of our institutions, tauntingly pointing to the demonstrations of a spirit of injustice and aggrandisement made by our country, in the midst of amicable negociation. Behold, said they, the conduct of those who are constantly reproaching kings. You saw how those admirers were astounded and hung their heads. You saw, too, when that illustrious man, who presides over us, adopted his pacific, moderate and just course, how they once more lifted up their heads, with exultation and delight beaming in their countenances. And you saw how those minions themselves were finally compelled to unite in the general praises bestowed upon our government. Beware how you forfeit this exalted character. Beware how you give a fatal sanction, in this infant period of our republic, scarcely yet two score years old, to military insubordination. Remember that Greece had her Alexander, Rome her Cæsar, England her Cromwell, France her Bonaparte, and, that if we would escape the rock on which they split, we must avoid their errors. . . .

He hoped gentlemen would deliberately survey the awful position on which we stand. They may bear down all opposition; they may even vote the general the public thanks; they may carry him triumphantly through this house. But, if they do, in my humble judgment, it will be a triumph of the principle of insubordination—a triumph of the military over the civil authority—a triumph over the powers of this house—a triumph over the constitution of the land. And he prayed most devoutly to heaven, that it might not prove, in its ultimate effects and consequences, a triumph over the liberties of the people.

6

HENRY CLAY

On the Tariff

March 30–31, 1824

Following the War of 1812, Henry Clay joined many younger members of the Republican Party in believing that the United States had almost suffered defeat on account of its material weaknesses. These leaders, who initially included John C. Calhoun and Andrew Jackson, began to move away from the traditional Jeffersonian aversion to centralized government and advocated federal measures to strengthen the American economy. For Clay, these included a protective tariff, aid to internal improvements, and later, a national bank.

The need for such measures grew more urgent, Clay believed, when the Panic of 1819 sent the American economy into a tailspin. Clay's proposed cure was a higher protective tariff to stimulate American manufacturing. If poor farmers could get new jobs in manufacturing and commerce, the remaining farmers could prosper by selling them food and raw materials. Clay's support for a higher tariff was a centerpiece of his campaign for the presidency in 1824.

Clay's speech to the committee[1] describes the contemporary American economy. What does he think is the cause of its distress? What does he mean by a "home market," and how does he think it would help?

Clay recognizes that many of his ideas were controversial. Slaveholding representatives were especially worried about his plan. How does Clay try to allay their concerns? Clay argues that the growth of manufacturing will

---

[1]Committee of the whole House.

James F. Hopkins et al., eds., *The Papers of Henry Clay*, 11 vols. (Lexington: University Press of Kentucky, 1959–1992), 3: 683–727.

*benefit agriculturists, including southern planters. Why did slaveholders con-
tinue to oppose his ideas?*

*Clay here reaches beyond purely economic arguments to appeal to Amer-
ican nationalism and the value of compromise between contending interests. How effective are these parts of the speech?*

... It is my intention, with the permission of the committee, to avail myself
also of this opportunity, to present to its consideration those general
views, as they appear to me, of the true policy of this country, which imperiously demand the passage of this bill. I am deeply sensible, Mr. Chairman, of the high responsibility of my present situation. But that responsibility inspires me with no other apprehension than that I shall be unable
to fulfil my duty; with no other solicitude than that I may, at least, in some
small degree, contribute to recal my country from the pursuit of a fatal
policy, which appears to me inevitably to lead to its impoverishment and
ruin. ...

Two classes of politicians divide the people of the United States. According to the system of one, the produce of foreign industry should be subjected to no other impost than such as may be necessary to provide a public revenue; and the produce of American industry should be left to sustain
itself, if it can, with no other than that incidental protection, in its competition, at home as well as abroad, with rival foreign articles. According to
the system of the other class, whilst they agree that the imposts should
be mainly, and may, under any modification, be safely relied on as a fit
and convenient source of public revenue, they would so adjust and arrange
the duties on foreign fabrics as to afford a gradual but adequate protection to American industry, and lessen our dependance on foreign nations,
by securing a certain, and, ultimately, a cheaper and better supply of our
own wants from our own abundant resources. Both classes are equally
sincere in their respective opinions, equally honest, equally patriotic, and
desirous of advancing the prosperity of the country. ...

In casting our eyes around us, the most prominent circumstance which
fixes our attention, and challenges our deepest regret, is, the general distress which pervades the whole country. It is forced upon us by numerous facts of the most incontestable character. It is indicated by the diminished exports of native produce; ... by our diminished commerce; by
successive unthreshed crops of grain, perishing in our barns and barn-
yards for the want of a market; by the alarming diminution of the circulating medium; by the numerous bankruptcies, not limited to the trading
classes, but extending to all orders of society; by an universal complaint

of the want of employment, and a consequent reduction of the wages of labor; by the ravenous pursuit after public situations, not for the sake of their honors, and the performance of their public duties, but as a means of private subsistence; by the reluctant resort to the perilous use of paper money; by the intervention of legislation in the delicate relation between debtor and creditor; and, above all, by the low and depressed state of the value of almost every description of the whole mass of the property of the nation, which has, on an average, sunk not less than about fifty per cent. within a few years. This distress pervades every part of the Union, every class of society; all feel it, though it may be felt, at different places, in different degrees. It is like the atmosphere which surrounds us—all must inhale it, and none can escape it. . . . What is the CAUSE of this widespreading distress, of this deep depression, which we behold stamped on the public countenance? . . .

. . . It is to be found in the fact that, during almost the whole existence of this government, we have shaped our industry, our navigation, and our commerce, in reference to an extraordinary war[2] in Europe, and to foreign markets, which no longer exist; in the fact that we have depended too much upon foreign sources of supply, and excited too little the native; in the fact that, whilst we have cultivated, with assiduous care, our foreign resources, we have suffered those at home to wither, in a state of neglect and abandonment. The consequence of the termination of the war of Europe, has been the resumption of European commerce, European navigation, and the extension of European agriculture and European industry, in all its branches. Europe, therefore, has no longer occasion to any thing like the same extent as that which she had during her wars, for American commerce, American navigation, the produce of American industry. Europe in commotion, and convulsed throughout all her members, is to America no longer the same Europe as she is now, tranquil, and watching with the most vigilant attention all her own peculiar interests, without regard to the operation of her policy upon us. The effect of this altered state of Europe upon us, has been to circumscribe the employment of our marine, and greatly to reduce the value of the produce of our territorial labor. The further effect of this twofold reduction has been to decrease the value of all property, whether on the land or on the ocean, and which I suppose to be about fifty per cent. And the still further effect

---

[2]The French Revolution and the wars of the Emperor Napoléon convulsed Europe for most of the years between 1791 and 1815. European agriculture was seriously disrupted during this period of conflict, and Americans prospered by supplying goods and services to the warring nations.

has been to diminish the amount of our circulating medium, in a proportion not less by its transmission abroad, or its withdrawal by the banking institutions, from a necessity which they could not control. . . . The greatest want of civilized society is a market for the sale and exchange of the surplus of the produce of the labor of its members. This market may exist at home or abroad, or both, but it must exist somewhere, if society prospers; and wherever it does exist, it should be competent to the absorption of the entire surplus of production. It is most desirable that there should be both a home and a foreign market. But, with respect to their relative superiority, I cannot entertain a doubt. The home market is first in order, and paramount in importance. The object of the bill under consideration, is to create this home market, and to lay the foundations of a genuine American policy. It is opposed; and it is incumbent upon the partisans of the foreign policy (terms which I shall use without any invidious intent) to demonstrate that the foreign market is an adequate vent for the surplus produce of our labor. But is it so? 1. Foreign nations cannot, if they would, take our surplus produce. If the source of supply, no matter of what, increases in a greater ratio than the demand for that supply, a glut of the market is inevitable, even if we suppose both to remain perfectly unobstructed. The duplication of our population takes place in terms of about twenty-five years. . . . Supposing the increase of our production to be in the same ratio, we should, every succeeding year, have, of surplus produce, four per cent. more than that of the preceding year, without taking into the account the differences of seasons which neutralize each other. . . . Now, the total foreign population, who consume our surplus produce, upon an average, do not double their aggregate number in a shorter term than that of about 100 years. Our powers of production increase then in a ratio four times greater than their powers of consumption. And hence their utter inability to receive from us our surplus produce.

But, 2dly, If they could, they will not. The policy of all Europe is adverse to the reception of our agricultural produce, so far as it comes into collision with its own; and, under that limitation, we are absolutely forbid to enter their ports, except under circumstances which deprive them of all value as a steady market. The policy of all Europe rejects those great staples of our country, which consist of objects of human subsistence. . . . Even Great Britain, to which we are its best customer, and from which we receive nearly one half in value of our whole imports, will not take from us articles of subsistence produced in our country cheaper than can be produced in Great Britain. In adopting this exclusive policy, the states of Europe do not inquire what is best for us, but what suits themselves, respectively. . . . They do not guide themselves by that romantic philanthropy, which we see displayed here, and which invokes us to continue to purchase the produce of foreign industry, without regard to the state or prosperity of our own, that foreigners may be pleased to purchase the few remaining articles of ours which their restrictive policy has not yet absolutely excluded from their consumption. . . .

Our agricultural is our greatest interest. It ought ever to be predominant. All others should bend to it. And, in considering what is for its advantage, we should contemplate it in all its varieties, of planting, farming, and grazing. Can we do nothing to invigorate it? nothing to correct the errors of the past, and to brighten the still more unpromising prospects which lie before us? We have seen, I think, the causes of the distresses of the country. We have seen, that an exclusive dependence upon the foreign market must lead to still severer distress, to impoverishment, to ruin. We must then change somewhat our course. We must give a new direction to some portion of our industry. We must speedily adopt a genuine American policy. Still cherishing a foreign market, let us create also a home market, to give further scope to the consumption of the produce of American industry. Let us counteract the policy of foreigners, and withdraw the support which we now give to their industry, and stimulate that of our own country. . . .

The creation of a home market is not only necessary to procure for our agriculture a just reward of its labors, but it is indispensable to obtain a supply of our necessary wants. If we cannot sell, we cannot buy. That portion of our population (and we have seen that it is not less than four-fifths,) which makes comparatively nothing that foreigners will buy, has nothing to make purchases with from foreigners. . . . It is in vain to tantalize us with the greater cheapness of foreign fabrics. There must be an ability to purchase, if an article be obtained, whatever may be the price, high or low, at which it was sold. And a cheap article is as much beyond the grasp of him who has no means to buy, as a high one. Even if it were true that the American manufacturer would supply consumption at dearer rates, it is better to have his fabrics than the unattainable foreign fabrics; for it is better to be ill supplied than not supplied at all. A coarse coat, which will communicate warmth and cover nakedness, is better than no coat.— The superiority of the home market results, 1st, from its steadiness and comparative certainty at all times; 2d, from the creation of reciprocal interests; 3d, from its greater security; and, lastly from an ultimate and not distant augmentation of consumption, and, consequently, of comfort, from increased quantity and reduced prices. But this home market, highly desirable as it is, can only be created and cherished by the PROTECTION of our own legislation against the inevitable prostration of our industry, which must ensue from the action of FOREIGN policy and legislation. . . .

. . . Labor is the source of all wealth; but it is not natural labor only. And the fundamental error of the gentleman from Virginia,[3] and of the school to which he belongs, in adducing, from our sparse population, our unfitness for the introduction of the arts, consists in their not sufficiently weighing the importance of the power of machinery. In former times, when but little comparative use was made of machinery, manual labor and the price of wages were circumstances of the greatest consideration. But it is far otherwise in these later times. Such are the improvements and the perfections in machinery, that, in analyzing the compound value of many fabrics, the element of natural labor is so inconsiderable as almost to escape detection. . . . Britain is herself the most striking illustration of the immense power of machinery. . . . A statistical writer of that country, several years ago, estimated the total amount of the artificial or machine labor of the nation, to be equal to that of one hundred millions of able-bodied laborers. Subsequent estimates of her artificial labor, at the present day, carry it to the enormous height of two hundred millions. But the population of the three kingdoms is 21,500,000. . . . Look at her immense subsidies! Behold her, standing unaided and alone, breasting the storm of Napoleon's colossal power, when all continental Europe owned and yielded to its irresistible sway; and, finally, contemplate her vigorous prosecution of the war, with and without allies, to its splendid termination, on the ever-memorable field of Waterloo! . . .

It [the tariff] has been treated as an imposition of burthens upon one part of the community by design for the benefit of another; as if, in fact, money were taken from the pockets of one portion of the people and put into the pockets of another. But, is that a fair representation of it? No man pays the duty assessed on the foreign article by compulsion, but voluntarily; and this voluntary duty, if paid, goes into the common exchequer, for the common benefit of all. Consumption has four objects of choice. 1. It may abstain from the use of the foreign article, and thus avoid the payment of the tax. 2. It may employ the rival American fabric. 3. It may engage in the business of manufacturing, which this bill is designed to foster. 4. Or it may supply itself from the household manufactures. But, it is said by the honorable gentleman from Virginia, that the South, owing to the character of a certain por-

---

[3]The gentleman from Virginia refers to Representative Philip P. Barbour, a strong opponent of the protective tariff.

tion of its population, cannot engage in the business of manufacturing. Now, I do not agree in that opinion to the extent in which it is asserted. The circumstance alluded to may disqualify the South from engaging in every branch of manufacture as largely as other quarters of the Union, but to some branches of it that part of our population is well adapted. It indisputably affords great facility in the household or domestic line.

But, if the gentleman's premises were true, could his conclusion be admitted? . . . The gentleman would have us abstain from adopting a policy called for by the interests of the greater and freer part of our population. But is that reasonable? Can it be expected that the interests of the greater part should be made to bend to the condition of the servile part of our population? That, in effect, would be to make us the slaves of slaves. . . . But, does not a perseverance in the foreign policy, as it now exists, in fact, make all parts of the Union, not planting, tributary to the planting parts? What is the argument? . . . The existing state of things . . . presents a sort of tacit compact between the cotton grower and the British manufacturer, the stipulations of which are, on the part of the cotton grower, that the whole of the United States, the other portions as well as the cotton growing, shall remain open and unrestricted in the consumption of British manufactures; and, on the part of the British manufacturer, that, in consideration thereof, he will continue to purchase the cotton of the South.

Thus, then, we perceive, that the proposed measure, instead of sacrificing the South to the other parts of the Union, seeks only to preserve them from being absolutely sacrificed under the operation of the tacit compact which I have described. Supposing the South to be actually incompetent, or disinclined to embark at all in the business of manufacturing, is not its interest, nevertheless, likely to be promoted by creating a new and an American source of supply for its consumption? Now foreign powers, and Great Britain principally, have the monopoly of the supply of Southern consumption. If this bill should pass, an American competitor in the supply of the South would be raised up, and ultimately, I cannot doubt, that it would be supplied cheaper and better. . . .

10. The next objection of the honorable gentleman from Virginia, which I shall briefly notice, is, that the manufacturing system is adverse to the genius of our government, in its tendency to the accumulation of large capitals in a few hands; in the corruption of the public morals, which is alleged to be incident to it; and in the consequent danger to the public liberty. The first part of the objection would apply to every lucrative business—to commerce, to planting, and to the learned professions. . . .

The best security against the demoralization of society, is the constant and profitable employment of its members. The greatest danger to public liberty is from idleness and vice. If manufactures form cities, so does commerce. And the disorders and violence which proceed from the contagion of the passions, are as frequent in one description of those communities as in the other. There is no doubt but that the yeomanry of a country is the safest depository of public liberty. In all time to come, and under any probable direction of the labor of our population, the agricultural class must be much the most numerous and powerful, and will ever retain, as it ought to retain, a preponderating influence in our councils. The extent and the fertility of our lands constitute an adequate security against an excess in manufactures; and also against oppression on the part of capitalists towards the laboring portions of the community....

Other and animating considerations invite us to adopt the policy of this system. Its importance, in connexion with the general defence in time of war, cannot fail to be duly estimated. Need I recal to our painful recollection the sufferings, for the want of an adequate supply of absolute necessaries, to which the defenders of their country's rights and our entire population were subjected during the late war? Or to remind the committee of the great advantage of a steady and unfailing source of supply, unaffected alike in war and in peace? Its importance, in reference to the stability of our Union, that paramount and greatest of all our interests, cannot fail warmly to recommend it, or at least to conciliate the forbearance of every patriot bosom. Now our people present the spectacle of a vast assemblage of jealous rivals, all eagerly rushing to the sea-board, jostling each other in their way, to hurry off to glutted foreign markets the perishable produce of their labor. The tendency of that policy, in conformity to which this bill is prepared, is to transform these competitors into friends and mutual customers; and, by the reciprocal exchanges of their respective productions, to place the confederacy upon the most solid of all foundations, the basis of common interest. And is not government called upon, by every stimulating motive, to adapt its policy to the actual condition and extended growth of our great republic? . . . Our policy should be modified . . ., so as to comprehend all, and sacrifice none. . . .

Even if the benefits of the policy were limited to certain sections of our country, would it not be satisfactory to behold American industry, wherever situated, active, animated, and thrifty, rather than persevere in a course which renders us subservient to foreign industry? But these benefits are twofold, direct, and collateral, and in the one shape or the other, they will diffuse themselves throughout the Union. All parts of the Union will participate, more or less, in both. As to the direct benefit, it is probable that the North and the East will enjoy the largest share. But the West and the South will also participate in them. Philadelphia, Baltimore, and Richmond, will divide with the Northern capitals the business of manufacturing. The latter city unites more advantages for its successful prosecution than any other place I know, Zanesville, in Ohio, only excepted. And where the direct benefit does not accrue, that will be enjoyed of supplying the raw material and provisions for the consumption of artisans. . . . You think the measure injurious to you; we believe our preservation depends upon its adoption. Our convictions, mutually honest, are equally strong. What is to be done? I invoke that saving spirit of mutual concession under which our blessed Constitution was formed, and under which alone it can be happily administered. I appeal to the South — to the high-minded, generous, and patriotic South — with which I have so often co-operated, in attempting to sustain the honor and to vindicate the rights of our country. Should it not offer, upon the altar of the public good, some sacrifice of its peculiar opinions? Of what does it complain? A possible temporary enhancement in the objects of consumption. Of what do we complain? A total incapacity, produced by the foreign policy, to purchase, at any price, necessary foreign objects of consumption. In such an alternative, inconvenient only to it, ruinous to us, can we expect too much from Southern magnanimity? The just and confident expectation of the passage of this bill has flooded the country with recent importations of foreign fabrics. If it should not pass, they will complete the work of destruction of our domestic industry. If it should pass, they will prevent any considerable rise in the price of foreign commodities, until our own industry shall be able to supply competent substitutes.

To the friends of the tariff I would also anxiously appeal. Every arrangement of its provisions does not suit each of you; you desire some further alterations; you would make it perfect. You want what you will never get. Nothing human is perfect. . . . If this bill do not pass, unquestionably no other can pass at this session, or probably during this Congress. And who will go home and say that he rejected all the benefits of this bill, because molasses has been subjected to the enormous additional duty of five cents per gallon? I call, therefore, upon the friends of the American policy, to yield somewhat of their own peculiar wishes, and not to reject the practicable in the idle pursuit after the unattainable. Let us imitate the illustrious example of the framers of the Constitution, and, always remembering that whatever springs from man partakes of his imperfections, depend upon experience to suggest, in future, the necessary amendments. . . .

7

EDWARD PATCHELL

Letter to Andrew Jackson

August 7, 1824

The leading candidates for president in 1824 were William H. Crawford of Georgia, John Quincy Adams of Massachusetts, Henry Clay of Kentucky, and Andrew Jackson of Tennessee. Crawford, Adams, and Clay were major players in national politics who did most of their campaigning in Washington. Only Andrew Jackson depended on his military reputation and his appeal to ordinary voters far from the seats of power. The following letter to Jackson from Edward Patchell[1] of Pittsburgh shows how favorably many grassroots voters viewed the general and his candidacy. Patchell describes an election for the office of brigadier general of the local unit of the Pennsylvania militia in which the different candidates were each associated with their favorite presidential candidate. Patchell regards his own victory in the election as a surrogate triumph for Jackson.

What sort of man was Edward Patchell? Why would he have favored Andrew Jackson for president? Why was he inclined to make a distinction between "the multitude" who favored Jackson and the "Office holders and office hunters" who favored other candidates?

My dear Sir, I had the honour of receiving your letter of the 16th may dated Washington City, which I woul[d] have on the instant promptly replyed to, but about that very period of time I had granted permission to my friends to use my name as a candidate for Brigadier General; . . . When a meeting was advertised to be held in the Courthouse, where there assembled upon the occasion upwards of one thousand of our citizens; the names of the several candidates ware put on nomination, and balletted for viva voice, when they ware severally hissed by nine tenths of the multitude; Untill my name was reached on the list, when

---

[1]Edward Patchell was a hat maker. Like Jackson's parents, he was born in north Ireland, and like Jackson himself, Patchell had little formal education.

John Spencer Bassett, ed., *The Correspondence of Andrew Jackson,* 7 vols. (Washington, D.C.: Carnegie Institution of Washington, 1926–1935), 3: 262–65.

shouts of Old Hickory resounded from all parts of the house, nine cheers for Old Hickory, was the word, "when the crowd burst in upon me . . ." and bore me out on their sholders into the public square; I assure you General I felt more proud of your nick name "than I now feel of the Generalship. . . . And I must confess had not it been for your sake I never would have yielded to become a candidate at this stage of life. Your friends here had applied to me at an early hour, I peremptorily declined the honour they purposed to confare on me; they then took up Major Piers, . . . "yet he . . . did not possess that digree of popularity which would warrant or justify the risque of your honour," which your friends here considered staked on the result of the Election; I therefore was again applyed to, and I gave my consent; And truely General, notwithstanding I have been Elected to that honourable post, I confess I am very unquallifyed to discharge the duties of any office whatever, as I have always throughout the whole course of my life" kept on the back ground well knowing my own imperfections . . . : I will beg leave to entertain you for a moment with a bare out line of my life, the part of the world" I was raised in, and the poor chance I had of receiving a polished education the alone accomplishment "which adorns the Genius of a promising youth.

My Father lived . . . a few miles below the City of Londonderry in the North of Ireland; He was a plain country farmer," and aspired no higher than many others of his good neighbours, thought if he sent his children to a common country schoolmaster for a few years "to learn Reading Writing and Arithmetick, that was all sufficient; I did not know the use of a classick Education at the time, being a miner; therefore since I have been in America" for the want of that all necessary accomplishment, I have stood in the rear rank, and never ventured in the front, untill Andrew Jackson the son of my dear countryman," was anounced a candidate for the first office in the peoples guift, And altho I well knew that my talents ware unadiquate to the task, yed I depended not only on my personal courage alone, but I trusted in my God, and your God, whome hath raised you up for to be a Saviour and a deliverance for his people. I considered you ware justly entitled to a nation's gratitude, and altho I well knew that I was not a polititian," yet nevertheless ware I to try" I could do something. . . . The first meeting which was held in the Courthouse in favour of your Election . . . was very numerous," much larger than any ever had been known heretofore—after the Chairman and Secretaries ware appointed" Mr. Baldwain stated the object of the meeting, and your name ware placed at the foot of the list; Wm. H. Crawford got one vote, H Clay five, J. Q. Adams two, J. C. Calhoun four, and Gen Andw Jackson upward of 1000, a resolution was then offered "that Henry

Baldwain be appointed to write an address" to the democratic republicans throughout the U. S. . . .

. . . I have reduced the *Lousie*[2] party here from 10,000 to something less than fifty, and they are chiefly the antient and notorious wire workers,[3] they are the Office holders and office hunters"; and all they can do now" is grin and shew thier teeth. They have made more than one attempt to stab you through my sides, in the collums of their Statesman;[4] But I stand here on too high ground for their arrows to reach me. General, I have never had the pleasure of seeing your face, and perhaps never may untill we meet in the Kingdom of Heaven," but you have my heart, and may that divine power" whoes almighty arm hath both defended and protected you" through every peral and danger" support and uphold your honour in old age and let the result of your pending Election" be what it may, give God the praise, his will be don on earth. . . .

I trust my dear Sir, that by this time you are fully sensible" that I have no possible motive in view" by becoming your friend and advocating your cause, for It is too well known that I am neither an office hunter, or an office holder, I assure you Sir, that when I have don all that I can to promote your interest, that I have don no more than what my heart tells me" is the bounden duty of every true and faithful American. . . . May God bless you Jackson. . . .

. . . Had I have been in possession of the Learning, talents and political knowledge of Henry Baldwain, I have vainity" to think that long err now, I would have reasoned the people into a sense of their duty. But Jackson, I must repeat it, I have done no more than my duty, and I even forbid you "return me thanks: And should we fail this Election, I will pray my God' to spare life" untill I see Andrew Jackson President of the U States, and then let me close my eyes in peace, adue. . . .

---

[2] *Lousie,* or "lousy." It is not clear why Patchell would call his opponents "lousy," except for his overall dislike of them.

[3] Wire workers: wire pullers or political manipulators; related to the current expression "to pull strings."

[4] Collums of their Statesman: that is, columns of the Pittsburgh *Statesman,* an anti-Jackson newspaper.

8

ANDREW JACKSON

Letter to L. H. Coleman

April 26, 1824

In 1824, Andrew Jackson received a letter from Dr. L. H. Coleman of Warrenton, North Carolina, asking his opinion of the tariff increases that Henry Clay had proposed in Congress (see Document 6). Candidates frequently received such letters, and it was understood that their answers would be published in the local press and perhaps republished by other newspapers around the country. Jackson therefore had to compose his answer carefully, since the published version would become a major part of his campaign literature. The tariff issue created complex political problems for Jackson because he had many supporters in Pennsylvania and New York who favored high tariffs and many southern supporters who opposed them. His own feelings about the matter were also complex. The tariff was the government's main source of operating revenue. Jackson wanted to keep the revenue high enough to repay the national debt, but he was also a southern planter who believed in low taxes and limited government. For the sake of his personal convictions and his political aspirations, Jackson needed to find a middle course on the tariff that would conform to his own principles and satisfy his northern supporters without alienating the South. The following reply to Dr. Coleman is his carefully worded response.

The letter to Dr. Coleman is above all a campaign document. How does Jackson use its wording to advance his candidacy? What reasons does he give for supporting a "judicious" level of protection? How are these similar to those of Henry Clay, as expressed in Document 6? How are they different? How does Jackson use military and patriotic concerns to make a case for tariff protection? Is the letter effective in its effort to appeal to high and low tariff supporters alike?

Sir: I had the honor this day to receive your letter of the 21st instant and with candor shall reply to it. My name has been brought before the nation by the people themselves without any agency of mine: for I wish it not to be forgotten that I have never solicited office, nor when called upon by

---

John Spencer Bassett, ed., *The Correspondence of Andrew Jackson,* 7 vols. (Washington, D.C.: Carnegie Institution of Washington, 1926–1935), 3: 249–51.

the constituted authorities have ever declined where I conceived my services would be beneficial to my country. But as my name has been brought before the nation for the first office in the gift of the people, it is incumbent on me, when asked, frankly to declare my opinion upon any political or national question pending before and about which the country feels an interest.

You ask my opinion on the Tariff. I answer, that I am in favor of a judicious examination and revision of it; and so far as the Tariff before us embraces the design of fostering, protecting, and preserving within ourselves the means of national defense and independence, particularly in a state of war, I would advocate and support it. The experience of the late war ought to teach us a lesson; and one never to be forgotten. If our liberty and republican form of government, procured for us by our revolutionary fathers, are worth the blood and treasure at which they were obtained, it surely is our duty to protect and defend them. . . .

Heaven smiled upon, and gave us liberty and independence. That same providence has blessed us with the means of national independence and national defense. If we omit or refuse to use the gifts which He has extended to us, we deserve not the continuation of His blessings. He has filled our mountains and our plains with minererals—with lead, iron, and copper, and given us a climate and soil for the growing of hemp and wool. These being the grand materials of our national defense, they ought to have extended to them adequate and fair protection, that our own manufactories and laborers may be placed on a fair competition with those of Europe; and that we may have within our own country a supply of those leading and important articles so essential to war. Beyond this, I look at the Tariff with an eye to the proper distribution of labor and revenue; and with a view to discharge our national debt. I am one of those who do not believe that a national debt is a national blessing, but rather a curse to a republic; inasmuch as it is calculated to raise around the administration a moneyed aristocracy dangerous to the liberties of the country.

This Tariff—I mean a judicious one—possesses more fanciful than real dangers. . . . Draw from agriculture the superabundant labor, employ it in mechanism and manufactures, thereby creating a home market for your breadstuffs, and distributing labor to a most profitable account, and benefits to the country will result. Take from agriculture in the United States six hundred thousand men, women, and children, and you at once give a home market for more bread stuffs than all Europe now furnishes us. In short, sir, we have been too long subject to the policy of the British merchants. It is time we should become a little more *Americanized,* and instead of feeding the paupers and laborers of Europe, feed our own, or else in a short time, by continuing our present policy, we shall all be paupers ourselves.

It is, therefore, my opinion that a careful Tariff is much wanted to pay our national debt, and afford us the means of that defense within ourselves on which the safety and liberty of the country depend; and last, though not least, give a proper distribution to our labor, which must prove beneficial to the happiness, independence, and wealth of the community. . . .

I have presented you my opinions freely, because I am without concealment, and should indeed despise myself if I could believe myself capable of acquiring the confidence of any by means so ignoble.

I am, sir, very respectfully, your obedient servant.

9

The First Volley:
Letters on the
"Corrupt Bargain" of 1824

Andrew Jackson received the greatest number of electoral votes in the presidential election of 1824, but because no candidate received a majority, the House of Representatives had to choose the president from among the three highest vote getters. When Henry Clay threw his support to the second-place finisher, John Quincy Adams of Massachusetts, Adams was elected by the House on February 9, 1825. Clay's decision was controversial because it violated his instructions from the Kentucky legislature and because Jackson supporters felt their candidate's level of support had won him the moral right to victory. To defend his actions, Clay wrote a letter to a friend in Virginia and asked him to publish it. When the letter became public, Jackson made a reply in another letter to a supporter in New York, and that letter also was published. Both letters are reprinted here.

Clay gives many reasons for supporting Adams. Why does he suggest that the election of a "military chieftain" would put America on "the fatal road which has conducted every other republic to ruin"? Describe the kinds of people that Clay's letter would have appealed to.

James F. Hopkins et al., eds., *The Papers of Henry Clay*, 11 vols. (Lexington: University Press of Kentucky, 1959–1992), 4: 45–46.

Evaluate Jackson's reply to Clay. How does the general imply that politicians like Clay pose a greater danger to the republic than a "military chieftain"? Which citizens would likely be more persuaded by Jackson's letter than by Clay's?

HENRY CLAY TO FRANCIS T. BROOKE
January 28, 1825

My Dear Sir: My position, in regard to the Presidential election, is highly critical, & such as to leave me no path on which I can move without censure; I have pursued, in regard to it, the rule which I always observe in the discharge of my public duty. I have interrogated my conscience as to what I ought to do, & that faithful guide tells me that I ought to vote for Mr. Adams. I shall fulfill its injunctions. Mr. Crawford's state of health, & the circumstances under which he presents himself to the house, appear to me to be conclusive against him. As a friend of liberty, & to the permanence of our institutions, I cannot consent, in this early stage of their existence, by contributing to the election of a military chieftain, to give the strongest guarranty that this republic will march in the fatal road which has conducted every other republic to ruin. I owe to our friendship this frank exposition of my intentions. I am, & shall continue to be, assailed by all the abuse, which partizan zeal, malignity, & rivalry can invent. I shall risk, without emotion, these effusions of malice, & remain unshaken in my purpose. What is a public man worth, if he will not expose himself, on fit occasions, for the good of his country?—

As to the result of the election, I cannot speak with absolute certainty; but there is every reason to believe that we shall avoid the dangerous precedent to which I allude.

Be pleased to give my respects to Mr. ...... & believe me always your cordial friend.

ANDREW JACKSON TO SAMUEL SWARTWOUT
February 22, 1825

My Dear Sir, . . .
Yesterday I recd. your communication adverting to the reasons and defence presented by Mr. Clay to Judge Brooks why duty and reflection imposed upon him the necessity of standing in opposition to me, because of my being as he is pleased to style me, "a Military Chieftain." I had before seen the letter; first when it appeared, I did entertain the opinion,

that perhaps some notice of it might be necessary. . . . I might yet consider some notice of it necessary; such a belief however I cannot entertain, without insulting the general testimonial with which by ninety-nine electers of the people I have been honored.

I am well aware that this term "Military Chieftain" has for sometime past been a cant phrase with Mr. Clay and certain of his retainers; but the vote with which by the people I have been honored, is enough to satisfy me, that the prejudice by them, sought to be produced availed but little. . . .

It is for an ingenuity stronger than mine to conceive what idea was intended to be conveyed by that term. It is very true that early in life, even in the days of boyhood, I contributed my mite to shake off the yoke of tyranny, and to build up the fabrick of free government; and when lately our country was involved in war, having the commission of Major Genl. of Militia in Tennessee, I made an appeal to the patriotism of the western citizens, when 3000 of them went with me to the field, to support her Eagles. If this can constitute me a "Military Chieftain" I am one. Aided by the patriotism of the western people, and an indulgent providence, it was my good fortune to protect our frontier border from the savages, and successfully to defend an important and vulnerable point of our Union. . . . Does this constitute a "Military Chieftain"? and are all our brave men in war, who go forth to defend their rights, and the rights of their country to be termed Military Chieftains, and therefore denounced? . . .

Mr. Clay never yet has risked himself for his country, sacrificed his repose, or made an effort to repel an invading foe; of course his "conscience" assured him that it was altogether wrong in any other man to lead his countrymen to battle and victory. He who fights, and fights successfully must according to his standard be held up as a "Military Chieftain": even Washington could he again appear among us might be so considered, because he dared to be a virtuous and successfull soldier, an honest statesman, and a correct man. It is only when overtaken by disaster and defeat, that any man is to be considered a safe politician and correct statesman. . . .

. . . It will be ascertained that I did not solicit the office of President. . . . No midnight taper burnt by me; no secret conclaves were held, or cabals entered into, to persuade any to a violation of pledges given, or of instructions received. By me no plans were concerted to impair the pure principles of our Republican institutions, or to frustrate that fundimental one which maintains the supremacy of the people's will; on the contrary, having never in any manner . . . interfered with the question, my conscience stands void of offence, and will go quietly with me, heedless of the insinuations of any, who thro management may seek an influence, not sanctioned by merit. . . .

10

WASHINGTON GAZETTE

"Mr. Clay and His Conscience"
February 11, 1825

Clay's public letter of January 28, 1825 (see Document 9) infuriated Jackson supporters. They felt that Clay's rejection of Jackson as a "military chieftain" not only insulted the general but, even worse, insulted the judgment of those who voted for him. The editor of Washington Gazette *reprinted Clay's letter with his own angry commentary. The editor was formerly a supporter of William H. Crawford but had come over to Jackson shortly before the vote in the House of Representatives.*

What are the editor's reasons for denouncing Clay and "his 'conscience'"? Why does he think that the will of the people is superior to the opinion of an individual? How do these ideas reflect American beliefs about "democracy"?

Mr. Clay, sensible of the indignation which would overtake him for his late conduct, has addressed to a friend in Virginia the following letter, and that friend has caused it to be inserted in the *Richmond Enquirer* of the 8th instant. It is but a thin disguise to a foul purpose. He, too, seizes upon the state of Mr. Crawford's health. He, too, puts on the semblance of apprehension of Gen. Jackson's military character. It will not do. Four states, whose delegations were on the spot, who had seen and conversed with Mr. Crawford, who are as good judges of his strength of mind and body as Mr. Clay, have attested, by their solemn votes, that both are good, and that Mr. Clay has misrepresented him. And what are "the circum-

From microfilm of the original, Library of Congress.

stances under which he presents himself to the House"? A minority of electoral votes. And did not Mr. Clay himself cling to a minority to the last moment? Did he not labor to exclude Mr. Crawford from the House, even by a plurality of one? And can any one doubt, if Mr. Clay had excluded Mr. Crawford, that he would have intrigued, with all his skill and dexterity, for the Presidency? No man doubts it. Then, as to Gen. Jackson—were not his military services, his great services to his country, the very cause why the People voted for him? They were. And Mr. Clay, in denouncing that Hero, sets himself up in judgment against the sense and the voice of the People—of the nation. He pretends to undervalue the minority of Mr. Crawford's electoral votes, and yet votes for Mr. Adams, who had a less number than General Jackson. His pretexts are too shallow to deceive any body. The selfish ambition of Henry Clay is visible in every line of his letter; and yet he has the boldness to appeal to his *"conscience"!* that conscience which, as a silent monitor, but too well informs him that he has caballed with Mr. Adams. What had we to fear from Gen. Jackson? He could not make war; for Congress alone can declare it. He could not raise and collect money, because that is the exclusive privilege of the same body. Checked on every side, what danger was there from this Hero which Mr. Clay attempted to brand as a mere "military chieftain"? Against whom did Gen. Jackson ever draw his sword but the enemies of his country?—Whom did he ever treat with harshness but the traitor? What expedition did he ever project but by the regular authority of government? And in what civil capacity has he ever failed to exercise a sound judgment and salutary discretion? If the People thought Gen. Jackson worthy, is it for Henry Clay to pronounce him unworthy? Is it for him to say to his fellow-citizens, "You shall not have the man you wish, but the man I will"? No.—Henry Clay himself has inflicted the deepest wound on the fundamental principle of our government. *He* has insulted and struck down the majesty of the People: *He* has impugned their sovereignty: *He* has interposed between the current of their sentiments and the object of their choice; and seeks to justify himself by stale electioneering excuses. A thousand "military chieftains" could not have done so much harm to our constitutional principles.—He has set a fatal example of corruption, which will open the way for future political adventurers. He has gambled away the rights of the People, and opened a course full of peril for free government. He has shewn to the foreign world that the Presidency may be bought and sold, like any other commodity in the market, and taught crowned heads, if they desire to subvert our liberties, where and how to apply their means.

11

MARGARET SMITH

Letter to Mrs. Kirkpatrick
March 11, 1829

Mrs. Margaret Bayard Smith was a leader of Washington's "high society," and her husband was the president of the local branch of the Bank of the United States. In 1829, she attended the first presidential inauguration of Andrew Jackson in the company of Francis Scott Key, author of "The Star Spangled Banner." Mrs. Smith left this vivid account of the day's events in a letter to her friend Mrs. Kirkpatrick.

Note the difference between the ceremony at the Capitol and the reception at the White House. Why did things go so much more smoothly at the former than the latter?

What sort of a person was Mrs. Smith? How did her social position affect her perception of the Jackson inauguration? In particular, note Mrs. Smith's attitudes toward "the people in all their majesty": At one point she calls them "sublime," and later she refers to "the rabble mob." What accounts for the difference? Why does she compare the crowd in the White House to the crowds who entered the palace of Versailles during the French Revolution? If Mrs. Smith had been able to vote, would she have been a Democrat or a National Republican?

. . . Thursday morning. I left the rest of this sheet for an account of the inauguration. It was not a thing of detail of a succession of small incidents. No, it was one grand whole, an imposing and majestic spectacle and to a reflective mind one of moral sublimity. Thousands and thousands of people, without distinction of rank, collected in an immense mass round the Capitol, silent, orderly and tranquil, with their eyes fixed on the front of that edifice, waiting the appearance of the President in the portico. The door from the Rotunda opens, preceded by the marshals, surrounded by the Judges of the Supreme Court, the old man with his grey locks, that crown of glory, advances, bows to the people, who greet him with a shout

---

Margaret Bayard Smith, *The First Forty Years of Washington Society* (New York: Scribners, 1906), 290–98.

that rends the air, the Cannons, from the heights around, from Alexandria and Fort Warburton proclaim the oath he has taken and all the hills reverberate the sound. It was grand, — it was sublime! An almost breathless silence, succeeded and the multitude was still, — listening to catch the sound of his voice, tho' it was so low, as to be heard only by those nearest to him. After reading his speech, the oath was administered to him by the Chief Justice. The Marshal presented the Bible. The President took it from his hands, pressed his lips to it, laid it reverently down, then bowed again to the people — Yes, to the people in all their majesty. And had the spectacle closed here, even Europeans must have acknowledged that a free people, collected in their might, silent and tranquil, restrained solely by a moral power, without a shadow around of military force, was majesty, rising to sublimity, and far surpassing the majesty of Kings and Princes, surrounded with armies and glittering in gold. . . .

A national salute was fired early in the morning, and ushered in the 4th of March. By ten oclock the Avenue was crowded with carriages of every description, from the splendid Barronet and coach, down to waggons and carts, filled with women and children, some in finery and some in rags, for it was the peoples President, and all would see him; the men all walked. . . . The terraces, the Balconies, the Porticos, seemed as we approached already filled. . . . It was a most exhilirating scene! Most of the ladies preferred being inside of the Capitol and the eastern portico, damp and cold as it was, had been filled from 9 in the morning by ladies who wished to be near the General when he spoke. Every room was filled and the windows crowded. . . . We stood on the South steps of the terrace; when the appointed hour came saw the General and his company advancing up the Avenue, slow, very slow, so impeded was his march by the crowds thronging around him. Even from a distance, he could be discerned from those who accompanied him, for he only was uncovered, (the Servant in presence of his Sovereign, the People). The south side of the Capitol hill was literally alive with the multitude, who stood ready to receive the hero and the multitude who attended him. "There, there, that is he," exclaimed different voices. "Which?" asked others. "He with the white head," was the reply. "Ah," exclaimed others, "there is the old man and his gray hair, there is the old veteran, there is Jackson." At last he enters the gate at the foot of the hill and turns to the road that leads round to the front of the Capitol. In a moment every one who until then had stood like statues gazing on the scene below them, rushed onward, to right, to left, to be ready to receive him in the front. Our party, of course, were more deliberate, we waited until the multitude had rushed past us and then left the terrace and walked round to the furthest side of the square, where there were no carriages to impede us, and entered it by the gate fronting the Capitol. Here was a clear space, and stationing ourselves on the central gravel walk we stood so as to have a clear, full view of the whole scene. The Capitol in all its grandeur and beauty. The Portico and grand steps leading to it, were filled with ladies. Scarlet, purple, blue, yellow, white draperies and waving plumes of every kind and colour, among the white marble pillars, had a fine effect. In the centre of the portico was a table covered with scarlet, behind it the closed door leading into the rotunda, below the Capitol and all around, a mass of living beings, not a ragged mob, but well dressed and well behaved respectable and worthy citizens. Mr. Frank Key, whose arm I had, and an old and frequent witness of great spectacles, often exclaimed, as well as myself, a mere novice, "It is beautiful, it is sublime!" ... At the moment the General entered the Portico and advanced to the table, the shout that rent the air, still resounds in my ears. When the speech was over, and the President made his parting bow, the barrier that had separated the people from him was broken down and they rushed up the steps all eager to shake hands with him. It was with difficulty he made his way through the Capitol and down the hill to the gateway that opens on the avenue. Here for a moment he was stopped. The living mass was impenetrable. After a while a passage was opened, and he mounted his horse which had been provided for his return (for he had walked to the Capitol) then such a cortege as followed him! Country men, farmers, gentlemen, mounted and dismounted, boys, women and children, black and white. Carriages, wagons and carts all pursuing him to the President's house.... We went Home, found your papa and sisters at the Bank, standing at the upper windows, where they had been seen by the President, who took off his hat to them, which they insisted was better than all we had seen.... In about an hour, the pavement was clear enough for us to walk. Your father, Mr. Wood, Mr. Ward, Mr. Lyon, with us, we set off to the President's House, but on a nearer approach found an entrance impossible, the yard and avenue was compact with living matter. The day was delightful, the scene animating, so we walked backward and forward at every turn meeting some new acquaintance and stopping to talk and shake hands.... [Finally] we effected our purpose. But what a scene did we witness! The *Majesty of the People* had disappeared, and a rabble, a mob, of boys, negros, women, children, scrambling, fighting, romping. What a pity what a pity! No arrangements had been made no police officers placed on duty and the whole house had been inundated by the rabble mob. We came too late. The President, after having been *literally* nearly pressed to death and almost suffocated and torn to pieces by the people in their eagerness to shake hands with Old Hickory, had retreated through the back way or south front and had escaped to his lodgings at Gadsby's. Cut glass and china to the amount of several thousand dollars had been broken in the struggle to get the refreshments, punch and other articles had been carried out in tubs and buckets, but had it been in hogsheads it would have been insufficient, ice-creams, and cake and lemonade, for 20,000 people, for it is said that number were there, tho' I think the estimate exaggerated. Ladies fainted, men were seen with bloody noses and such a scene of confusion took place as is impossible to describe, — those who got in could not get out by the door again, but had to scramble out of windows. At one time, the President who had retreated and retreated until he was pressed against the wall, could only be secured by a number of gentlemen forming round him and making a kind of barrier of their own bodies, and the pressure was so great that Col Bomford who was one said that at one time he was afraid they should have been pushed down, or on the President. It was then the windows were thrown open, and the torrent found an outlet, which otherwise might have proved fatal.

This concourse had not been anticipated and therefore not provided against. Ladies and gentlemen, only had been expected at this Levee, not the people en masse. But it was the People's day, and the People's President and the People would rule. God grant that one day or other, the People, do not put down all rule and rulers. I fear, enlightened Freemen as they are, they will be found, as they have been found in all ages and countries where they get the Power in their hands, that of all tyrants, they are the most ferocious, cruel and despotic. The noisy and disorderly rabble in the President's House brought to my mind descriptions I had read, of the mobs in the Tuileries and at Versailles. . . .

. . . Col. Bomford has been here, just now and given me an account of the Ball, which he says was elegant, splendid and in perfect order. The President and his family were not there. The Vice President and lady and the members of the new cabinet were. Mrs. Bomford was in her grand costume, — scarlet velvet richly trimmed with gold embroidery, the large Ruby, set in diamonds, for which Col. Bomford has refused five thousand dollars, and which I believe you have seen, she wore in her turban. . . . During all this bustle in the city, Mr. Adams was quietly fixed at Meridian Hill, to which place he and his family had removed some days before. . . . Everybody is in a state of agitation, — gloomy or glad. A *universal removal* in the departments is apprehended, and many are quaking and trembling, where *all* depends on their places.

The city, so crowded and bustling, by tomorrow will be silent and deserted, for people are crowding away as eagerly as they crowded here. . . .

12

ANDREW JACKSON

Excerpt on Indian Removal
from the First Annual Message

December 8, 1829

Following the example of Thomas Jefferson, nineteenth-century presidents did not appear yearly before Congress to make a State of the Union address. Instead they sent Congress a detailed annual message in written form, spelling out their policy objectives for the coming year. Jackson used a portion of his first annual message to spell out his policy toward Native Americans.

In 1829, there were still dozens of Indian tribes living on their own lands between the Appalachian Mountains and the Mississippi River. Jackson's proposals were primarily aimed at the Cherokees, Creeks, Choctaws, Chickasaws, and Seminoles — the so-called Five Civilized Tribes who inhabited large parts of Georgia, Alabama, Mississippi, and Florida. Unlike most of the tribes to the north of the Ohio, these tribes were comparatively large and well organized. Their lands were quite valuable, and they had made notable progress in adopting those aspects of white culture and technology that would enable them to protect their political independence as well as survive and compete in a modern economy. Of the five, the Cherokees had modernized the most, adopting a written constitution and a written language and creating a professional armed guard to enforce tribal laws and protect tribal lands from white incursions. Some Cherokees were cotton planters who owned African American slaves, and others were beginning to mine gold on their lands in Georgia.

The Cherokees' actions had aroused intense resentment among white Georgians. Whites coveted Indian lands and feared the power of nonwhite people in a slaveholding society. State leaders also opposed the creation of an independent Cherokee republic inside state borders. They demanded that Cherokees give up their tribal lands and sovereignty and submit to the laws of Georgia. In effect, this policy would leave the Cherokees with no defense against any form of white assault.

Jackson's solution was to offer the Indians a chance to exchange their lands

James D. Richardson, comp., *A Compilation of the Messages and Papers of the Presidents, 1789–1897*, 10 vols. (Washington, D.C.: Government Printing Office, 1897), 2: 456–59.

in the East for equivalent territories beyond the Mississippi. In the West, Indians would live beyond the borders of any existing state, and the continued existence of tribal governments and communal land ownership would not conflict with rival claims about states' rights and private property. Jackson also claimed that Indians would be protected from harmful contact with white society. He would not require them to move, he said, but if they remained in the East, they would lose most of their lands and the right to govern themselves as independent tribes. In most southern states, they would also be denied the right to vote and to testify in court against white people.

How do Jackson's policies reflect his experience as an Indian fighter? His residence in the South and West? Note the president's constitutional argument. Are there contradictions apparent in Jackson's language or ideas? Was tribal sovereignty truly incompatible with states' rights? Was removal likely to be as noncompulsory in practice as Jackson claimed?

The condition and ulterior destiny of the Indian tribes within the limits of some of our States have become objects of much interest and importance. It has long been the policy of Government to introduce among them the arts of civilization, in the hope of gradually reclaiming them from a wandering life. This policy has, however, been coupled with another wholly incompatible with its success. Professing a desire to civilize and settle them, we have at the same time lost no opportunity to purchase their lands and thrust them farther into the wilderness. By this means they have not only been kept in a wandering state, but been led to look upon us as unjust and indifferent to their fate. Thus, though lavish in its expenditures upon the subject, Government has constantly defeated its own policy, and the Indians in general, receding farther and farther to the west, have retained their savage habits. A portion, however, of the Southern tribes, having mingled much with the whites and made some progress in the arts of civilized life, have lately attempted to erect an independent government within the limits of Georgia and Alabama. These States, claiming to be the only sovereigns within their territories, extended their laws over the Indians, which induced the latter to call upon the United States for protection.

Under these circumstances the question presented was whether the General Government had a right to sustain those people in their pretensions. The Constitution declares that "no new State shall be formed or erected within the jurisdiction of any other State" without the consent of its legislature. If the General Government is not permitted to tolerate the erection of a confederate State within the territory of one of the members of this Union against her consent, much less could it allow a foreign and independent government to establish itself there. Georgia became a member of the Confederacy which eventuated in our Federal Union as a sovereign State, always asserting her claim to certain limits, which, having been originally defined in her colonial charter and subsequently recognized in the treaty of peace, she has ever since continued to enjoy. . . . Alabama was admitted into the Union on the same footing with the original States, with boundaries which were prescribed by Congress. There is no constitutional, conventional, or legal provision which allows them less power over the Indians within their borders than is possessed by Maine or New York. . . . If the principle involved . . . be abandoned, it will follow that the objects of this Government are reversed, and that it has become a part of its duty to aid in destroying the States which it was established to protect.

Actuated by this view of the subject, I informed the Indians inhabiting parts of Georgia and Alabama that their attempt to establish an independent government would not be countenanced by the Executive of the United States, and advised them to emigrate beyond the Mississippi or submit to the laws of those States.

Our conduct toward these people is deeply interesting to our national character. Their present condition, contrasted with what they once were, makes a most powerful appeal to our sympathies. Our ancestors found them the uncontrolled possessors of these vast regions. By persuasion and force they have been made to retire from river to river and from mountain to mountain, until some of the tribes have become extinct and others have left but remnants to preserve for awhile their once terrible names. Surrounded by the whites with their arts of civilization, which by destroying the resources of the savage doom him to weakness and decay, the fate of the Mohegan, the Narragansett, and the Delaware is fast overtaking the Choctaw, the Cherokee, and the Creek. That this fate surely awaits them if they remain within the limits of the States does not admit of a doubt. Humanity and national honor demand that every effort should be made to avert so great a calamity. It is too late to inquire whether it was just in the United States to include them and their territory within the bounds of new States, whose limits they could control. That step can not be retraced. A State can not be dismembered by Congress or restricted in the exercise of her constitutional power. But the people of those States and of every State, actuated by feelings of justice and a regard for our national honor, submit to you the interesting question whether something can not be done, consistently with the rights of the States, to preserve this much-injured race.

As a means of effecting this end I suggest for your consideration the propriety of setting apart an ample district west of the Mississippi, and without the limits of any State or Territory now formed, to be guaranteed to the Indian tribes as long as they shall occupy it, each tribe having a distinct control over the portion designated for its use. There they may be secured in the enjoyment of governments of their own choice, subject to no other control from the United States than such as may be necessary to preserve peace on the frontier and between the several tribes. There the benevolent may endeavor to teach them the arts of civilization, and, by promoting union and harmony among them, to raise up an interesting commonwealth, destined to perpetuate the race and to attest the humanity and justice of this Government.

This emigration should be voluntary, for it would be as cruel as unjust to compel the aborigines to abandon the graves of their fathers and seek a home in a distant land. But they should be distinctly informed that if they remain within the limits of the States they must be subject to their laws. In return for their obedience as individuals they will without doubt be protected in the enjoyment of those possessions which they have improved by their industry. . . . Submitting to the laws of the States, and receiving, like other citizens, protection in their persons and property, they will ere long become merged in the mass of our population. . . .

13

THEODORE FRELINGHUYSEN

On Indian Removal

April 9, 1830

National Republicans rejected Jackson's constitutional thinking on the Indian question. Senator Theodore Frelinghuysen passionately defended the Indians' rights to stay in their ancestral homelands, arguing that their natural rights to the land predated both the "State sovereignty" of Georgia and the constitutional power of the federal government. A deeply religious Christian, Frelinghuysen argued that the forcible dispossession of the Indians was a sin that God would punish. While Jackson's policy of territorial expansion appealed to Americans' admiration of power, growth, and indi-

Register of Debates in Congress, 21st Cong., 1st sess., 309–20.

vidual self-assertion, Frelinghuysen appealed to the equally powerful tradition that America must hold itself to a high moral standard in its national conduct.

In the end, Jackson's policy prevailed in a series of very close votes, but Frelinghuysen's argument laid the groundwork for a vision of America's mission of moral and physical improvement that later exerted powerful influence in Henry Clay's Whig Party. When Clay ran for president in 1844, Theodore Frelinghuysen was his vice presidential running mate on the Whig ticket.

What legal argument does Frelinghuysen present here to defend the rights of Indian tribes to remain within the boundaries of existing states? How is this different from Jackson's argument in Document 8? Frelinghuysen also claims that the proposed removal of the Indians would not be truly voluntary. Why? Though supporters claimed that Indian removal would be a humanitarian policy, Frelinghuysen denies it. What are his reasons? How do Frelinghuysen's own religious values shape his attitude to Indian removal? What sorts of white Americans would be likely to take his side of this dispute with President Jackson?

. . . I now proceed to the discussion of those principles which, in my humble judgment, fully and clearly sustain the claims of the Indians to all their political and civil rights, as by them asserted. And here, I insist that, by immemorial possession, as the original tenants of the soil, they hold a title beyond and superior to the British Crown and her colonies, and to all adverse pretensions of our confederation and subsequent Union. God, in his providence, planted these tribes on this Western continent, so far as we know, before Great Britain herself had a political existence. I believe, sir, it is not now seriously denied that the Indians are men, endowed with kindred faculties and powers with ourselves; that they have a place in human sympathy, and are justly entitled to a share in the common bounties of a benignant Providence. And, with this conceded, I ask in what code of the law of nations, or by what process of abstract deduction, their rights have been extinguished? . . .

In the light of natural law, can a reason for a distinction exist in the mode of enjoying that which is my own? If I use it for hunting, may another take it because he needs it for agriculture? I am aware that some writers have, by a system of artificial reasoning, endeavored to justify, or rather excuse the encroachments made upon Indian territory; and they denominate these abstractions the law of nations, and, in this ready way, the question is despatched. Sir, as we trace the sources of this law, we find its authority to depend either upon the conventions or common consent of nations. And when, permit me to inquire, were the Indian tribes ever consulted on the establishment of such a law? Whoever represented them or their interests in any Congress of nations, to confer upon the public rules of intercourse, and the proper foundations of dominion and property? The plain matter of fact is, that all these partial doctrines have resulted from the selfish plans and pursuits of more enlightened nations; and it is not matter for any great wonder, that they should so largely partake of a mercenary and exclusive spirit toward the claims of the Indians.

It is, however, admitted, sir, that, when the increase of population and the wants of mankind demand the cultivation of the earth, a duty is thereby devolved upon the proprietors of large and uncultivated regions, of devoting them to such useful purposes. But such appropriations are to be obtained by fair contract, and for reasonable compensation. . . . Several years ago, official reports to Congress stated the amount of Indian grants to the United States to exceed two hundred and fourteen millions of acres. Yes, sir, we have acquired, and now own, more land as the fruits of their bounty than we shall dispose of at the present rate to actual settlers in two hundred years. For, very recently, it has been ascertained, on this floor, that our public sales average not more than about one million of acres annually. . . . As the tide of our population has rolled on, we have added purchase to purchase. The confiding Indian listened to our professions of friendship: we called him brother, and he believed us. Millions after millions he has yielded to our importunity, until we have acquired more than can be cultivated in centuries—and yet we crave more. We have crowded the tribes upon a few miserable acres on our Southern frontier: it is all that is left to them of their once boundless forests: and still, like the horse-leech, our insatiated cupidity cries, give! give! . . .

. . . Our ancestors found these people, far removed from the commotions of Europe, exercising all the rights, and enjoying the privileges, of free and independent sovereigns of this new world. They were not a wild and lawless horde of banditti,[1] but lived under the restraints of government, patriarchal in its character, and energetic in its influence. They had chiefs, head men, and councils. The white men, the authors of all their wrongs, approached them as friends—they extended the olive branch; and, being then a feeble colony and at the mercy of the native tenants of the soil, by presents and professions, propitiated their good will. The Indian yielded a slow, but substantial confidence; granted to the colonists an abiding place; and suffered them to grow up to man's estate beside

---

[1]Banditti are bandits.

him. He never raised the claim of elder title: as the white man's wants increased, he opened the hand of his bounty wider and wider. By and by, conditions are changed. His people melt away; his lands are constantly coveted; millions after millions are ceded. The Indian bears it all meekly; he complains, indeed, as well he may; but suffers on: and now he finds that this neighbor, whom his kindness had nourished, has spread an adverse title over the last remains of his patrimony, barely adequate to his wants, and turns upon him, and says, "away! we cannot endure you so near us! These forests and rivers, these groves of your fathers, these firesides and hunting grounds, are ours by the right of power, and the force of numbers." Sir, let every treaty be blotted from our records, and in the judgment of natural and unchangeable truth and justice, I ask, who is the injured, and who is the aggressor? Let conscience answer, and I fear not the result. . . . Do the obligations of justice change with the color of the skin? Is it one of the prerogatives of the white man, that he may disregard the dictates of moral principles, when an Indian shall be concerned? No, sir. . . .

. . . Sir, the Cherokees . . . have no part in this controversy. They hold by better title than either Georgia or the Union. They have nothing to do with State sovereignty, or United States, sovereignty. They are above and beyond both. True, sir, they have made treaties with both, but not to acquire title or jurisdiction; these they had before — ages before the evil hour to them, when their white brothers fled to them for an asylum. They treated to secure protection and guarantee for subsisting powers and privileges; and so far as those conventions raise obligations, they are willing to meet, and always have met, and faithfully performed them; and now expect from a great people, the like fidelity to plighted covenants. . . .

. . . A few pence of duty on tea, that invaded no fireside, excited no fears, disturbed no substantial interest whatever, awakened in the American colonies a spirit of firm resistance; and how was the tea tax met, sir? Just as it should be. There was lurking beneath this trifling imposition of duty, a covert assumption of authority, that led directly to oppressive exactions. "No taxation without representation," became our motto. We would neither pay the tax nor drink the tea. Our fathers buckled on their armor, and, from the water's edge, repelled the encroachments of a misguided cabinet. We successfully and triumphantly contended for the very rights and privileges that our Indian neighbors now implore us to protect and preserve to them. Sir, this thought invests the subject under debate with most singular and momentous interest. We, whom God has exalted to the very summit of prosperity — whose brief career forms the brightest page in history; the wonder and praise of the world; freedom's hope, and her consolation; we, about to turn traitors to our principles and our fame —

about to become the oppressors of the feeble, and to cast away our birthright! Sir, I hope for better things. . . .

It is not surprising that our agents advertised the War Department, that if the General Government refused to interfere, and the Indians were left to the law of the States, they would soon exchange their lands and remove. To compel, by harsh and cruel penalties, such exchange, is the broad purpose of this act of Georgia, and nothing is wanting to fill up the picture of this disgraceful system, but to permit the bill before us to pass without amendment or proviso. Then it will all seem fair on our statute books. It legislates for none but those who may choose to remove, while we know that grinding, heart-breaking exactions are set in operation elsewhere, to drive them to such a choice. By the modification I have submitted, I beg for the Indian the poor privilege of the exercise of his own will. But the law of Georgia is not yet satisfied. The last section declares, "that no Indian, or descendant of any Indian, residing within the Creek or Cherokee nations of Indians, shall be deemed a competent witness in any Court of this State, to which a white person may be a party, except such white person resides within the said nation." It did not suffice to rob these people of the last vestige of their own political rights and liberties; the work was not complete until they were shut out of the protection of Georgia laws. For, sir, after the first day of June next, a gang of lawless white men may break into the Cherokee country, plunder their habitations, murder the mother with the children, and all in the sight of the wretched husband and father, and no law of Georgia will reach the atrocity. It is vain to tell us, sir, that murder may be traced by circumstantial probabilities. The charge against this State is, you have, by force and violence, stripped these people of the protection of their government, and now refuse to cast over them the shield of your own. The outrage of the deed is, that you leave the poor Indian helpless and defenceless, and in this cruel way hope to banish him from his home. Sir, if this law be enforced, I do religiously believe that it will awaken tones of feeling that will go up to God, and call down the thunders of his wrath.

The end, however, is to justify the means. "The removal of the Indian tribes to the west of the Mississippi is demanded by the dictates of humanity." This is a word of conciliating import. But it often makes its way to the heart under very doubtful titles, and its present claims deserve to be rigidly questioned. Who urges this plea? They who covet the Indian lands—who wish to rid themselves of a neighbor that they despise, and whose State pride is enlisted in rounding off their territories. . . .

It is alleged that the Indians cannot flourish in the neighborhood of a white population, that whole tribes have disappeared under the influence of this propinquity. As an abstract proposition, it implies reproach somewhere. Our virtues certainly have not such deadly and depopulating power. It must, then, be our vices that possess these destructive energies—and shall we commit injustice, and put in, as our plea for it, that our intercourse with the Indians has been so demoralizing that we must drive them from it to save them? . . .

Sir, had we devoted the same care to elevate their moral condition that we have to degrade them, the removal of the Indian would not now seek for an apology in the suggestions of humanity. But I waive this, and, as to the matter of fact, how stands the account? Wherever a fair experiment has been made, the Indians have readily yielded to the influence of moral cultivation. Yes, sir, they flourish under this culture, and rise in the scale of being. They have shown themselves to be highly susceptible of improvement, and the ferocious feelings and habits of the savage are soothed and reformed by the mild charities of religion. They can very soon be taught to understand and appreciate the blessings of civilization and regular government. . . .

It is further maintained, "that one of the greatest evils to which the Indians are exposed is, that incessant pressure of population, that forces them from seat to seat, without allowing time for moral and intellectual improvement." Sir, this is the very reason—the deep, cogent, reason, which I present to the Senate, now to raise the barrier against the pressure of population, and with all the authority of this nation, command the urging tide "thus far and no farther." Let us save them now, or we never shall. For, is it not clear as the sunbeam, sir, that a removal will aggravate their woes? If the tide is nearly irresistible at this time, when a few more years shall fill the regions beyond the Arkansas with many more millions of enterprising white men, will not an increased impulse be given, that shall sweep the red men away into the barren prairies, or the Pacific of the West? Such, I fear, will be their doom. . . .

. . . Is this the time, sir, to break up this peaceful community, to put out their council fires, to annul their laws and customs, to crush the rising hopes of their youth, and to drive the desponding and discouraged Indian to despair? Let it be called a sickly humanity—every freeman in the land, that has one spark of the spirit of his fathers, will feel and denounce it to be an unparallelled stretch of cruel injustice. And, if the deed be done, sir, how it is regarded in Heaven will, sooner or later, be known on earth; for this is the judgment-place of public sins. . . .

Sir, if we abandon these aboriginal proprietors of our soil, these early allies and adopted children of our forefathers, how shall we justify it to our country? to all the glory of the past, and the promise of the future? Her good name is worth all else besides that contributes to her greatness. . . .

How shall we justify this trespass to ourselves? Sir, we may deride it, and laugh it to scorn now; but the occasion will meet every man, when he must look inward, and make honest inquisition there. Let us beware how, by oppressive encroachments upon the sacred priveleges of our Indian neighbors, we minister to the agonies of future remorse.

I have, in my humble measure, attempted to discharge a public and most solemn duty towards an interesting portion of my fellow men. Should it prove to have been as fruitless as I know it to be below the weight of their claims, yet even then, sir, it will have its consolations. Defeat in such a cause is far above the triumphs of unrighteous power; and in the language of an eloquent writer—"I had rather receive the blessing of one poor Cherokee, as he casts his last look back upon his country, for having, though in vain, attempted to prevent his banishment, than to sleep beneath the marble of all the Cæsars."

14

ANDREW JACKSON

Veto of the Maysville Road
1830

In the 1824 campaign, Andrew Jackson supported federally sponsored "national" projects of internal improvement. When he became president, however, he became convinced that internal improvement projects were draining the federal treasury and preventing the repayment of the national debt. He also believed that vote swapping for internal improvements would open Congress to corruption and the destruction of republican values. And though he did not say so, he had no desire to build a federal road for the constituents of Henry Clay. Finally, he knew that his southern supporters had begun to worry that "broad construction" of the constitution could eventually lead to federal measures against slavery, and he wished to assure them of his support for states' rights. For all these reasons, Jackson decided to veto the bill to purchase stock

James D. Richardson, comp., *A Compilation of the Messages and Papers of the Presidents, 1789–1897,* 10 vols. (Washington, D.C.: Government Printing Office, 1897), 2: 483–93.

*in the Maysville, Washington, Paris, and Lexington Turnpike Road Company,
linking Clay's hometown of Lexington, Kentucky, with the Ohio River.*

*Why does Jackson distinguish here between allowing the federal govern-
ment to build roads under its own jurisdiction and allowing it to grant money
to the states for this purpose? Jackson insists that federal appropriations to
the states can be made only for projects that are national, not local. Does
the president think it is easy or reasonable to draw a clear line between
national and local projects? Does the Maysville Road qualify as a national
project? Why?*

*Jackson moves beyond legalistic arguments, declaring that "the preser-
vation and success of the republican principle rest with us." Why does he
think that a constitutional amendment is necessary for a program of federally financed internal improvements? Why does Jackson suggest that the
repayment of the national debt is more important than rapid construction
of internal improvements? How would Jackson's interpretation of the Constitution affect federal spending today?*

To the House of Representatives.

Gentlemen: I have maturely considered the bill proposing to authorize
"a subscription of stock in the Maysville, Washington, Paris, and Lexington Turnpike Road Company," and now return the same to the House
of Representatives, in which it originated, with my objections to its passage.

Sincerely friendly to the improvement of our country by means of
roads and canals, I regret that any difference of opinion in the mode of
contributing to it should exist between us; and if in stating this difference
I go beyond what the occasion may be deemed to call for, I hope to find
an apology in the great importance of the subject, an unfeigned respect
for the high source from which this branch of it has emanated, and an
anxious wish to be correctly understood by my constituents in the discharge of all my duties. . . .

. . . I have given . . . all the reflection demanded by a just regard for the
interests of those of our fellow-citizens who have desired its passage, and
by the respect which is due to a coordinate branch of the Government,
but I am not able to view it in any other light than as a measure of purely
local character. . . . It has no connection with any established system of
improvements; is exclusively within the limits of a State, . . . and even as
far as the State is interested conferring partial instead of general advantages.

Considering the magnitude and importance of the power, and the embarrassments to which, from the very nature of the thing, its exercise must necessarily be subjected, the real friends of internal improvement ought not to be willing to confide it to accident and chance. What is properly *national* in its character or otherwise is an inquiry which is often extremely difficult of solution. . . . The question regards the character of the work, not that of those by whom it is to be accomplished. Notwithstanding the union of the Government with the corporation by whose immediate agency any work of internal improvement is carried on, the inquiry will still remain, Is it national and conducive to the benefit of the whole, or local and operating only to the advantage of a portion of the Union?

. . . Besides many minor considerations, there are two prominent views of the subject which have made a deep impression upon my mind, which, I think, are well entitled to your serious attention, and will, I hope, be maturely weighed by the people.

From the official communication submitted to you it appears that if no adverse and unforeseen contingency happens in our foreign relations and no unusual diversion be made of the funds set apart for the payment of the national debt we may look with confidence to its entire extinguishment in the short period of four years. The extent to which this pleasing anticipation is dependent upon the policy which may be pursued in relation to measures of the character of the one now under consideration must be obvious to all, and equally so that the events of the present session are well calculated to awaken public solicitude upon the subject. By the statement from the Treasury Department and those from the clerks of the Senate and House of Representatives, herewith submitted, it appears that the bills which have passed into laws, and those which in all probability will pass before the adjournment of Congress, anticipate appropriations which, with the ordinary expenditures for the support of Government, will exceed considerably the amount in the Treasury for the year 1830. Thus, whilst we are diminishing the revenue by a reduction of the duties on tea, coffee, and cocoa the appropriations for internal improvement are increasing beyond the available means of the Treasury. And if to this calculation be added the amounts contained in bills which are pending before the two Houses, it may be safely affirmed that $10,000,000 would not make up the excess over the Treasury receipts, unless the payment of the national debt be postponed and the means now pledged to that object applied to those enumerated in these bills. Without a well-regulated system of internal improvement this exhausting mode of appropriation is not likely to be avoided, and the plain consequence must be either a continuance of the national debt or a resort to additional taxes.

... The preservation and success of the republican principle rest with us. To elevate its character and extend its influence rank among our most important duties, and the best means to accomplish this desirable end are those which will rivet the attachment of our citizens to the Government of their choice by the comparative lightness of their public burthens and by the attraction which the superior success of its operations will present to the admiration and respect of the world. Through the favor of an overruling and indulgent Providence our country is blessed with general prosperity and our citizens exempted from the pressure of taxation, which other less favored portions of the human family are obliged to bear; yet it is true that many of the taxes collected from our citizens through the medium of imposts have for a considerable period been onerous. In many particulars these taxes have borne severely upon the laboring and less prosperous classes of the community, being imposed on the necessaries of life, and this, too, in cases where the burthen was not relieved by the consciousness that it would ultimately contribute to make us independent of foreign nations for articles of prime necessity by the encouragement of their growth and manufacture at home. They have been cheerfully borne because they were thought to be necessary to the support of Government and the payment of the debts unavoidably incurred in the acquisition and maintenance of our national rights and liberties. . . . When the national debt is paid, the duties upon those articles which we do not raise may be repealed with safety, and still leave, I trust, without oppression to any section of the country, an accumulating surplus fund, which may be beneficially applied to some well-digested system of improvement.

... Assuming these suggestions to be correct, will not our constituents require the observance of a course by which they can be effected? Ought they not to require it? With the best disposition to aid, as far as I can conscientiously, in furtherance of works of internal improvement, my opinion is that the soundest views of national policy at this time point to such a course. Besides the avoidance of an evil influence upon the local concerns of the country, how solid is the advantage which the Government will reap from it in the elevation of its character! How gratifying the effect of presenting to the world the sublime spectacle of a Republic of more than 12,000,000 happy people, in the fifty-fourth year of her existence, after having passed through two protracted wars—the one for the acquisition and the other for the maintenance of liberty—free from debt and with all her immense resources unfettered! What a salutary influence would not such an exhibition exercise upon the cause of liberal principles and free government throughout the world! Would we not ourselves find in its effect an additional guaranty that our political institutions will be transmitted to the most remote posterity without decay? . . .

In the other view of the subject, and the only remaining one which it is my intention to present at this time, is involved the expediency of embarking in a system of internal improvement without a previous amendment of the Constitution explaining and defining the precise powers of the Federal Government over it.[1] Assuming the right to appropriate money to aid in the construction of national works to be warranted by the cotemporaneous and continued exposition of the Constitution, its insufficiency for the successful prosecution of them must be admitted by all candid minds. If we look to usage to define the extent of the right, that will be found so variant and embracing so much that has been overruled as to involve the whole subject in great uncertainty and to render the execution of our respective duties in relation to it replete with difficulty and embarrassment. . . .

. . . I will not detain you with professions of zeal in the cause of internal improvements . . . for I do not suppose there is an intelligent citizen who does not wish to see them flourish. But though all are their friends, but few, I trust, are unmindful of the means by which they should be promoted; none certainly are so degenerate as to desire their success at the cost of that sacred instrument with the preservation of which is indissolubly bound our country's hopes. . . . When an honest observance of constitutional compacts can not be obtained from communities like ours, it need not be anticipated elsewhere, and the cause in which there has been so much martyrdom, and from which so much was expected by the friends of liberty, may be abandoned, and the degrading truth that man is unfit for self-government admitted. And this will be the case if *expediency* be made a rule of construction in interpreting the Constitution. . . .

But I do not entertain such gloomy apprehensions. If it be the wish of the people that the construction of roads and canals should be conducted by the Federal Government, it is not only highly expedient, but indispensably necessary, that a previous amendment of the Constitution, delegating the necessary power and defining and restricting its exercise with reference to the sovereignty of the States, should be made. Without it nothing extensively useful can be effected. The right to exercise as much jurisdiction as is necessary to preserve the works and to raise

---

[1]The U.S. Constitution was never amended to permit federal expenditures for internal improvements, but changes in prevailing constitutional interpretation after the Civil War eventually supplanted arguments like the one Jackson makes here.

funds by the collection of tolls to keep them in repair can not be dispensed with. . . .

If it be the desire of the people that the agency of the Federal Government should be confined to the appropriation of money in aid of such undertakings, in virtue of State authorities, then the occasion, the manner, and the extent of the appropriations should be made the subject of constitutional regulation. This is the more necessary in order that they may be equitable among the several States, promote harmony between different sections of the Union and their representatives, preserve other parts of the Constitution from being undermined by the exercise of doubtful powers. . . .

That a constitutional adjustment of this power upon equitable principles is in the highest degree desirable can scarcely be doubted, nor can it fail to be promoted by every sincere friend to the success of our political institutions. . . . The time has never yet been when the patriotism and intelligence of the American people were not fully equal to the greatest exigency, and it never will when the subject calling forth their interposition is plainly presented to them. To do so with the questions involved in this bill, and to urge them to an early, zealous, and full consideration of their deep importance, is, in my estimation, among the highest of our duties. . . .

In presenting these opinions I have spoken with the freedom and candor which I thought the occasion for their expression called for, and now respectfully return the bill which has been under consideration for your further deliberation and judgment.

15

ANDREW JACKSON

Bank Veto

July 10, 1832

The charter of the Bank of the United States would not expire until 1836, but Henry Clay decided to make it an issue in the presidential election of 1832. He introduced a bill to grant the Bank a new charter, essentially daring Jackson to veto it in an election year. If Jackson signed the bill, Clay would

James D. Richardson, comp., *A Compilation of the Messages and Papers of the Presidents, 1789–1897,* 10 vols. (Washington, D.C.: Government Printing Office, 1897), 2: 577–91.

win a policy victory. If Jackson vetoed the bill, Clay would use the issue against him in his own campaign for the presidency. Jackson's political goal in the veto message was to escape this trap by killing the Bank with powerful language that would lead most American voters to support his decision. As you read the veto message, ask yourself how Jackson goes about his task. What are his principal arguments against the Bank? How convincing are they? What kinds of voters would be likely to believe them? In particular, how does Jackson enlist American patriotism against the Bank? Is this consistent with his earlier positions? Why does Jackson call the Bank unconstitutional?

Above all, Jackson attacks the Bank as a violation of the principle of equal rights. He says the charter would give "a gratuity of many millions to the stockholders." He also says that it would "make the rich richer and the potent more powerful." How does Jackson describe "equal protection and equal benefits" in the final paragraphs of the veto message? Does he make any allowances for legitimate kinds of inequality among citizens? In his opinion, why is the Bank charter an illegitimate form of inequality?

What kinds of changes were occurring in American society that might incline some citizens to agree with Jackson's charges? What kinds of citizens would be likely to reject his analysis?

Finally, try to form your own opinion about the Bank of the United States. Was it appropriate for a democracy to give so much power to a private corporation? Did the economic benefits of the Bank outweigh its disadvantages? Are Jackson's moral, constitutional, and economic arguments sound or far-fetched?

To the Senate:

The bill "to modify and continue" the act entitled "An act to incorporate the subscribers to the Bank of the United States" was presented to me on the 4th July instant. Having considered it with that solemn regard to the principles of the Constitution which the day was calculated to inspire, and come to the conclusion that it ought not to become a law, I herewith return it to the Senate, in which it originated, with my objections.

A bank of the United States is in many respects convenient for the Government and useful to the people. Entertaining this opinion, and deeply impressed with the belief that some of the powers and privileges possessed by the existing bank are unauthorized by the Constitution, subversive of the rights of the States, and dangerous to the liberties of the people, I felt it my duty at an early period of my Administration to call the attention of Congress to the practicability of organizing an institution combining all its advantages and obviating these objections. I sincerely regret that in the act before me I can perceive none of those modifications of the bank charter which are necessary, in my opinion, to make it compatible with justice, with sound policy, or with the Constitution of our country.

The present corporate body, denominated the president, directors, and company of the Bank of the United States, will have existed at the time this act is intended to take effect twenty years. It enjoys an exclusive privilege of banking under the authority of the General Government, a monopoly of its favor and support, and, as a necessary consequence, almost a monopoly of the foreign and domestic exchange. The powers, privileges, and favors bestowed upon it in the original charter, by increasing the value of the stock far above its par value, operated as a gratuity of many millions to the stockholders.

An apology may be found for the failure to guard against this result in the consideration that the effect of the original act of incorporation could not be certainly foreseen at the time of its passage. The act before me proposes another gratuity to the holders of the same stock, and in many cases to the same men, of at least seven millions more. This donation finds no apology in any uncertainty as to the effect of the act. On all hands it is conceded that its passage will increase at least 20 or 30 per cent more the market price of the stock, subject to the payment of the annuity of $200,000 per year secured by the act, thus adding in a moment one-fourth to its par value. It is not our own citizens only who are to receive the bounty of our Government. More than eight millions of the stock of this bank are held by foreigners. By this act the American Republic proposes virtually to make them a present of some millions of dollars. . . .

Every monopoly and all exclusive privileges are granted at the expense of the public, which ought to receive a fair equivalent. The many millions which this act proposes to bestow on the stockholders of the existing bank must come directly or indirectly out of the earnings of the American people. It is due to them, therefore, if their Government sell monopolies and exclusive privileges, that they should at least exact for them as much as they are worth in open market. . . . The present value of the monopoly . . . is $17,000,000, and this the act proposes to sell for three millions, payable in fifteen annual installments of $200,000 each.

It is not conceivable how the present stockholders can have any claim to the special favor of the Government. . . .

But this act does not permit competition in the purchase of this monopoly. It seems to be predicated on the erroneous idea that the present stockholders have a prescriptive right not only to the favor but to the bounty of Government. It appears that more than a fourth part of the stock is held by foreigners and the residue is held by a few hundred of our own citizens, chiefly of the richest class. For their benefit does this act exclude the whole American people from competition in the purchase of this monopoly and dispose of it for many millions less than it is worth. . . .

. . . If our Government must sell monopolies, it would seem to be its duty to take nothing less than their full value, and if gratuities must be made once in fifteen or twenty years let them not be bestowed on the subjects of a foreign government nor upon a designated and favored class of men in our own country. It is but justice and good policy, as far as the nature of the case will admit, to confine our favors to our own fellow-citizens, and let each in his turn enjoy an opportunity to profit by our bounty. In the bearings of the act before me upon these points I find ample reasons why it should not become a law. . . .

The ninth section of the act recognizes principles of worse tendency than any provision of the present charter.

It enacts that "the cashier of the bank shall annually report to the Secretary of the Treasury the names of all stockholders who are not resident citizens of the United States, and on the application of the treasurer of any State shall make out and transmit to such treasurer a list of stockholders residing in or citizens of such State, with the amount of stock owned by each." Although this provision, taken in connection with a decision of the Supreme Court,[1] surrenders, by its silence, the right of the States to tax the banking institutions created by this corporation under the name of branches throughout the Union, it is evidently intended to be construed as a concession of their right to tax that portion of the stock which may be held by their own citizens and residents. . . . As it is only the stock *held* in the States and not that *employed* within them which would be subject to taxation, and as the names of foreign stockholders are not to be reported to the treasurers of the States, it is obvious that the stock held by them will be exempt from this burden . . . [and] will be worth 10 or 15 per cent more to foreigners than to citizens of the United States. . . .

. . . As little stock is held in the West, it is obvious that the debt of the people in that section to the bank is principally a debt to the Eastern and foreign stockholders; that the interest they pay upon it is carried into the Eastern States and into Europe, and that it is a burden upon their indus-

---

[1] *Osborn v. Bank of the United States,* 9 Wheaton 738 (1824). Henry Clay had successfully argued for the Bank in this case.

try and a drain of their currency, which no country can bear without inconvenience and occasional distress. . . . More than half a million . . . [dollars] does not stop in the Eastern States, but passes on to Europe to pay the dividends of the foreign stockholders. In the principle of taxation recognized by this act the Western States find no adequate compensation for this perpetual burden on their industry and drain of their currency. The branch bank at Mobile made last year $95,140, yet under the provisions of this act the State of Alabama can raise no revenue from these profitable operations, because not a share of the stock is held by any of her citizens. . . . The tendency of the plan of taxation which this act proposes will be to place the whole United States in the same relation to foreign countries which the Western States now bear to the Eastern. When by a tax on resident stockholders the stock of this bank is made worth 10 or 15 per cent more to foreigners than to residents, most of it will inevitably leave the country.

Thus will this provision in its practical effect deprive the Eastern as well as the Southern and Western States of the means of raising a revenue from the extension of business and great profits of this institution. It will make the American people debtors to aliens in nearly the whole amount due to this bank, and send across the Atlantic from two to five millions of specie every year to pay the bank dividends.

. . . Of the twenty-five directors of this bank five are chosen by the Government and twenty by the citizen stockholders. From all voice in these elections the foreign stockholders are excluded by the charter. . . . The entire control of the institution would necessarily fall into the hands of a few citizen stockholders, and the . . . temptation to designing men [would be] to secure that control in their own hands by monopolizing the remaining stock. There is danger that a president and directors would then be able to elect themselves from year to year, and without responsibility or control manage the whole concerns of the bank during the existence of its charter. It is easy to conceive that great evils to our country and its institutions might flow from such a concentration of power in the hands of a few men irresponsible to the people.

Is there no danger to our liberty and independence in a bank that in its nature has so little to bind it to our country? The president of the bank has told us that most of the State banks exist by its forbearance. Should its influence become concentered, as it may under the operation of such an act as this, in the hands of a self-elected directory whose interests are identified with those of the foreign stockholders, will there not be cause to tremble for the purity of our elections in peace and for the independence of our country in war? Their power would be great whenever they might choose to exert it. . . . But if any private citizen or public functionary should interpose to curtail its powers or prevent a renewal of its privileges, it can not be doubted that he would be made to feel its influence.

Should the stock of the bank principally pass into the hands of the subjects of a foreign country, and we should unfortunately become involved in a war with that country, what would be our condition? . . . Controlling our currency, receiving our public moneys, and holding thousands of our citizens in dependence, it would be more formidable and dangerous than the naval and military power of the enemy.

If we must have a bank with private stockholders, every consideration of sound policy and every impulse of American feeling admonishes that it should be *purely American*. . . . So abundant is domestic capital that competition in subscribing for the stock of local banks has recently led almost to riots. . . . Instead of sending abroad the stock of the bank in which the Government must deposit its funds and on which it must rely to sustain its credit in times of emergency, it would rather seem to be expedient to prohibit its sale to aliens under penalty of absolute forfeiture.

It is maintained by the advocates of the bank that its constitutionality in all its features ought to be considered as settled by precedent and by the decision of the Supreme Court. To this conclusion I can not assent. Mere precedent is a dangerous source of authority, and should not be regarded as deciding questions of constitutional power except where the acquiescence of the people and the States can be considered as well settled. . . .

. . . The Congress, the Executive, and the Court must each for itself be guided by its own opinion of the Constitution. Each public officer who takes an oath to support the Constitution swears that he will support it as he understands it, and not as it is understood by others. It is as much the duty of the House of Representatives, of the Senate, and of the President to decide upon the constitutionality of any bill or resolution which may be presented to them for passage or approval as it is of the supreme judges when it may be brought before them for judicial decision. The opinion of the judges has no more authority over Congress than the opinion of Congress has over the judges, and on that point the President is independent of both. The authority of the Supreme Court must not, therefore, be permitted to control the Congress or the Executive when acting in their legislative capacities, but to have only such influence as the force of their reasoning may deserve.

But in the case relied upon the Supreme Court have not decided that all the features of this corporation are compatible with the Constitution. . . .

... Under the decision of the Supreme Court, ... it is the exclusive province of Congress and the President to decide whether the particular features of this act are *necessary* and *proper* in order to enable the bank to perform conveniently and efficiently the public duties assigned to it as a fiscal agent, and therefore constitutional, or *unnecessary* and *improper,* and therefore unconstitutional.

Without commenting on the general principle affirmed by the Supreme Court, let us examine the details of this act in accordance with the rule of legislative action which they have laid down. It will be found that many of the powers and privileges conferred on it can not be supposed necessary for the purpose for which it is proposed to be created, and are not, therefore, means necessary to attain the end in view, and consequently not justified by the Constitution. . . .

It can not be *necessary* to the character of the bank as a fiscal agent of the Government that its private business should be exempted from that taxation to which all the State banks are liable, nor can I conceive it *"proper"* that the substantive and most essential powers reserved by the States shall be thus attacked and annihilated as a means of executing the powers delegated to the General Government. It may be safely assumed that none of those sages who had an agency in forming or adopting our Constitution ever imagined that any portion of the taxing power of the States not prohibited to them nor delegated to Congress was to be swept away and annihilated as a means of executing certain powers delegated to Congress. . . .

... That a bank of the United States, competent to all the duties which may be required by the Government, might be so organized as not to infringe on our own delegated powers or the reserved rights of the States I do not entertain a doubt. Had the Executive been called upon to furnish the project of such an institution, the duty would have been cheerfully performed. In the absence of such a call it was obviously proper that he should confine himself to pointing out those prominent features in the act presented which in his opinion make it incompatible with the Constitution and sound policy. . . .

The bank is professedly established as an agent of the executive branch of the Government, and its constitutionality is maintained on that ground. Neither upon the propriety of present action nor upon the provisions of this act was the Executive consulted. It has had no opportunity to say that it neither needs nor wants an agent clothed with such powers and favored by such exemptions. There is nothing in its legitimate functions which makes it necessary or proper. . . .

It is to be regretted that the rich and powerful too often bend the acts of government to their selfish purposes. Distinctions in society will always exist under every just government. Equality of talents, of education, or of wealth can not be produced by human institutions. In the full enjoyment of the gifts of Heaven and the fruits of superior industry, economy, and virtue, every man is equally entitled to protection by law; but when the laws undertake to add to these natural and just advantages artificial distinctions, to grant titles, gratuities, and exclusive privileges, to make the rich richer and the potent more powerful, the humble members of society—the farmers, mechanics, and laborers—who have neither the time nor the means of securing like favors to themselves, have a right to complain of the injustice of their Government. There are no necessary evils in government. Its evils exist only in its abuses. If it would confine itself to equal protection, and, as Heaven does its rains, shower its favors alike on the high and the low, the rich and the poor, it would be an unqualified blessing. In the act before me there seems to be a wide and unnecessary departure from these just principles.

Nor is our Government to be maintained or our Union preserved by invasions of the rights and powers of the several States. In thus attempting to make our General Government strong we make it weak. Its true strength consists in leaving individuals and States as much as possible to themselves—in making itself felt, not in its power, but in its beneficence; not in its control, but in its protection; not in binding the States more closely to the center, but leaving each to move unobstructed in its proper orbit.

Experience should teach us wisdom. Most of the difficulties our Government now encounters and most of the dangers which impend over our Union have sprung from an abandonment of the legitimate objects of Government by our national legislation, and the adoption of such principles as are embodied in this act. Many of our rich men have not been content with equal protection and equal benefits, but have besought us to make them richer by act of Congress. By attempting to gratify their desires we have in the results of our legislation arrayed section against section, interest against interest, and man against man, in a fearful commotion which threatens to shake the foundations of our Union. It is time to pause in our career to review our principles, and if possible revive that devoted patriotism and spirit of compromise which distinguished the sages of the Revolution and the fathers of our Union. If we can not at once, in justice to interests vested under improvident legislation, make our Government what it ought to be, we can at least take a stand against all new grants of monopolies and exclusive privileges, against any prostitution of our Government to the advancement of the few at the expense of the many, and in favor of compromise and gradual reform in our code of laws and system of political economy.

I have now done my duty to my country. If sustained by my fellow-citizens, I shall be grateful and happy; if not, I shall find in the motives which impel me ample grounds for contentment and peace. In the difficulties which surround us and the dangers which threaten our institutions there is cause for neither dismay nor alarm. For relief and deliverance let us firmly rely on that kind Providence which I am sure watches with peculiar care over the destinies of our Republic, and on the intelligence and wisdom of our countrymen. Through *His* abundant goodness and *their* patriotic devotion our liberty and Union will be preserved.

16

HENRY CLAY

On the American System

February 2, 3, and 6, 1832

Henry Clay utterly rejected Andrew Jackson's analysis of the effects of the Bank of the United States. By 1832, he had become the leading opponent of Jackson's program in Congress as well as the National Republican nominee for the presidential election of 1832. As an alternative to Jackson's program of states' rights, minimal government, and homespun simplicity, Clay put together a program he called the "American System." It included a high protective tariff, a strong Bank of the United States, and federal support for internal improvements by distribution of the proceeds from the sale of public lands. He introduced the plan in this 1832 speech to the Senate that spelled out his vision for American progress.

What are the main parts of the American System, and how do they fit together? What kinds of values does Clay appeal to when he argues for its adoption? How are they different from the values Jackson expressed in the Bank veto? How do the two arguments suggest different visions for the country's future?

Calvin Colton, ed., *The Life, Correspondence, and Speeches of Henry Clay,* 6 vols. (New York: Barnes, 1857), 5: 439–86.

*Southerners, especially South Carolinians, warned that a higher tariff
could lead to dissolution of the Union. Clay disagrees here and insists that
high tariffs would strengthen the Union. Why does he think so? How does
the American System reflect Clay's strong love of the Union?*

. . . In one sentiment, Mr. President, expressed by the honorable gentleman from South Carolina (General Hayne), though perhaps not in the
sense intended by him, I entirely concur. I agree with him, that the decision on the system of policy embraced in this debate, involves the future
destiny of this growing country. One way, I verily believe, it would lead
to deep and general distress, general bankruptcy, and national ruin, without benefit to any part of the Union; the other, the existing prosperity will
be preserved and augmented, and the nation will continue rapidly to
advance in wealth, power, and greatness, without prejudice to any section of the confederacy.

Thus viewing the question, I stand here as the humble but zealous
advocate, not of the interests of one State, or seven States only, but of the
whole Union. . . .

Eight years ago, it was my painful duty to present to the other House
of Congress an unexaggerated picture of the general distress pervading
the whole land. We must all yet remember some of its frightful features.
We all know that the people were then oppressed, and borne down by an
enormous load of debt; that the value of property was at the lowest point
of depression; that ruinous sales and sacrifices were everywhere made
of real estate; that stop laws, and relief laws, and paper money were
adopted, to save the people from impending destruction; that a deficit in
the public revenue existed, which compelled government to seize upon,
and divert from its legitimate object, the appropriations to the sinking
fund, to redeem the national debt; and that our commerce and navigation were threatened with a complete paralysis. *In short, sir, if I were to
select any term of seven years since the adoption of the present Constitution
which exhibited a scene of the most wide-spread dismay and desolation, it
would be exactly that term of seven years which immediately preceded the
establishment of the tariff of 1824.*

I have now to perform the more pleasing task of exhibiting an imper-
fect sketch of the existing state of the unparalleled prosperity of the country. On a general survey, we behold cultivation extended, the arts flourishing, the face of the country improved, our people fully and profitably
employed, and the public countenance exhibiting tranquillity, contentment, and happiness. And if we descend into particulars, we have the

agreeable contemplation of a people out of debt; land rising slowly in value, but in a secure and salutary degree; a ready though not extravagant market for all the surplus productions of our industry; innumerable flocks and herds browsing and gamboling on ten thousand hills and plains, covered with rich and verdant grasses; our cities expanded, and whole villages springing up, as it were, by enchantment; our exports and imports increased and increasing; our tonnage, foreign and coastwise, swelling and fully occupied; the rivers of our interior animated by the perpetual thunder and lightning of countless steamboats; the currency sound and abundant; the public debt of two wars nearly redeemed; and, to crown all, the public treasury overflowing, embarrassing Congress, not to find subjects of taxation, but to select the objects which shall be liberated from the impost. *If the term of seven years were to be selected, of the greatest prosperity which this people have enjoyed since the establishment of their present Constitution, it would be exactly that period of seven years which immediately followed the passage of the tariff of 1824.*

This transformation of the condition of the country from gloom and distress to brightness and prosperity, has been mainly the work of American legislation, fostering American industry, instead of allowing it to be controlled by foreign legislation, cherishing foreign industry. The foes of the American system, in 1824, with great boldness and confidence, predicted, . . . the ruin of the public revenue, and the creation of a necessity to resort to direct taxation. . . . Every prediction which they made has failed, utterly failed. Instead of the ruin of the public revenue, with which they then sought to deter us from the adoption of the American system, we are now threatened with its subversion, by the vast amount of the public revenue produced by that system. . . .

While we thus behold the entire failure of all that was foretold against the system, it is a subject of just felicitation to its friends, that all their anticipations of its benefits have been fulfilled, or are in progress of fulfillment. . . .

It is now proposed to abolish the system, to which we owe so much of the public prosperity, and it is urged that the arrival of the period of the redemption of the public debt has been confidently looked to as presenting a suitable occasion to rid the country of the evils with which the system is alleged to be fraught. . . . But the people of the United States have not coupled the payment of their public debt with the destruction of the protection of their industry against foreign laws and foreign industry. They have been accustomed to regard the extinction of the public debt as relief from a burden, and not as the infliction of a curse. If it is to be attended or followed by the subversion of the American system, and an exposure of our establishments and our productions to the unguarded consequences of the selfish policy of foreign powers, the payment of the public debt will be the bitterest of curses. . . .

If the system of protection be founded on principles erroneous in theory, pernicious in practice, above all, if it be unconstitutional, as is alleged, it ought to be forthwith abolished, and not a vestige of it suffered to remain. But before we sanction this sweeping denunciation, let us look a little at this system, its magnitude, its ramifications, its duration, and the high authorities which have sustained it. . . . Why, sir, there is scarcely an interest, scarcely a vocation in society, which is not embraced by the beneficence of this system.

It comprehends our coasting tonnage and trade, from which all foreign tonnage is absolutely excluded.

It includes all our foreign tonnage, with the inconsiderable exception made by treaties of reciprocity with a few foreign powers.

It embraces our fisheries, and all our hardy and enterprising fishermen.

It extends to almost every mechanic art. . . . The mechanics . . . enjoy a measure of protection adapted to their several conditions, varying from twenty to fifty per cent. The extent and importance of some of these artisans may be estimated by a few particulars. The tanners, curriers, boot and shoemakers, and other workers in hides, skins, and leather, produce an ultimate value per annum of forty millions of dollars; the manufacturers of hats and caps produce an annual value of fifteen millions; the cabinet-makers, twelve millions; the manufacturers of bonnets and hats for the female sex, lace, artificial flowers, combs, and so forth, seven millions; and the manufacturers of glass, five millions. . . .

It affects the cotton planter himself, and the tobacco planter, both of whom enjoy protection.

The total amount of the capital vested in sheep, the land to sustain them, wool, woolen manufactures, and woolen fabrics, and the subsistence of the various persons directly or indirectly employed in the growth and manufacture of the article of wool, is estimated at one hundred and sixty-seven millions of dollars, and the number of persons at one hundred and fifty thousand.

The value of iron, considered as a raw material, and of its manufacturers, is estimated at twenty-six millions of dollars per annum. Cotton goods, exclusive of the capital vested in the manufacture, and of the cost of the raw material, are believed to amount, annually, to about twenty millions of dollars.

These estimates have been carefully made, by practical men of undoubted character, who have brought together and embodied their information. Anxious to avoid the charge of exaggeration, they have sometimes placed their estimates below what was believed to be the actual amount of these interests. . . .

. . . And are we not bound deliberately to consider whether we can proceed to this work of destruction without a violation of the public faith? The people of the United States have justly supposed that the policy of protecting their industry against foreign legislation and foreign industry was fully settled . . . by repeated and deliberate acts of government, performed at distant and frequent intervals. In full confidence that the policy was firmly and unchangeably fixed, thousands upon thousands have invested their capital, purchased a vast amount of real and other estate, made permanent establishments, and accommodated their industry. Can we expose to utter and irretrievable ruin this countless multitude, without justly incurring the reproach of violating the national faith?

I shall not discuss the constitutional question. Without meaning any disrespect to those who raise it, if it be debatable, it has been sufficiently debated. . . .

. . . It is true, the question was not debated in 1816; and why not? Because it was not debatable; it was then believed not fairly to arise. . . . What was not dreamed of before, or in 1816, and scarcely thought of in 1824, is now made, by excited imaginations, to assume the imposing form of a serious constitutional barrier. . . .

When gentlemen have succeeded in their design of an immediate or gradual destruction of the American system, what is their substitute? Free trade! Free trade! The call for free trade is as unavailing, as the cry of a spoiled child in its nurse's arms, for the moon, or the stars that glitter in the firmament of heaven. It never has existed, it never will exist. Trade implies at least two parties. To be free, it should be fair, equal, and reciprocal. . . . We may break down all barriers to free trade on our part, but the work will not be complete, until foreign powers shall have removed theirs. There would be freedom on one side, and restriction, prohibitions, and exclusions, on the other. . . .

Gentlemen deceive themselves. It is not free trade that they are recommending to our acceptance. It is, in effect, the British colonial system that we are invited to adopt; and, if their policy prevail, it will lead substantially to the recolonization of these States under the commercial dominion of Great Britain. . . .

I will now, Mr. President, proceed to a more particular consideration of the arguments urged against the protective system, and an inquiry into its practical operation, especially on the cotton-growing country. . . . It is alleged that the system operates prejudicially to the cotton planter, by diminishing the foreign demand for his staple; that we can not sell to Great Britain unless we buy from her; that the import duty is equivalent to an export duty, and falls upon the cotton grower; that South Carolina pays a disproportionate quota of the public revenue; that an abandonment of the protective policy would lead to an augmentation of our exports, of an amount not less than one hundred and fifty millions of dollars; and, finally, that the South can not partake of the advantages of manufacturing, if there be any. Let us examine these various propositions in detail. First, that the foreign demand for cotton is diminished, and that we can not sell to Great Britain unless we buy from her. . . .

The argument comprehends two errors, one of fact and the other of principle. It assumes that we do not in fact purchase of Great Britain. What is the true state of the case? There are certain, but very few articles which it is thought sound policy requires that we should manufacture at home, and on these the tariff operates. But with respect to all the rest, and much the larger number of articles of taste, fashion, and utility, they are subject to no other than revenue duties, and are freely introduced. I have before me from the Treasury a statement of our imports from England, Scotland, and Ireland, . . . from which it will appear that . . . the last year's importation . . . will probably be the greatest in the whole term of eleven years.

Now, if it be admitted that there is a less amount of the protected articles imported from Great Britain, she may be, and probably is, compensated for the deficiency, by the increased consumption in America of the articles of her industry not falling within the scope of the policy of our protection. The establishment of manufactures among us excites the creation of wealth, and this gives new powers of consumption, which are gratified by the purchase of foreign objects. A poor nation can never be a great consuming nation. Its poverty will limit its consumption to bare subsistence.

The erroneous principle which the argument includes, is, that it devolves on us the duty of taking care that Great Britain shall be enabled to purchase from us without exacting from Great Britain the corresponding duty. If it be true on one side that nations are bound to shape their policy in reference to the ability of foreign powers, it must be true on both sides of the Atlantic. . . .

But, does Great Britain practice toward us upon the principles which we are now required to observe in regard to her? The exports to the United Kingdom . . . fall short of the amount of imports by upward of forty-six millions of dollars. . . . It is surprising how we have been able to sustain, for so long a time, a trade so very unequal. . . . Great Britain constantly acts on the maxim of buying only what she wants and can not produce, and selling to foreign nations the utmost amount she can. In conformity with this maxim, she excludes articles of prime necessity, produced by us, equally if not more necessary than any of her industry which we tax, although the admission of those articles would increase our ability to purchase from her, according to the argument of gentlemen. . . .

But if there were a diminution of the British demand for cotton equal to the loss of a market for the few British fabrics which are within the scope of our protective policy, the question would still remain, whether the cotton-planter is not amply indemnified by the creation of additional demand elsewhere? With respect to the cotton-grower, it is the totality of the demand, and not its distribution, which affects his interests. If any system of policy will augment the aggregate of the demand, that system is favorable to his interests, although its tendency may be to vary the theater of the demand. It could not, for example, be injurious to him, if, instead of Great Britain continuing to receive the entire quantity of cotton which she now does, two or three hundred thousand bales of it were taken to the other side of the channel, and increased to that extent the French demand. It would be better for him, because it is always better to have several markets than one. Now if, instead of a transfer to the opposite side of the channel, of those two or three hundred thousand bales, they are transported to the northern States, can that be injurious to the cotton-grower? Is it not better for him? Is it not better to have a market at home, unaffected by war, or other foreign causes, for that amount of his staple? . . .

. . . By its existence at home, the circle of those exchanges is created, which reciprocally diffuses among all who are embraced within it the productions of their respective industry. The cotton-grower sells the raw material to the manufacturer; he buys the iron, the bread, the meal, the coal, and the countless number of objects of his consumption from his fellow-citizens, and they in turn purchase his fabrics. . . . The main argument of gentlemen is founded upon the idea of mutual ability resulting from mutual exchanges. They would furnish an ability to foreign nations by purchasing from them, and I, to our own people, by exchanges at home. If the American manufacture were discontinued, and that of England were to take its place, how would she sell the additional quantity of twenty-four millions of cotton goods, which we now make? To us? That has been shown to be impracticable. To other foreign nations? She has already pushed her supplies to them to the utmost extent. The ultimate consequence would then be to diminish the total consumption of cotton, to say nothing now of the reduction of price that would take place by throwing into the ports of Great Britain the two hundred thousand bales, which, no longer being manufactured in the United States, would go thither. . . .

. . . It is contended, in the last place, that the South can not, from physical and other causes, engage in the manufacturing arts. I deny the premises, and I deny the conclusion. I deny the fact of inability; and, if it existed, I deny the conclusion, that we must, therefore, break down our manufactures, and nourish those of foreign countries. The South possesses, in an extraordinary degree, two of the most important elements of manufacturing industry — water-power and labor. The former gives to our whole country a most decided advantage over Great Britain. But a single experiment, stated by the gentleman from South Carolina, in which a faithless slave put the torch to a manufacturing establishment, has discouraged similar enterprises. We have in Kentucky the same description of population, and we employ them, almost exclusively, in many of our hemp manufactories. . . .

Let it be supposed, however, that the South can not manufacture; must those parts of the Union which can, be therefore prevented? Must we support those of foreign countries? . . .

I regret, Mr. President, that one topic has, I think, unnecessarily been introduced into this debate. I allude to the charge brought against the manufacturing system, as favoring the growth of aristocracy. . . . The joint-stock companies of the North, as I understand them, are nothing more than associations, sometimes of hundreds, by means of which the small earnings of many are brought into a common stock, and the associates, obtaining corporate privileges, are enabled to prosecute, under one superintending head, their business to better advantage. Nothing can be more essentially democratic or better devised to counterpoise the influence of individual wealth. In Kentucky, almost every manufactory known to me, is in the hands of enterprising and self-made men, who have acquired whatever wealth they possess by patient and diligent labor. Comparisons are odious, and but in defense would not be made by me. But is there more tendency to aristocracy in a manufactory, supporting hundreds of freemen, or in a cotton plantation, with its not less numerous slaves, sustaining perhaps only two white families—that of the master and the overseer? . . .

I could extend and dwell on the long list of articles—the hemp, iron, lead, coal, and other items—for which a demand is created in the home market by the operation of the American system; but I should exhaust the patience of the Senate. Where, where should we find a market for all these articles, if it did not exist at home? What would be the condition of the largest portion of our people, and of the territory, if this home market were annihilated? How could they be supplied with objects of prime necessity? What would not be the certain and inevitable decline in the price of all these articles, but for the home market? . . .

But if all this reasoning were totally fallacious; if the price of manufactured articles were really higher, under the American system, than without it, I should still argue that high or low prices were themselves relative—relative to the ability to pay them. It is in vain to tempt, to tantalize us with the lower prices of European fabrics than our own, if we have nothing wherewith to purchase them. If, by the home exchanges, we can be supplied with necessary, even if they are dearer and worse, articles of American production than the foreign, it is better than not to be supplied at all. And how would the large portion of our country, which I have described, be supplied, but for the home exchanges? A poor people, destitute of wealth or of exchangeable commodities, has nothing to purchase foreign fabrics with. To them they are equally beyond their reach, whether their cost be a dollar or a guinea. It is in this view of the matter that Great Britain, by her vast wealth, her excited and protected industry, is enabled to bear a burden of taxation, which, when compared to that of other nations, appears enormous, but which, when her immense riches are compared to theirs, is light and trival. The gentleman from South Carolina has drawn a lively and flattering picture of our coasts, bays, rivers, and harbors; and he argues that these proclaimed the design of Providence, that we should be a commercial people. I agree with him. We differ only as to the means. He would cherish the foreign, and neglect the internal trade. I would foster both. . . . By penetrating the bosoms of our mountains, and extracting from them their precious treasures; by cultivating the earth, and securing a home market for its rich and abundant products; by employing the water with which we are blessed; by stimulating and protecting our native industry, in all its forms; we shall but nourish and promote the prosperity of commerce, foreign and domestic.

I have hitherto considered the question in reference only to a state of peace; but a season of war ought not to be entirely overlooked. We have enjoyed nearly twenty years of peace; but who can tell when the storm of war shall again break forth? Have we forgotton, so soon, the privations to which not merely our brave soldiers and our gallant tars[1] were subjected, but the whole community, during the last war, for the want of absolute necessaries? To what an enormous price they rose! And how inadequate the supply was at any price! . . . It would be easy to show that the higher prices of peace . . . were more than compensated by the lower prices of war, during which, supplies of all essential articles are indispensable to its vigorous, effectual, and glorious prosecution. I conclude this part of the argument with the hope that my humble exertions have not been altogether unsuccessful in showing,

First, that the policy which we have been considering ought to continue to be regarded as the genuine American system.

Secondly, that the free trade system, which is proposed as its substitute, ought really to be considered as the British colonial system.

Thirdly, that the American system is beneficial to all parts of the Union, and absolutely necessary to much the larger portion.

Fourthly, that the price of the great staple of cotton, and of all our chief productions of agriculture, has been sustained and upheld, and a decline averted, by the protective system.

Fifthly, that if the foreign demand for cotton has been at all diminished by the operation of that system, the diminution has been more than compensated in the additional demand created at home.

Sixthly, that the constant tendency of the system, by creating competition among ourselves, and between American and European industry, reciprocally acting upon each other, is to reduce prices of manufactured objects.

Seventhly, that in point of fact, objects within the scope of the policy of protection have greatly fallen in price.

Eighthly, that if, in a season of peace, these benefits are experienced, in a season of war, when the foreign supply might be cut off, they would be much more extensively felt.

Ninthly, and finally, that the substitution of the British colonial system for the American system, without benefiting any section of the Union, by subjecting us to a foreign legislation, regulated by foreign interests, would lead to the prostration of our manufactories, general impoverishment, and ultimate ruin. . . .

---

[1]Sailors were called "tars" because tar was used to waterproof wooden ships and their rigging, and tar frequently marked hair, skin, and clothing.

... But, sir, it is impossible to conceal from our view the facts, that there is a great excitement in South Carolina; that the protective system is openly and violently denounced in popular meetings; and that the Legislature itself has declared its purpose of resorting to counteracting measures. . . . The great principle which lies at the foundation of all free governments, is, that the majority must govern; from which there is or can be no appeal but to the sword. That majority ought to govern wisely, equitably, moderately, and constitutionally, but govern it must, subject only to that terrible appeal. If ever one or several States, being a minority, can, by menacing a dissolution of the Union, succeed in forcing an abandonment of great measures, deemed essential to the interests and prosperity of the whole, the Union from that moment is practically gone. . . . I would intreat the patriotic people of South Carolina . . . to pause, solemnly pause! and contemplate the frightful precipice which lies directly before them. To retreat may be painful and mortifying to their gallantry and pride, but it is to retreat to the Union, to safety, and to those brethren with whom, or with whose ancestors, they, or their ancestors, have won, on fields of glory, imperishable renown. To advance, is to rush on certain and inevitable disgrace and destruction. . . .

The danger to our Union does not lie on the side of persistence in the American system, but on that of its abandonment. . . . What would be the condition of this Union, if Pennsylvania and New York, those mammoth members of our confederacy, were firmly persuaded that their industry was paralyzed, and their prosperity blighted, by the enforcement of the British colonial system, under the delusive name of free trade? . . . But . . . let them feel that a foreign system is to predominate, and the sources of their subsistence and comfort dried up; let New England and the West, and the middle States, all feel that they too are the victims of a mistaken policy, and let these vast portions of our country despair of any favorable change, and then indeed might we tremble for the continuance and safety of this Union. . . .

And now, sir, I would address a few words to the friends of the American system in the Senate. The revenue must, ought to be, reduced. The country will not, after by the payment of the public debt ten or twelve millions of dollars become unnecessary, bear such an annual surplus. Its distribution would form a subject of perpetual contention. . . . But the revenue ought to be reduced, so as to accommodate it to the fact of the payment of the public debt. . . . Let us then adopt the measure before us, which will benefit all classes—the farmer, the professional man, the merchant, the manufacturer, the mechanic; and the cotton planter more than all. A few months ago there was no diversity of opinion as to the expediency of this measure. All, then, seemed to unite in the selection of these objects for a repeal of duties which were not produced within the country. Such a repeal did not touch our domestic industry, violated no principle, offended no prejudice.

Can we not all, whatever may be our favorite theories, cordially unite on this neutral ground? When that is occupied, let us look beyond it, and see if any thing can be done in the field of protection, to modify, to improve it, or to satisfy those who are opposed to the system. Our southern brethren believe that it is injurious to them, and ask its repeal. We believe that its abandonment will be prejudicial to them, and ruinous to every other section of the Union. However strong their convictions may be, they are not stronger than ours. Between the points of the preservation of the system and its absolute repeal, there is no principle of union. If it can be shown to operate immoderately on any quarter; if the measure of protection to any article can be demonstrated to be undue and inordinate, it would be the duty of Congress to interpose and apply a remedy. And none will co-operate more heartily than I shall in the performance of that duty. It is quite probable that beneficial modifications of the system may be made without impairing its efficacy. But to make it fulfill the purposes of its institution, the measure of protection ought to be adequate. If it be not, all interests will be injuriously affected. The manufacturer, crippled in his exertions, will produce less perfect and dearer fabrics, and the consumer will feel the consequence. This is the spirit, and these are the principles only, on which it seems to me that a settlement of the great question can be made, satisfactorily to all parts of our Union.

17

ANDREW JACKSON

Nullification Proclamation
December 10, 1832

The Tariffs of 1828 and 1832 stirred resentment in all the southern states and passionate outrage in South Carolina. These protective tariffs were intended to subsidize the growth of manufacturing industries everywhere in the country, but southerners believed that they could not benefit from the tariff because their soil, climate, and above all, their "institutions" (meaning slavery) were better suited to agriculture. Despairing of congressional relief, the state of South Carolina finally nullified the two federal tariffs in 1832, proclaiming them unconstitutional and requiring state officials to prevent their collection in South Carolina. The Ordinance of Nullification concluded by threatening the secession of South Carolina if the federal government attempted to overturn its operation.

Nullification presented a strong challenge to Andrew Jackson. He believed in states' rights, strict construction, and decentralized government. In the areas where he felt the Constitution did give the federal government supreme power, however, he fully supported protecting federal prerogatives and had no intention of allowing nullification to succeed. When South Carolina issued its Ordinance of Nullification, he responded with a Proclamation that spelled out his views on the nature of the Union.

As a constitutional idea, nullification was based on the belief that the Constitution had been formed by a compact of states and that the states retained the right to decide whether the acts of the central government conformed to the original agreement. Why does Jackson here reject this view, calling the United States "a government, not a league"? In Jackson's view, does the idea of nullification have implications for the principle of majority rule? for democracy? Does he make a convincing case for the idea of perpetual American union?

Does the proclamation indicate that Jackson was ready to resort to force in political disputes? How would his arguments be used again in future political controversies? Do you think Henry Clay would have agreed with the ideas expressed in this proclamation?

James D. Richardson, comp., *A Compilation of the Messages and Papers of the Presidents, 1789–1897,* 10 vols. (Washington, D.C.: Government Printing Office, 1897), 2: 640–56.

... Whereas the ... [nullification] ordinance prescribes to the people of South Carolina a course of conduct in direct violation of their duty as citizens of the United States, contrary to the laws of their country, subversive of its Constitution,[1] and having for its object the destruction of the Union—that Union which, coeval with our political existence, led our fathers, without any other ties to unite them than those of patriotism and a common cause, through a sanguinary struggle to a glorious independence; that sacred Union, hitherto inviolate, which, perfected by our happy Constitution, has brought us, by the favor of Heaven, to a state of prosperity at home and high consideration abroad rarely, if ever, equaled in the history of nations:

To preserve this bond of our political existence from destruction, to maintain inviolate this state of national honor and prosperity, and to justify the confidence my fellow-citizens have reposed in me, I, Andrew Jackson, President of the United States, have thought proper to issue this my proclamation, stating my views of the Constitution and laws applicable to the measures adopted by the convention of South Carolina and to the reasons they have put forth to sustain them, declaring the course which duty will require me to pursue, and, appealing to the understanding and patriotism of the people, warn them of the consequences that must inevitably result from an observance of the dictates of the convention. . . .

The ordinance is founded, not on the indefeasible right of resisting acts which are plainly unconstitutional and too oppressive to be endured, but on the strange position that any one State may not only declare an act of Congress void, but prohibit its execution; that they may do this consistently with the Constitution; that the true construction of that instrument permits a State to retain its place in the Union and yet be bound by no other of its laws than those it may choose to consider as constitutional. It is true, they add, that to justify this abrogation of a law it must be palpably contrary to the Constitution; but it is evident that to give the right of resisting laws of that description, cou-

---

[1]Jackson cited no specific clause of the U.S. Constitution to support these views, but he probably believed that nullification was a direct violation of Article VI, which declares that "This Constitution and the laws of the United States which shall be made in pursuance thereof ... shall be the supreme law of the land; and the judges in every State shall be bound thereby, anything in the Constitution or laws of any State to the contrary notwithstanding." Without endorsing Chief Justice John Marshall's view that the United States Supreme Court held the exclusive right to make final and binding interpretation of the Constitution, Jackson intended to show that nullification subverted the implicit constitutional principle of majority rule.

pled with the uncontrolled right to decide what laws deserve that character, is to give the power of resisting all laws; for as by the theory there is no appeal, the reasons alleged by the State, good or bad, must prevail. . . .

If this doctrine had been established at an earlier day, the Union would have been dissolved in its infancy. The excise law in Pennsylvania, the embargo and nonintercourse law in the Eastern States, the carriage tax in Virginia, were all deemed unconstitutional, and were more unequal in their operation than any of the laws now complained of; but, fortunately, none of those States discovered that they had the right now claimed by South Carolina. The war into which we were forced to support the dignity of the nation and the rights of our citizens might have ended in defeat and disgrace, instead of victory and honor, if the States who supposed it a ruinous and unconstitutional measure had thought they possessed the right of nullifying the act by which it was declared and denying supplies for its prosecution. . . . The discovery of this important feature in our Constitution was reserved to the present day. To the statesmen of South Carolina belongs the invention, and upon the citizens of that State will unfortunately fall the evils of reducing it to practice.

If the doctrine of a State veto upon the laws of the Union carries with it internal evidence of its impracticable absurdity, our constitutional history will also afford abundant proof that it would have been repudiated with indignation had it been proposed to form a feature in our Government.

In our colonial state, although dependent on another power, we very early considered ourselves as connected by common interest with each other. Leagues were formed for common defense, and before the declaration of independence we were known in our aggregate character as *the United Colonies of America.* That decisive and important step was taken jointly. We declared ourselves a nation by a joint, not by several acts, and when the terms of our Confederation were reduced to form it was in that of a solemn league of several States, by which they agreed that they would collectively form one nation for the purpose of conducting some certain domestic concerns and all foreign relations. In the instrument forming that Union is found an article which declares that "every State shall abide by the determinations of Congress on all questions which by that Confederation should be submitted to them."[2]

---

[2]Articles of Confederation, Article XIII: "Every State shall abide by the determinations of the United States in Congress assembled on all questions which by this confederation are submitted to them."

Under the Confederation, then, no State could legally annul a decision of the Congress or refuse to submit to its execution; but no provision was made to enforce these decisions. . . . They had no judiciary, no means of collecting revenue.

But the defects of the Confederation need not be detailed. Under its operation we could scarcely be called a nation. We had neither prosperity at home nor consideration abroad. This state of things could not be endured, and our present happy Constitution was formed, but formed in vain if this fatal doctrine prevails. It was formed for important objects that are announced in the preamble, made in the name and by the authority of the people of the United States, whose delegates framed and whose conventions approved it. The most important among these objects—that which is placed first in rank, on which all the others rest—is *"to form a more perfect union."* Now, . . . can it be conceived that an instrument made for the purpose of *"forming a more perfect union"* . . . could be so constructed by the assembled wisdom of our country as to substitute for that Confederation a form of government dependent for its existence on the local interest, the party spirit, of a State, or of a prevailing faction in a State? Every man of plain, unsophisticated understanding who hears the question will give such an answer as will preserve the Union. . . .

I consider, then, the power to annul a law of the United States, assumed by one State, *incompatible with the existence of the Union, contradicted expressly by the letter of the Constitution, unauthorized by its spirit, inconsistent with every principle on which it was founded, and destructive of the great object for which it was formed.*

After this general view of the leading principle, we must examine the particular application of it which is made in the ordinance.

The preamble rests its justification on these grounds: It assumes as a fact that the obnoxious laws, although they purport to be laws for raising revenue, were in reality intended for the protection of manufactures, which purpose it asserts to be unconstitutional; that the operation of these laws is unequal; that the amount raised by them is greater than is required by the wants of the Government; and, finally, that the proceeds are to be applied to objects unauthorized by the Constitution. These are the only causes alleged to justify an open opposition to the laws of the country and a threat of seceding from the Union if any attempt should be made to enforce them. The first virtually acknowledges that the law in question was passed under a power expressly given by the Constitution to lay and collect imposts; but its constitutionality is drawn in question from the *motives* of those who passed it. . . . How is that [motive] to be ascertained? . . . Admit this doctrine, and you give to the States an uncontrolled right to decide, and every law may be annulled under this pretext. . . .

The next objection is that the laws in question operate unequally. This objection may be made with truth to every law that has been or can be passed. The wisdom of man never yet contrived a system of taxation that would operate with perfect equality. If the unequal operation of a law makes it unconstitutional, and if all laws of that description may be abrogated by any State for that cause, then, indeed, is the Federal Constitution unworthy of the slightest effort for its preservation. We have hitherto relied on it as the perpetual bond of our Union; we have received it as the work of the assembled wisdom of the nation; we have trusted to it as to the sheet anchor of our safety in the stormy times of conflict with a foreign or domestic foe; we have looked to it with sacred awe as the palladium of our liberties, and with all the solemnities of religion have pledged to each other our lives and fortunes here and our hopes of happiness hereafter in its defense and support. Were we mistaken, my countrymen, in attaching this importance to the Constitution of our country? Was our devotion paid to the wretched, inefficient, clumsy contrivance which this new doctrine would make it? Did we pledge ourselves to the support of an airy nothing—a bubble that must be blown away by the first breath of disaffection? Was this self-destroying, visionary theory the work of the profound statesmen, the exalted patriots, to whom the task of constitutional reform was intrusted? Did the name of Washington sanction, did the States deliberately ratify, such an anomaly in the history of fundamental legislation? No; we were not mistaken. The letter of this great instrument is free from this radical fault. Its language directly contradicts the imputation; its spirit, its evident intent, contradicts it. No; we did not err. Our Constitution does not contain the absurdity of giving power to make laws and another to resist them. The sages whose memory will always be reverenced have given us a practical and, as they hoped, a permanent constitutional compact. The Father of his Country did not affix his revered name to so palpable an absurdity. Nor did the States, when they severally ratified it, do so under the impression that a veto on the laws of the United States was reserved to them or that they could exercise it by implication. . . . The Constitution is still the object of our reverence, the bond of our Union, our defense in danger, the source of our prosperity in peace. It shall descend, as we have received it, uncorrupted by sophistical construction, to our posterity; and the sacrifices of local interest, of State prejudices, of personal animosities, that were made to bring it into existence, will again be patriotically offered for its support. . . .

Here is a law of the United States, not even pretended to be unconstitutional, repealed by the authority of a small majority of the voters of a single State. Here is a provision of the Constitution which is solemnly abrogated by the same authority.

... The ordinance ... not only ... [asserts] the right to annul the laws of which it complains, but to enforce it by a threat of seceding from the Union if any attempt is made to execute them.

This right to secede is deduced from the nature of the Constitution, which, they say, is a compact between sovereign States who have preserved their whole sovereignty and therefore are subject to no superior; that because they made the compact they can break it when in their opinion it has been departed from by the other States. Fallacious as this course of reasoning is, it enlists State pride and finds advocates in the honest prejudices of those who have not studied the nature of our Government sufficiently to see the radical error on which it rests.

The people of the United States formed the Constitution, acting through the State legislatures in making the compact, to meet and discuss its provisions, and acting in separate conventions when they ratified those provisions; but the terms used in its construction show it to be a Government in which the people of all the States, collectively, are represented. We are *one people* in the choice of President and Vice-President. ... The candidates having the majority of all the votes are chosen. The electors of a majority of States may have given their votes for one candidate, and yet another may be chosen. The people, then, and not the States, are represented in the executive branch.

In the House of Representatives there is this difference, that the people of one State do not, as in the case of President and Vice-President, all vote for the same officers. The people of all the States do not vote for all the members, each State electing only its own representatives. But this creates no material distinction. When chosen, they are all representatives of the United States, not representatives of the particular State from which they come. They are paid by the United States, not by the State; nor are they accountable to it for any act done in the performance of their legislative functions; and however they may in practice, as it is their duty to do, consult and prefer the interests of their particular constituents when they come in conflict with any other partial or local interest, yet it is their first and highest duty, as representatives of the United States, to promote the general good.

The Constitution of the United States, then, forms a *government,* not a league; and whether it be formed by compact between the States or in any other manner, its character is the same. ... Each State, having expressly parted with so many powers as to constitute, jointly with the other States, a single nation, can not, from that period, possess any right to secede, because such secession does not break a league, but destroys the unity of a nation; and any injury to that unity is not only a breach which would result from the contravention of a compact, but it is an offense against the whole Union. To say that any State may at pleasure secede from the Union is to say that the United States are not a nation, because it would be a solecism to contend that any part of a nation might dissolve its connection with the other parts, to their injury or ruin, without committing any offense. Secession, like any other revolutionary act, may be morally justified by the extremity of oppression; but to call it a constitutional right is confounding the meaning of terms, and can only be done through gross error or to deceive those who are willing to assert a right, but would pause before they made a revolution or incur the penalties consequent on a failure.

Because the Union was formed by a compact, it is said the parties to that compact may, when they feel themselves aggrieved, depart from it; but it is precisely because it is a compact that they can not. A compact is an agreement or binding obligation. . . . A league between independent nations generally has no sanction [against a breach] other than a moral one; or if it should contain a penalty, as there is no common superior it can not be enforced. A government, on the contrary, always has a sanction, express or implied; and in our case it is both necessarily implied and expressly given. An attempt, by force of arms, to destroy a government is an offense, . . . and such government has the right by the law of self-defense to pass acts for punishing the offender. . . .

. . . No one, fellow-citizens, has a higher reverence for the reserved rights of the States than the Magistrate who now addresses you. No one would make greater personal sacrifices or official exertions to defend them from violation; but equal care must be taken to prevent, on their part, an improper interference with or resumption of the rights they have vested in the nation. The line has not been so distinctly drawn as to avoid doubts in some cases of the exercise of power. Men of the best intentions and soundest views may differ in their construction of some parts of the Constitution; but there are others on which dispassionate reflection can leave no doubt. Of this nature appears to be the assumed right of secession. It rests, as we have seen, on the alleged undivided sovereignty of the States and on their having formed in this sovereign capacity a compact which is called the Constitution, from which, because they made it, they have the right to secede. Both of these positions are erroneous, and some of the arguments to prove them so have been anticipated. . . .

Fellow-citizens of my native State, let me not only admonish you, as the First Magistrate of our common country, not to incur the penalty of its laws, but use the influence that a father would over his children whom he saw rushing to certain ruin. In that paternal language, with that paternal feeling, let me tell you, my countrymen, that you are deluded by men who are either deceived themselves or wish to deceive you.... They are not champions of liberty, emulating the fame of our Revolutionary fathers, nor are you an oppressed people, contending, as they repeat to you, against worse than colonial vassalage. You are free members of a flourishing and happy Union. There is no settled design to oppress you. You have indeed felt the unequal operation of laws which may have been unwisely, not unconstitutionally, passed; but that inequality must necessarily be removed. At the very moment when you were madly urged on to the unfortunate course you have begun a change in public opinion had commenced....

I have urged you to look back to the means that were used to hurry you on to the position you have now assumed and forward to the consequences it will produce. Something more is necessary. Contemplate the condition of that country of which you still form an important part. Consider its Government, uniting in one bond of common interest and general protection so many different States, giving to all their inhabitants the proud title of *American citizen,* protecting their commerce, securing their literature and their arts, facilitating their intercommunication, defending their frontiers, and making their name respected in the remotest parts of the earth. Consider the extent of its territory, its increasing and happy population, its advance in arts which render life agreeable, and the sciences which elevate the mind! See education spreading the lights of religion, morality, and general information into every cottage in this wide extent of our Territories and States. Behold it as the asylum where the wretched and the oppressed find a refuge and support. Look on this picture of happiness and honor and say, *We too are citizens of America.* Carolina is one of these proud States; her arms have defended, her best blood has cemented, this happy Union. And then add, if you can, without horror and remorse, This happy Union we will dissolve; this picture of peace and prosperity we will deface; this free intercourse we will interrupt; these fertile fields we will deluge with blood; the protection of that glorious flag we renounce; the very name of Americans we discard.... But the dictates of a high duty oblige me solemnly to announce that you can not succeed. The laws of the United States must be executed. I have no discretionary power on the subject; my duty is emphatically pronounced in the Constitution. Those who told you that you might peaceably prevent their execution deceived you; they could not have been deceived themselves. They know that a forcible opposition could alone prevent the execution of the laws, and they know that such opposition must be repelled. Their object is disunion. But be not deceived by names. Disunion by armed force is *treason*. Are you really ready to incur its guilt? If you are, on the heads of the instigators of the act be the dreadful consequences; on their heads be the dishonor, but on yours may fall the punishment. . . . It is yet in your power to disappoint them. There is yet time to show that the descendants of the Pinckneys, the Sumpters, the Rutledges, and of the thousand other names which adorn the pages of your Revolutionary history will not abandon that Union to support which so many of them fought and bled and died. . . . Snatch from the archives of your State the disorganizing edict of its convention. . . . Declare that you will never take the field unless the star-spangled banner of your country shall float over you; that you will not be stigmatized when dead, and dishonored and scorned while you live, as the authors of the first attack on the Constitution of your country. Its destroyers you can not be. You may disturb its peace, you may interrupt the course of its prosperity, you may cloud its reputation for stability; but its tranquillity will be restored, its prosperity will return, and the stain upon its national character will be transferred and remain an eternal blot on the memory of those who caused the disorder. . . .

May the Great Ruler of Nations grant that the signal blessings with which He has favored ours may not, by the madness of party or personal ambition, be disregarded and lost; and may His wise providence bring those who have produced this crisis to see the folly before they feel the misery of civil strife, and inspire a returning veneration for that Union which, if we may dare to penetrate His designs, He has chosen as the only means of attaining the high destinies to which we may reasonably aspire.

In testimony whereof I have caused the seal of the United States to be hereunto affixed, having signed the same with my hand.

Done at the city of Washington, this 10th day of December, A.D. 1832, and of the Independence of the United States the fifty-seventh.

18

HENRY CLAY

On the Compromise Tariff

February 12, 1833

Henry Clay was a great friend of the tariff and also a believer in a strong federal government. He had no respect for the doctrines of nullification but had long since retreated from the warlike temperament that had once led him to clamor for war with Britain (see Document 4). He believed that the great and lasting interests of the United States were all mutually compatible. Instead of going to war over the tariff, he helped to arrange a compromise that would preserve protection for nine years and then lower the tariff to a level that provided no more than the minimal revenue needs of the federal government. In the following speech, he spells out the values that led supporters to call him the "Great Compromiser."

What are the main provisions of the Compromise Tariff? What advantages do they offer to the supporters of protection? to the nullifiers?

Many South Carolinians admitted that worries about the future of slavery lay beneath their campaign for states' rights and nullification. How does Clay attempt to use these worries to remind South Carolina of the advantages of the Union?

What are the differences between Clay's approach to the tariff crisis and Jackson's? Both men appeal to the value of union: How is Clay's view of the Union different from Jackson's?

... I rise, sir, on this occasion, actuated by no motives of a private nature, by no personal feelings, and for no personal objects; but exclusively in obedience to a sense of the duty which I owe to my country. . . . When I survey, sir, the whole face of our country, I behold all around me evidences of the most gratifying prosperity, a prospect which would seem to be without a cloud upon it, were it not that through all parts of the country there exist great dissensions and unhappy distinctions, which, if they can possibly be relieved and reconciled by any broad scheme of legislation adapted to all interests, and regarding the feelings of all sections, ought to be quieted. . . .

Calvin Colton, ed., *The Life, Correspondence, and Speeches of Henry Clay*, 6 vols. (New York: Barnes, 1857), 5: 537–50.

In presenting the modification of the tariff laws, which I am now about to submit, I have two great objects in view. My first object looks to the tariff. I am compelled to express the opinion . . . that . . . the tariff stands in imminent danger. If it should be preserved during this session, it must fall at the next session. . . . But in my opinion, sir, the sudden repeal of the tariff policy would bring ruin and destruction on the whole people of this country. There is no evil, in my opinion, equal to the consequences which would result from such a catastrophe.

What, sir, are the complaints which unhappily divide the people of this great country? On the one hand it is said, by those who are opposed to the tariff, that it unjustly taxes a portion of the people, and paralyzes their industry; . . . that there is to be no end to the system; which, right or wrong, is to be urged to their inevitable ruin. And what is the just complaint, on the other hand, of those who support the tariff? It is, that the policy of the government is vacillating and uncertain, and that there is no stability in our legislation. . . . On one side we are urged to repeal a system which is fraught with ruin; on the other side, the check now imposed on enterprise, and the state of alarm in which the public mind has been thrown, render all prudent men desirous, looking ahead a little way, to adopt a state of things, on the stability of which they may have reason to count. Such is the state of feeling on the one side and on the other. I am anxious to find out some principle of mutual accommodation, to satisfy, as far as practicable, both parties—to increase the stability of our legislation; and at some distant day—but not too distant, when we take into view the magnitude of the interests which are involved—to bring down the rate of duties to that revenue standard, for which our opponents have so long contended. The basis on which I wish to found this modification is one of time; and the several parts of the bill to which I am about to call the attention of the Senate, are founded on this basis. I propose to give protection to our manufactured articles, adequate protection for a length of time, . . . securing the stability of legislation, and allowing time for a gradual reduction on one side, and on the other proposing to reduce the duties to that revenue standard, for which the opponents of the system have so long contended. I will now proceed to lay the provisions of the bill before the Senate, with a view to draw their attention to the true character of the bill. . . .

. . . The most that can be objected to the bill by those with whom I co-operate to support the protective system, is, that, in consideration of nine and a half years of peace, certainty, and stability, the manufacturers relinquished some advantages which they now enjoy. . . . After the accumulation of capital and skill, the manufacturers will stand alone, unaided by the government, in competition with the imported articles from any quarter. Now give us time; cease all fluctuations and agitations, for nine years, and the manufacturers in every branch will sustain themselves against foreign competition. . . . If the tariff be overthrown, as may be its fate next session, the country will be plunged into extreme distress and agitation. I want harmony. . . . I delight not in this perpetual turmoil. Let us have peace, and become once more united as a band of brothers. . . .

. . . All parties may find in this measure some reasons for objection. And what human measure is there which is free from objectionable qualities? It has been remarked, and justly remarked, by the great father of our country himself, that if that great work which is the charter of our liberties . . . had been submitted, article by article, to all the different States composing this Union, that the whole would have been rejected; and yet when the whole was presented together, it was accepted as a whole. I will admit that my friends do not get all they could wish for; and the gentlemen on the other side do not obtain all they might desire; but both will gain all that in my humble opinion is proper to be given in the present condition of this country. It may be true that there will be loss and gain in this measure. But how is this loss and gain distributed? Among our countrymen. What we lose, no foreign land gains; and what we gain, will be no loss to any foreign power. It is among ourselves the distribution takes place. The distribution is founded on that great principle of compromise and concession which lies at the bottom of our institutions, which gave birth to the Constitution itself. . . .

It remains for me now to touch another topic. . . . When I came to take my seat on this floor, I had supposed that a member of this Union had taken an attitude of defiance and hostility against the authority of the general government. I had imagined that she had arrogantly required that we should abandon at once a system which had long been the settled policy of this country. Supposing that she had manifested this feeling, and taken up this position, I had in consequence, felt a disposition to hurl defiance back again, and to impress upon her the necessity of the performance of her duties as a member of this Union. But since my arrival here, I find that South Carolina does not contemplate force, for it is denied and denounced by that State. She disclaims it; and asserts that she is merely making an experiment. . . . Her appeal is not to arms, but to another power; not to the sword, but to the law. . . . She disclaims any intention of resorting to force unless we should find it indispensable to execute the laws of the Union by applying force to her. It seems to me the aspect of the attitude of South Carolina has changed; or rather, the new light which

I have obtained, enables me to see her in a different attitude; and I have not truly understood her until she passed her laws, by which it was intended to carry her ordinance into effect. Now, I venture to predict that the State to which I have referred must ultimately fail in her attempt. . . . From one end to the other of this continent, by acclamation, as it were, nullification has been put down, and put down in a manner more effectually than by a thousand wars or a thousand armies—by the irresistible force, by the mighty influence of public opinion. Not a voice beyond the single State of South Carolina has been heard in favor of the principle of nullification, which she has asserted by her own ordinance; and I will say, that she must fail in her lawsuit. . . .

. . . South Carolina must perceive the embarrassments of her situation. She must be desirous—it is unnatural to suppose that she is not—to remain in the Union. What! a State whose heroes in its gallant ancestry fought so many glorious battles along with those of the other States of this Union—a State with which this confederacy is linked by bonds of such a powerful character! I have sometimes fancied what would be her condition if she goes out of this Union; if her five hundred thousand people should at once be thrown upon their own resources. She is out of the Union. What is the consequence? She is an independent power. What then does she do? She must have armies and fleets, and an expensive government; have foreign missions; she must raise taxes; enact this very tariff which has driven her out of the Union, in order to enable her to raise money, and to sustain the attitude of an independent power. If she should have no force, no navy to protect her, she would be exposed to piratical incursions. Their neighbor, St. Domingo, might pour down a horde of pirates on her borders, and desolate her plantations. She must have her embassies; therefore must she have a revenue. And let me tell you, there is another consequence, an inevitable one: she has a certain description of persons recognized as property south of the Potomac, and west of the Mississippi, which would be no longer recognized as such, except within their own limits. This species of property would sink to one half of its present value, for it is Louisiana and the south-western States which are her great market.

But I will not dwell on this topic any longer. I say it is utterly impossible that South Carolina ever desired, for a moment, to become a separate and independent State. . . . I would repeat, that under all the circumstances of the case, the condition of South Carolina is only one of the elements of a combination, the whole of which, together, constitutes a motive of action which renders it expedient to resort, during the present session of Congress, to some measure in order to quiet and tranquilize the country.

If there be any who want civil war, who want to see the blood of any portion of our countrymen spilt, I am not one of them. I wish to see war of no kind; but, above all, I do not desire to see civil war. When war begins, whether civil or foreign, no human sight is competent to foresee when, or how, or where it is to terminate. But when a civil war shall be lighted up in the bosom of our own happy land, and armies are marching, and commanders are winning their victories, and fleets are in motion on our coast, tell me, if you can, tell me, if any human being can tell its duration. God alone knows where such a war would end. In what a state will our institutions be left? In what a state our liberties? I want no war; above all, no war at home.

Sir, I repeat, that I think South Carolina has been rash, intemperate, and greatly in the wrong; but I do not want to disgrace her, nor any other member of this Union. No: I do not desire to see the luster of one single star dimmed of that glorious confederacy which constitutes our political sun; still less do I wish to see it blotted out, and its light obliterated forever....

In conclusion, allow me to intreat and implore each individual member of this body to bring into the consideration of this measure which I have had the honor of proposing, the same love of country which, if I know myself, has actuated me, and the same desire of restoring harmony to the Union, which has prompted this effort. If we can forget for a moment—but that would be asking too much of human nature—if we could suffer, for one moment, party feelings and party causes—and, as I stand here before my God, I declare I have looked beyond those considerations, and regarded only the vast interests of this united people— I should hope that under such feelings, and with such dispositions, we may advantageously proceed to the consideration of this bill, and heal, before they are yet bleeding, the wounds of our distracted country.

19

HENRY CLAY

On the Removal of the Deposits

December 26, 1833

President Jackson's war against the Bank of the United States was not concluded by his veto of its recharter in 1832. The Bank continued to do business under its old charter, which did not expire until 1836. In the aftermath of the veto, President Jackson began to worry that the existing Bank would use its funds to bribe Congress, corrupt public opinion, and thereby obtain a recharter despite his opposition. To prevent this possibility, Jackson decided to order the secretary of the treasury to withdraw the government's money from the BUS and deposit it in a series of state banks that became known as the "pet banks." Since the government was the Bank's largest depositor, Jackson hoped that the loss of these funds would destroy the Bank's power to influence Congress with loans and bribes and thus destroy its ability to undermine the democratic process.

Secretary of the Treasury William J. Duane thought this plan was dangerous and believed that he had the right to make independent decisions about the safekeeping of the government's funds. After a long and tedious negotiation that ended when Duane flatly refused to obey Jackson's orders, the president fired him and replaced him with a new secretary who would follow instructions. He explained his actions in a paper read to the cabinet on September 18, 1833.

The removal of the deposits enraged Jackson's critics as nothing else he had ever done. They agreed with the discharged Duane that the secretary of the treasury was an independent official who was not subject to direct control by the president. They feared that giving the president complete authority over government funds would concentrate too much power in the hands of one man. Above all, they resented Jackson's seeming defiance of the legal guidelines for the storage of the government's money.

Henry Clay took the lead in denouncing Jackson's actions in this famous two-day speech that began on December 26, 1833. In it, Clay introduces two resolutions censuring Jackson's conduct and then defends them in great detail. His critique of Jackson's alleged tyranny inspired opponents to call themselves "Whigs" after the British political faction that had opposed the

---

Calvin Colton, ed., *The Life, Correspondence, and Speeches of Henry Clay,* 6 vols. (New York: A. Barnes, 1857), 5: 576–620.

unlimited powers of the Crown. By the spring of 1834, Jackson's enemies were calling themselves "Whigs" in local election campaigns, and the Whig Party emerged as the principal vehicle for anti-Jackson political activity.

Why does Henry Clay begin this speech by stating that the United States was "in the midst of a revolution"? Why does he call it "hitherto bloodless"?

Clay argues that the president has no power to require the removal of the federal deposits. What are his reasons? How does the argument reflect Clay's views on the supremacy of law?

Clay also critically reviews Jackson's own reasons for deposit removal. Why would Jackson fear that the Bank was dangerous to "the morals of the people" and "the purity of the elective franchise"? How does Clay reject these arguments? Why does he think that Jackson's actions threaten to destroy republican government?

Resolved, that by dismissing the late Secretary of the Treasury, because he would not, contrary to his sense of his own duty, remove the money of the United States in deposit with the bank of the United States and its branches, in conformity with the president's opinion; and by appointing his successor to effect such removal, which has been done, the president has assumed the exercise of a power over the treasury of the United States not granted to him by the Constitution and laws, and dangerous to the liberties of the people.

Resolved, that the reasons assigned by the Secretary of the Treasury for the removal of the money of the United States, deposited in the bank of the United States and its branches, communicated to Congress on the 3d of December, 1833, are unsatisfactory and insufficient.

We are in the midst of a revolution, hitherto bloodless, but rapidly tending toward a total change of the pure republican character of the government, and to the concentration of all power in the hands of one man. The powers of Congress are paralyzed, except when exerted in conformity with his will, by frequent and an extraordinary exercise of the executive veto, not anticipated by the founders of our Constitution, and not practiced by any of the predecessors of the present chief magistrate. . . . The constitutional participation of the Senate in the appointing power is virtually abolished by the constant use of the power of removal from office, without any known cause, . . . How often have we, senators, felt that the check of the Senate, instead of being, as the Constitution intended, a salutary control, was an idle ceremony? . . .

The judiciary has not been exempt from the prevailing rage for innovation. Decisions of the tribunals, deliberately pronounced, have been contemptuously disregarded. And the sanctity of numerous treaties openly violated. Our Indian relations, coeval with the existence of the government, and recognized and established by numerous laws and treaties, have been subverted, the rights of the helpless and unfortunate aborigines trampled in the dust, and they brought under subjection to unknown laws, in which they have no voice, promulgated in an unknown language. The most extensive and most valuable public domain that ever fell to the lot of one nation, is threatened with a total sacrifice. The general currency of the country—the life-blood of all its business—is in the most imminent danger of universal disorder and confusion. The power of internal improvement lies crushed beneath the veto. The system of protection of American industry was snatched from impending destruction at the last session; but we are now coolly told by the Secretary of the Treasury, without a blush, "that it is understood to be conceded on all hands, that the tariff for protection merely is to be finally abandoned." By the 3d of March, 1837, if the progress of innovation continues, there will be scarcely a vestige remaining of the government and its policy, as they existed prior to the 3d of March, 1829. In a term of eight years, a little more than equal to that which was required to establish our liberties, the government will have been transformed into an elective monarchy—the worst of all forms of government.

Such is a melancholy but faithful picture of the present condition of our public affairs. It is not sketched or exhibited to excite, here or elsewhere, irritated feeling. I have no such purpose. I would, on the contrary, implore the Senate and the people to discard all passion and prejudice, and to look calmly, but resolutely, upon the actual state of the Constitution and the country. Although I bring into the Senate the same unabated spirit, and the same firm determination which have ever guided me in the support of civil liberty, and the defense of our Constitution, I contemplate the prospect before us with feelings of deep humiliation and profound mortification. . . .

Mr. President, when Congress adjourned, at the termination of the last session, there was one remnant of its powers, that over the purse, left untouched. The two most important powers of civil government are, those of the sword and the purse. The first, with some restriction, is confided by the Constitution to the executive, and the last to the legislative department. If they are separate, and exercised by different responsible departments, civil liberty is safe; but if they are united in the hands of the same individual, it is gone. . . .

Up to the period of the termination of the last session of Congress, the exclusive constitutional power of Congress over the treasury of the

United States had never been contested. Among its earliest acts was one to establish the treasury department, which provided for the appointment of a treasurer who was required to give bond and security in a very large amount, "to receive and keep the money of the United States, and to disburse the same, upon warrants drawn by the Secretary of the Treasury, countersigned by the comptroller, recorded by the register, and not otherwise." Prior to the establishment of the present bank of the United States, no treasury or place had been provided and designated by law for the safe-keeping of the public moneys, but the treasurer was left to his own discretion and responsibility. When the existing bank was established, it was provided that the public moneys should be deposited with it, and consequently that bank became the treasury of the United States. . . . Its safety was drawn in question by the chief magistrate, and an agent was appointed, a little more than a year ago, to investigate its ability. He reported to the executive, that it was perfectly safe. His apprehensions of its solidity were communicated by the president to Congress, and a committee was appointed to examine the subject. They, also, reported in favor of its security. And, finally, among the last acts of the House of Representatives, prior to the close of the last session, was the adoption of a resolution, manifesting its entire confidence in the ability and solidity of the bank.

After all these testimonies to the perfect safety of the public moneys, in the place appointed by Congress, who could have supposed that the place would have been changed? Who could have imagined, that within sixty days of the meeting of Congress, and, as it were, in utter contempt of its authority, the change should have been ordered? Who would have dreamed, that the treasurer should have thrown away the single key to the treasury, over which Congress held ample control, and accepted in lieu of it some dozens of keys, over which neither Congress nor he has any adequate control? Yet, sir, all this has been done; and it is now our solemn duty—to inquire, first by whose authority it has been ordered? and, secondly, whether the order has been given in conformity with the Constitution and laws of the United States?

I agree, sir, and I am happy whenever I can agree with the president, as to the immense importance of these questions. He says, in a paper which I hold in my hand, that he looks upon the pending question as involving higher consideration than the "mere transfer of a sum of money from one bank to another. Its decision may affect the character of our government for ages to come." And with him, I view it as of transcendent importance, both in its consequences and the great principles which the question involves. . . . It involves the distribution of power by the executive, and the taking away a power from Congress which it was never before doubted to possess—the power over the public purse. Entertaining these views, I shall not, to-day, at least, examine the reasons assigned by the president, or by the Secretary of the Treasury; for if the president had no power to perform the act, no reasons however cogent or strong, which he can assign as urging him to the accomplishment of his purpose, no reasons, can sanctify an unconstitutional and illegal act.

The first question, sir, which I intimated it to be my purpose to examine, was, by whose direction was this change of the deposits made? . . .

Sir, is there a senator here who will tell me that this removal was not made by the president? . . .

And has the president any power over the treasury by the Constitution? None, sir—none. The Constitution requires that no money shall be drawn from the treasury except by appropriation, thus placing it entirely under the control of Congress. But the president himself says—"upon him has been devolved, by the Constitution and the suffrages of the American people, the duty of superintending the operation of the executive departments of the government, and seeing that the laws are faithfully executed." Sir, the president, in another part of this same paper, refers to the same suffrages of the American people, as the source of some new powers over and above those in the Constitution, or at least as expressive of their approbation of the exercise of them. Sir, I differ from the president on this point; . . . His re-election resulted from his presumed merits generally, and the confidence and attachment of the people; and from the unworthiness of his competitor; nor was it intended thereby to express their approbation of all the opinions he was known to hold. . . . Sir, the truth is, that the re-election of the president proves as little an approbation by the people of all the opinions he may hold, even if he had ever unequivocally expressed what those opinions were . . . as it would prove that if the president had a carbuncle . . . they meant, by re-electing him, to approve of his carbuncle. But the president says, that the duty "has been devolved upon him," to remove the deposits, "by the Constitution and the suffrages of the American people." Sir, does he mean to say that these suffrages created of themselves a new source of power? That he derived an authority from them which he did not hold as from any other source? If he means that their suffrages made him the president of the United States, and that, as president, he may exercise every power pertaining to that office under the Constitution and the laws, there are none who can controvert it; but then there could be no need to add the suffrages to the Constitution. But his language is, "the suffrages of the American people and the Constitution." Sir, I deny it. There is not a syllable in the Constitution which imposes any such duty upon him. There is nothing of any such thing; no color to the idea. . . .

Though the president is mistaken in his assertion, that the Constitution devolves upon the president the superintendence of the departments, there is one clause of that instrument which he has very correctly quoted, and which makes it his duty to "see that the laws are faithfully executed," as it is mine now to examine what authority he obtains by this clause in the case before us. Under it, the most enormous pretensions have been set up for the president. . . .

What . . . it will be asked, does this clause, that the president shall see that the laws are faithfully executed, mean? Sir, it means nothing more nor less than this, that if resistance is made to the laws, he shall take care that resistance shall cease. . . . We have established a system in which power has been carefully divided among different departments of the government. And we have been told a thousand times that this division is indispensable as a safeguard to civil liberty. We have designated the departments, and have established in each officers to examine the powers belonging to each. The president, it is true, presides over the whole; his eye surveys the whole extent of the system in all its movements. But has he power to enter into the courts, for example, and tell them what is to be done? Or may he come here, and tell us the same? Or when we have made a law, can he withhold the power necessary to its practical effect? He moves, it is true, in a high, a glorious sphere. It is his to watch over the whole with a paternal eye; and, when any one wheel of the vast machine is for a time interrupted by the occurrence of invasion or rebellion, it is his care to propel its movements, and to furnish it with the requisite means of performing its appropriate duty in its own place.

. . . If the doctrine be indeed true, then it is most evident that there is no longer any other control over our affairs than that exerted by the president. If it be true, that when a duty is by law specifically assigned to a particular officer, the president may go into his office and control him in the manner of performing it, then is it most manifest that all barriers for the safety of the treasury are gone. Sir, it is that union of the purse and the sword, in the hand of one man, which constitutes the best definition of tyranny which our language can give. . . .

Now, sir, let us trace some of the other sources of the exercise of this power, or motives for it, or by whatever name they are to be called. He says to Mr. Duane:

"The president repeats, that he begs the cabinet to consider the proposed measure as his own, in the support of which he shall require no one of them to make a sacrifice of opinion or principle. Its responsibility has been assumed, after the most mature deliberation and reflection, as necessary to preserve the morals of the people, the freedom of the press, and the purity of the elective franchise."

The morals of the people! What part of the Constitution has given to the president any power over "the morals of the people?" None. It does not give such power even over religion, the presiding and genial influence over every true system of morals. No, sir, it gives him no such power.

And what is the next step? To-day he claims a power as necessary to the morals of the people; to-morrow he will claim another, as still more indispensable to our religion. And the president might in this case as well have said that he went into the office of the Secretary of the Treasury, and controlled his free exercise of his authority as secretary, because it was necessary to preserve "the religion of the people!" I ask for the authority. Will any one of those gentlemen here, who consider themselves as the vindicators of the executive, point me to any clause of the Constitution which gives to the present President of the United States any power to preserve "the morals of the people?" . . .

But "the purity of the elective franchise," also, the president has very much at heart. And here, again, I ask what part of the Constitution gives him any power over that "franchise?" Look, sir, at the nature of the exercise of this power! If it was really necessary that steps should be taken to preserve the purity of the press or the freedom of elections, what ought the president to have done? Taken the matter into his own hands? No, sir; it was his duty to recommend to Congress the passage of laws for the purpose, under suitable sanctions; laws which the courts of the United States would execute. We could not have been worse off under such laws, (however exceptionable they might be), than we are now. We could then, sir, have reviewed the laws, and seen whether Congress or the president had properly any power over this matter; or whether the article of the Constitution which forbids that the press shall be touched, and declares that religion shall be sacred from all the powers of legislation, applied in the case or not. This the president has undertaken to do of himself, without the shadow of authority, either in the Constitution or the laws. . . .

Such, sir, are the powers on which the president relies to justify his seizure of the treasury of the United States. I have examined them one by one; and they all fail, utterly fail, to bear out the act. We are irresistibly brought to the conclusion, that the removal of the public money from the bank of the United States has been effected by the displacement from the head of the treasury department of one who would not remove them, and putting in his stead another person, who would; and, secondly, that the president has no color of authority in the Constitution or the laws for the act which he has undertaken to perform. . . .

And where now, sir, is the public treasury? Who can tell? It is certainly without a local habitation, if it be not without a name. And where is the money of the people of the United States? Floating about in treasury drafts or checks to the amount of millions, placed in the hands of tottering banks, to enable them to pay their own debts, instead of being appropriated to the service of the people. These checks are scattered to the winds by the treasurer of the United States, who is required by law to let out money from the treasury, on warrants signed by the Secretary of the Treasury, countersigned, registered, and so forth, and not otherwise. . . .

Thus, sir, the people's money is put into a bank here, and a bank there, in regard to the solvency of which we know nothing, and it is placed there to be used in the event of certain contingences — contingences of which neither the treasurer nor the secretary have yet deigned to furnish us any account.

Where was the oath of office of the treasurer, when he ventured thus to sport with the people's money? Where was the Constitution, which forbids money to be drawn from the treasury without appropriation by law? Where was the treasurer's bond, when he thus cast about people's money? Sir, his bond is forfeited. I do not pretend to any great knowledge of the law, but give me an intelligent and unpacked jury, and I will undertake to prove to him that he has forfeited the penalty of his bond.

Mr. President, the people of the United States are indebted to the president for the boldness of this movement; and as one among the humblest of them, I profess my obligations to him. He has told the Senate, in his message refusing an official copy of his cabinet paper, that it has been published for the information of the people. As a part of the people, the Senate, if not in their official character, have a right to its use. In that extraordinary paper, he has proclaimed, that the measure is his own; and that he has taken upon himself the responsibility of it. In plain English, he has proclaimed an open, palpable, and daring usurpation!

For more than fifteen years, Mr. President, I have been struggling to avoid the present state of things. I thought I perceived in some proceedings, during the conduct of the Seminole war, a spirit of defiance to the Constitution and to all law. With what sincerity and truth, with what earnestness and devotion to civil liberty, I have struggled, the searcher of all human hearts best knows. With what fortune, the bleeding Constitution of my country now fatally attests.

I have, nevertheless, persevered; and under every discouragement during the short time that I expect to remain in the public councils I will persevere. And if a bountiful Providence would allow an unworthy sinner to approach the throne of grace, I would beseech Him, as the greatest favor He could grant to me here below, to spare me until I live to behold the people rising in their majesty, with a peaceful and constitutional exercise of their power, to expel the Goths from Rome; to rescue the public treasury from pillage, to preserve the Constitution of the United States; to uphold the Union against the danger of the concentration and consolidation of all power in the hands of the executive; and to sustain the liberties of the people of this country against the imminent perils to which they now stand exposed. . . .

And now, Mr. President, what, under all these circumstances, is it our duty to do? Is there a senator who can hesitate to affirm, in the language of the resolution, that the president has assumed a dangerous power over the treasury of the United States, not granted to him by the Constitution and the laws; and that the reasons assigned for the act, by the Secretary of the Treasury, are insufficient and unsatisfactory?

The eyes and the hopes of the American people are anxiously turned to Congress. They feel that they have been deceived and insulted; their confidence abused; their interests betrayed; and their liberties in danger. They see a rapid and alarming concentration of all power in one man's hands. . . . The question is no longer what laws will Congress pass, but what will the executive not veto? The president, and not Congress, is addressed for legislative action. . . . We behold the usual incidents of approaching tyranny. The land is filled with spies and informers; and detraction and denunciation are the orders of the day. People, especially official incumbents in this place, no longer dare speak in the fearless tones of manly freedom, but in the cautious whispers of trembling slaves. The premonitory symptons of despotism are upon us; and if Congress do not apply an instantaneous and effective remedy, the fatal collapse will soon come on, and we shall die—ignobly die! base, mean, and abject slaves— the scorn and contempt of mankind—unpitied, unwept, unmourned!

20

ANDREW JACKSON

Protest against Censure Resolutions

April 15, 1834

The Senate eventually passed a modified version of Clay's resolution condemning Jackson's conduct in the removal of deposits from the Bank of the United States. The censure drew a strong protest from Old Hickory, who claimed that the Senate was trying to impeach him without going through the proper constitutional procedure. More important, he fought back against the idea that the president lacked the authority to give orders to cabinet secretaries or to fire them at will. For the most part, Jackson's arguments in favor of a strong presidency became generally accepted by later generations.

What are Jackson's grounds here for arguing that the president must have the power to give orders to the cabinet and to dismiss them at will? What does he mean by declaring that "the President is the direct representative of the American people, but the Secretaries are not"? Why does he think that it would undermine republican government if the president submitted to a censure by the Senate? Why does he think that a strong democracy requires a strong presidency?

To the Senate of the United States:

It appears by the published Journal of the Senate that on the 26th of December last a resolution was offered by a member of the Senate, which after a protracted debate was on the 28th day of March last modified by the mover and passed by the votes of twenty-six Senators out of forty-six who were present and voted, in the following words, viz:

> *Resolved.* That the President, in the late Executive proceedings in relation to the public revenue, has assumed upon himself authority and power not conferred by the Constitution and laws, but in derogation of both.

Having had the honor, through the voluntary suffrages of the American people, to fill the office of the President of the United States during the period which may be presumed to have been referred to in this resolution,

---

James D. Richardson, comp., *A Compilation of the Messages and Papers of the Presidents, 1789–1897,* 10 vols. (Washington, D.C.: Government Printing Office, 1897), 3: 69–94.

it is sufficiently evident that the censure it inflicts was intended for myself. Without notice, unheard and untried, I thus find myself charged on the records of the Senate, and in a form hitherto unknown in our history, with the high crime of violating the laws and Constitution of my country.

It can seldom be necessary for any department of the Government, when assailed in conversation or debate or by the strictures of the press or of popular assemblies, to step out of its ordinary path for the purpose of vindicating its conduct or of pointing out any irregularity or injustice in the manner of the attack; but when the Chief Executive Magistrate is, by one of the most important branches of the Government in its official capacity, in a public manner, and by its recorded sentence, but without precedent, competent authority, or just cause, declared guilty of a breach of the laws and Constitution, it is due to his station, to public opinion, and to a proper self-respect that the officer thus denounced should promptly expose the wrong which has been done.

In the present case, moreover, there is even a stronger necessity for such a vindication. By an express provision of the Constitution, before the President of the United States can enter on the execution of his office he is required to take an oath or affirmation in the following words:

> I do solemnly swear (or affirm) that I will faithfully execute the office of President of the United States and will to the best of my ability preserve, protect, and defend the Constitution of the United States.

The duty of defending so far as in him lies the integrity of the Constitution would indeed have resulted from the very nature of his office, but by thus expressing it in the official oath or affirmation, which in this respect differs from that of any other functionary, the founders of our Republic have attested their sense of its importance and have given to it a peculiar solemnity and force. Bound to the performance of this duty by the oath I have taken, by the strongest obligations of gratitude to the American people, and by the ties which unite my every earthly interest with the welfare and glory of my country, and perfectly convinced that the discussion and passage of the above-mentioned resolution were not only unauthorized by the Constitution, but in many respects repugnant to its provisions and subversive of the rights secured by it to other coordinate departments, I deem it an imperative duty to maintain the supremacy of that sacred instrument and the immunities of the department intrusted to my care by all means consistent with my own lawful powers, with the rights of others, and with the genius of our civil institutions. To this end I have caused this my *solemn protest* against the aforesaid proceedings to be placed on the files of the executive department and to be transmitted to the Senate. . . .

Under the Constitution of the United States the powers and functions of the various departments of the Federal Government and their responsibilities for violation or neglect of duty are clearly defined or result by necessary inference. . . . Each of . . . [the three branches] is the coequal of the other two, and all are the servants of the American people, without power or right to control or censure each other in the service of their common superior, save only in the manner and to the degree which that superior has prescribed.

The responsibilities of the President are numerous and weighty. He is liable to impeachment for high crimes and misdemeanors, and on due conviction to removal from office and perpetual disqualification; and notwithstanding such conviction, he may also be indicted and punished according to law. He . . . is also accountable at the bar of public opinion for every act of his Administration. Subject only to the restraints of truth and justice, the free people of the United States have the undoubted right . . . to discuss his official conduct and to express and promulgate their opinions concerning it. Indirectly also his conduct may come under review in either branch of the Legislature, or in the Senate when acting in its executive capacity, and so far as the executive or legislative proceedings of these bodies may require it, it may be exercised by them. These are believed to be the proper and only modes in which the President of the United States is to be held accountable for his official conduct.

Tested by these principles, the resolution of the Senate is wholly unauthorized by the Constitution, and in derogation of its entire spirit. It assumes that a single branch of the legislative department may for the purposes of a public censure, and without any view to legislation or impeachment, take up, consider, and decide upon the official acts of the Executive. But in no part of the Constitution is the President subjected to any such responsibility, and in no part of that instrument is any such power conferred on either branch of the Legislature. . . .

The President of the United States, therefore, has been by a majority of his constitutional triers accused and found guilty of an impeachable offense, but in no part of this proceeding have the directions of the Constitution been observed. . . .

In this view . . . the resolution . . . must certainly be regarded . . . simply as an official rebuke or condemnatory sentence, too general and indefinite to be easily repelled, but yet sufficiently precise to bring into discredit the conduct and motives of the Executive. . . . And it is not too much to say of the whole of these proceedings that if they shall be approved and sustained by an intelligent people, then will that great contest . . . [for] the right of every citizen to a notice before trial, to a hearing before conviction, and to an impartial tribunal for deciding on the charge have been waged in vain.

If the resolution had been left in its original form it is not to be presumed that it could ever have received the assent of a majority of the Senate, for the acts therein specified as violations of the Constitution and laws were clearly within the limits of the Executive authority. . . . It is therefore due to the occasion that a condensed summary of the views of the Executive in respect to them should be here exhibited.

By the Constitution "the executive power is vested in a President of the United States." Among the duties imposed upon him, and which he is sworn to perform, is that of "taking care that the laws be faithfully executed." Being thus made responsible for the entire action of the executive department, it was but reasonable that the power of appointing, overseeing, and controlling those who execute the laws—a power in its nature executive—should remain in his hands. . . .

The executive power vested in the Senate is neither that of "nominating" nor "appointing." It is merely a check upon the Executive power of appointment. If individuals are proposed for appointment by the President by them deemed incompetent or unworthy, they may withhold their consent and the appointment can not be made. They check the action of the Executive, but can not in relation to those very subjects act themselves nor direct him. Selections are still made by the President, and the negative given to the Senate, without diminishing his responsibility, furnishes an additional guaranty to the country that the subordinate executive as well as the judicial offices shall be filled with worthy and competent men.

The whole executive power being vested in the President, who is responsible for its exercise, it is a necessary consequence that he should have a right to employ agents of his own choice to aid him in the performance of his duties, and to discharge them when he is no longer willing to be responsible for their acts. In strict accordance with this principle, the power of removal, which, like that of appointment, is an original executive power, is left unchecked by the Constitution in relation to all executive officers, for whose conduct the President is responsible, while it is taken from him in relation to judicial officers, for whose acts he is not responsible. . . .

Thus was it settled by the Constitution, the laws, and the whole practice of the Government that the entire executive power is vested in the President of the United States; that as incident to that power the right of appointing and removing those officers who are to aid him in the execution of the laws, with such restrictions only as the Constitution prescribes, is vested in the President; that the Secretary of the Treasury is one of those officers; that the custody of the public property and money is an Executive function which, in relation to the money, has always been exercised through the Secretary of the Treasury and his subordinates; that in the performance of these duties he is subject to the supervision and control of the President, and in all important measures having relation to them consults the Chief Magistrate and obtains his approval and sanction; that the law establishing the bank did not, as it could not, change the relation between the President and the Secretary . . . , and that all departments of the Government, and the nation itself, approved or acquiesced in these acts and principles as in strict conformity with our Constitution and laws.

During the last year the approaching termination, according to the provisions of its charter and the solemn decision of the American people, of the Bank of the United States made it expedient, and its exposed abuses and corruptions made it, in my opinion, the duty of the Secretary of the Treasury, to place the moneys of the United States in other depositories. The Secretary did not concur in that opinion, and declined giving the necessary order and direction. So glaring were the abuses and corruptions of the bank, so evident its fixed purpose to persevere in them, and so palpable its design by its money and power to control the Government and change its character, that I deemed it the imperative duty of the Executive authority, by the exertion of every power confided to it by the Constitution and laws, to check its career and lessen its ability to do mischief, even in the painful alternative of dismissing the head of one of the Departments. At the time the removal was made other causes sufficient to justify it existed, but if they had not the Secretary would have been dismissed for this cause only.

His place I supplied by one whose opinions were well known to me. . . . In accordance with the views long before expressed by him he proceeded, with my sanction, to make arrangements for depositing the moneys of the United States in other safe institutions.

The resolution of the Senate as originally framed and as passed, if it refers to these acts, presupposes a right in that body to interfere with this exercise of Executive power. If the principle be once admitted, it is not difficult to perceive where it may end. If by a mere denunciation like this resolution the President should ever be induced to act in a matter of official duty contrary to the honest convictions of his own mind in compliance with the wishes of the Senate, the constitutional independence of the executive department would be as effectually destroyed and its power as effectually transferred to the Senate as if that end had been accomplished by an amendment of the Constitution. . . . It has already been maintained . . . that the Secretary of the Treasury is the officer of Congress and independent of the President; that the President has no right to control him, and consequently none to remove him. With the same propriety and on similar grounds may the Secretary of State, the Secretaries of War and the Navy, and the Postmaster-General each in succession be declared independent of the President, the subordinates of Congress, and removable only with the concurrence of the Senate. Followed to its consequences, this principle will be found effectually to destroy one coordinate department of the Government, to concentrate in the hands of the Senate the whole executive power, and to leave the President as powerless as he would be useless—the shadow of authority after the substance had departed.

. . . Nearly forty-five years had the President exercised, without a question as to his rightful authority, those powers for the recent assumption of which he is now denounced. The vicissitudes of peace and war had attended our Government; violent parties, watchful to take advantage of any seeming usurpation on the part of the Executive, had distracted our councils; frequent removals, or forced resignations in every sense tantamount to removals, had been made of the Secretary and other officers of the Treasury, and yet in no one instance is it known that any man, whether patriot or partisan, had raised his voice against it as a violation of the Constitution. The expediency and justice of such changes in reference to public officers of all grades have frequently been the topic of discussion, but the constitutional right of the President to appoint, control, and remove the head of the Treasury as well as all other Departments seems to have been universally conceded. And what is the occasion upon which other principles have been first officially asserted? The Bank of the United States, a great moneyed monopoly, had attempted to obtain a renewal of its charter by controlling the elections of the people and the action of the Government. . . . This, with its corruption of the press, its violation of its charter, its exclusion of the Government directors from its proceedings, its neglect of duty and arrogant pretensions, made it, in the opinion of the President, incompatible with the public interest and the safety of our institutions that it should be longer employed as the fiscal agent of the Treasury. A Secretary of the Treasury . . . refused to do what his superior in the executive department considered the most imperative of his duties, and became in fact, however innocent his motives, the protector of the bank. And on this occasion it is discovered for the first time that those who framed the Constitution misunderstood it; that the First Congress and all its successors have been under a delusion; that the practice of near forty-five years is but a continued usurpation; that the Secretary of the Treasury is not responsible to the President, and that to remove him is a violation of the Constitution and laws for which the President deserves to stand forever dishonored on the journals of the Senate. . . .

. . . The President is the direct representative of the American people, but the Secretaries are not. If the Secretary of the Treasury be independent of the President in the execution of the laws, then is there no direct responsibility to the people in that important branch of this Government to which is committed the care of the national finances. And it is in the power of the Bank of the United States, or any other corporation, body of men, or individuals, if a Secretary shall be found to accord with them in opinion or can be induced in practice to promote their views, to control through him the whole action of the Government (so far as it is exercised by his Department) in defiance of the Chief Magistrate elected by the people and responsible to them.

But the evil tendency of the particular doctrine adverted to . . . the practice by the Senate of the unconstitutional power of arraigning and censuring the official conduct of the Executive in the manner recently pursued. Such proceedings are eminently calculated to unsettle the foundations of the Government, to disturb the harmonious action of its different departments, and to break down the checks and balances by which the wisdom of its framers sought to insure its stability and usefulness.

The honest differences of opinion which occasionally exist between the Senate and the President in regard to matters in which both are obliged to participate are sufficiently embarrassing; but if the course recently adopted by the Senate shall hereafter be frequently pursued, it is not only obvious that the harmony of the relations between the President and the Senate will be destroyed, but that other and graver effects will ultimately ensue. If the censures of the Senate be submitted to by the President, the confidence of the people in his ability and virtue and the character and usefulness of his Administration will soon be at an end, and the real power of the Government will fall into the hands of a body holding their offices for long terms, not elected by the people and not to them directly responsible. If, on the other hand, the illegal censures of the Senate should be resisted by the President, collisions and angry controversies might ensue, discreditable in their progress and in the end compelling the people to adopt the conclusion either that their Chief Magistrate was unworthy of their respect or that the Senate was chargeable with calumny and injustice. Either of these results would impair public confidence in the perfection of the system and lead to serious alterations of its framework or to the practical abandonment of some of its provisions.

The influence of such proceedings on the other departments of the Government, and more especially on the States, could not fail to be extensively pernicious. . . . All the independent departments of the Government, and the States which compose our confederated Union, instead of attending to their appropriate duties and leaving those who may offend to be reclaimed or punished in the manner pointed out in the Constitution, would fall to mutual crimination and recrimination and give to the people confusion and anarchy instead of order and law, until at length some form of aristocratic power would be established on the ruins of the Constitution or the States be broken into separate communities.

Far be it from me to charge or to insinuate that the present Senate of the United States intend in the most distant way to encourage such a result. It is not of their motives or designs, but only of the tendency of their acts, that it is my duty to speak. . . . It is due to the high trust with which I have been charged, to those who may be called to succeed me in it, to the representatives of the people whose constitutional prerogative has been unlawfully assumed, to the people and to the States, and to the Constitution they have established that I should not permit its provisions to be broken down by such an attack on the executive department without at least some effort "to preserve, protect, and defend" them. With this view, and for the reasons which have been stated, I do hereby *solemnly protest* against the aforementioned proceedings of the Senate as unauthorized by the Constitution, contrary to its spirit and to several of its express provisions, subversive of that distribution of the powers of government which it has ordained and established, destructive of the checks and safeguards by which those powers were intended on the one hand to be controlled and on the other to be protected, and calculated by their immediate and collateral effects, by their character and tendency, to concentrate in the hands of a body not directly amenable to the people a degree of influence and power dangerous to their liberties and fatal to the Constitution of their choice.

The resolution of the Senate contains an imputation upon my private as well as upon my public character, and as it must stand forever on their journals, I can not close this substitute for that defense which I have not been allowed to present in the ordinary form without remarking that I have lived in vain if it be necessary to enter into a formal vindication of my character and purposes from such an imputation. In vain do I bear upon my person enduring memorials of that contest in which American liberty was purchased; in vain have I since periled property, fame, and life in defense of the rights and privileges so dearly bought; in vain am I now, without a personal aspiration or the hope of individual advantage, encountering responsibilities and dangers from which by mere inactivity in relation to a single point I might have been exempt, if any serious doubts can be entertained as to the purity of my purposes and motives. . . . The only ambition I can feel is to acquit myself to Him to whom I must soon render an account of my stewardship, to serve my fellowmen, and live respected and honored in the history of my country. No; the ambition which leads me on is an anxious desire and a fixed determination to return to the people unimpaired the sacred trust they have confided to my charge; to heal the wounds of the Constitution and preserve it from further violation; to persuade my countrymen, so far as I may, that it is not in a splendid government supported by powerful monopolies and aristocratical establishments that they will find happiness or their liberties protection, but in a plain system, void of pomp, protecting all and granting favors to none, dispensing its blessings, like the dews of Heaven, unseen and unfelt save in the freshness and beauty they contribute to produce. It is such a government that the genius of our people requires; such an one only under which our States may remain for ages to come united, prosperous, and free. If the Almighty Being who has hitherto sustained and protected me will but vouchsafe to make my feeble powers instrumental to such a result, I shall anticipate with pleasure the place to be assigned me in the history of my country, and die contented with the belief that I have contributed in some small degree to increase the value and prolong the duration of American liberty.

To the end that the resolution of the Senate may not be hereafter drawn into precedent with the authority of silent acquiescence on the part of the executive department, and to the end also that my motives and views in the Executive proceedings denounced in that resolution may be known to my fellow-citizens, to the world, and to all posterity, I respectfully request that this message and protest may be entered at length on the journals of the Senate.

21

ANDREW JACKSON

Letter to Tilghman A. Howard

August 20, 1833

President Jackson firmly believed that the majority of enfranchised Americans supported his economic policies. He blamed opposition to his program on the efforts of a small, self-interested minority of wealthy persons and corporations that sought to gain control of the government and enrich themselves further at public expense. In the following letter to a political activist in Indiana, he calls these interests "the predatory portion of the community" and explains how the "many" could defend themselves against the machinations of the "few." By following the example of Pennsylvania and other states, Jackson supporters could form themselves into well-drilled units of a national Democratic Party that would unite at the polls to defeat all opposing candidates. No one must be allowed to form a splinter group that claimed loyalty to Jacksonian principles but dissented from a particular local candidate or cause because divisions among the Democrats could spell defeat.

What attitude does Jackson express in this letter to the men and institutions that were promoting the Market Revolution? Whom does he have in mind when he refers to "the predatory portion of the community"? Why does he use such language? What does Jackson mean by the "primitive simplicity and purity" of American institutions? Why do you suppose he prefers to describe reforms as a return to original perfection?

What does Jackson mean by "the great radical principle of freedom"? How does he think equality would make Americans more free? How would strict party discipline promote this result?

Dear Sir. . . . I thank you for the kind estimate you have made of my public life. I feel very sensibly, how much I owe to the favor of that public, (which you justly call "the greatest nation of freemen on earth") for "the last seal of approbation with which it has stamped my career." The people have over valued my Services, greatly overpaid, in their affectionate and grateful enthusiasm all the labors of my life and have only con-

---

John Spencer Bassett, ed., *The Correspondence of Andrew Jackson,* 7 vols. (Washington, D.C.: Carnegie Institution of Washington, 1926–1935), 5: 165–66.

sidered in their recompense, what I have wished to do, not what I have done for my country. The high station to which I have been again called by their suffrages, has no other attractions for me, than as it manifests the approbation of my fellow citizens, and furnishes the opportunity to make some requital by devoting my latest energies, in the endeavor to secure, as far as it is possible for me, their power permanently over their Government. If I can restore to our institutions their primitive simplicity and purity, can only succeed in banishing those extraneous corrupting influences which tend to fasten monopoly and aristocracy on the constitution and to make the Government an engine of oppression to the people instead of the agent of their will, I may then look back to the honors conferred upon me, with feelings of just pride — with the consciousness that they have not been bestowed altogether in vain.

I look to the overthrow of those systems, (which have been engrafted on our Government to bring in a new and controlling influence, not springing from the popular will,) as the principal means of defeating the machinations of the men, from whom you apprehend future distractions to our country. It is only when they can identify themselves with privileged joint stock Companies, with the Stockholders in a national Bank or the log rolling system of Internal Improvements, Squandering the taxes raised on the whole people, in benefitting particular classes and maintaining a personal influence by partial legislation in congress, that these men have the power to be mischievous. It is immaterial whether artful intriguing and ambitious persons, are enabled, to divert the treasures of a country to the purpose of creating a standing army or of embodying political forces, to act in concert against the unsuspecting undisciplined classes of the community. The *trained Band,* whether of military or political mercenaries, is but too apt to prevail. And whenever polit[i]cal machinery is successfully employed to destroy the great radical principle of freedom — equality among the people in the rights conferred by the Government — then aspiring individuals can avail themselves of the selfish, interested classes to aid in promoting an ambition which is naturally prone to multiply the advantages and increase the strength of the predatory portion of the community. My great hope of avoiding the evils of which you speak, arises from the prospect of being able to restore the equilibrium of the Government; equality in the condition of the people, so far as it depends on legislation.

It will undoubtedly, as you observe, form a part of the policy of the disappointed as well as some of the aspiring politicians "to cut up the party" which has sustained the Administration, by coalitions between distinguished individuals. Creating divisions among the people as to men, is one of the artifices, essential to the success of the *few* over the *many.* It is therefore of the utmost importance, that the majority should adopt some means to prevent such divisions. The Democratic party of Pennsylvania, and of several other states, have adopted the plan of calling Conventions of Delegates, elected by the people themselves and charged with their instructions for the purpose of selecting candidates for important trusts and of thus producing concert among the friends of the same principles. This plan has had the most beneficial operation, in preventing distractions among the people of these states in selecting agents to give effect to their wishes, and in maintaining their control in the Government. It strikes me that this is the only mode by which the people, will be able long to retain in their own hands, the election of President and Vice President. It is doubtless, as you say, the design of those who are opposed to the principles and measures of the present administration, to divide the majority supporting it, by dissentions as to individuals and to bring the election of President again into the House of Representatives, in the hope, that it may there be decided by the sinister influences, to which I have already adverted. I trust the good sense of the people will prevent such result. . . .

accept the assurance of my high respect and esteem and my best wishes for your health and prosperity.

22

ANDREW JACKSON

Letter to Joseph Conn Guild

April 24, 1835

By 1835, Jackson was nearing the end of his second term in office, and he was appalled that some of his self-described "friends" in Tennessee were opposing the election of Vice President Martin Van Buren as his successor. Judge Hugh Lawson White, a former Jackson supporter, proclaimed himself more faithful to the spirit of the original Jackson movement than Van Buren, an unpopular New Yorker, and Jackson's enemies throughout were using the White candidacy to organize a southern Whig Party.

In the following letter to a Tennessee politician, Joseph Conn Guild,

John Spencer Bassett, ed., *The Correspondence of Andrew Jackson,* 7 vols. (Washington, D.C.: Carnegie Institution of Washington, 1926–1935), 5: 338–41.

Jackson throws himself against this effort to usurp his movement. In it, he emphasizes the importance of party discipline and organization more strongly than ever and directly connects his movement to the Democratic-Republican Party of Thomas Jefferson.

As in the letter to Tilghman Howard (see Document 21), Jackson associates his party with "the will of the people," or democracy itself, and declares his determination to "secur[e] its permanent ascendancy." What do you think he means by this? What experiences did Jackson have as president that reinforced his support for strong political party organization? Why does he think "that whichever party makes the President, must give direction to his administration" and "it is as true in politics as morals, that those who are not for us are against us"?

Jackson also calls his opponents "the aristocracy" and "the Office Holders." Why does he do this? How did his views continue to shape American feelings about democracy?

My Dear Sir, . . . I have read with attention your letter and duly prize and approve the principles you avow, and to *inforce* those principles you most justly remark "that it is not so important to the great Republican party, who of that party we elevate to the Presidency, as to deprive the opposition of making him for us." It is certain that whichever party makes the President, must give direction to his administration. No chief magistrate in this country can become a Dictator. No one can carry on this Govt. without support, and the Head of it must rely for support on the party by whose suffrages he is elected, or, he must betray the expectations of those who invest him with power to obtain support from their adversaries. Your doctrine, then, that the opposition should not be allowed by the Republicans *to make a President for them,* is based *on honor,* as well as *patriotism.* With the truth and principle of a Patriot then, for your guide and the public good your end, I wish you success with all my heart.

You tell me that "every opponent of my administration is strongly in favor of Judge White." This is what I expected. The opponents of popular rights have been invited by the Meetings nominating him to unite in his support to *"destroy the landmarks of party."* This suits precisely the views of the ever vigilant enemies of the cause of Republicanism. Their great object now is to divide the Republican party and bring the election of President and vice president into Congress. There wielding the power of the Bank, the opposition are sure to succeed. Whoever is elected by them, must come *in upon terms* and be, not the President of the people, but of the politicians.

It is as true in politics as morals, that those who are not for us are against us. It is impossible to serve two masters. All, then, who lend themselves to promote the designs of the opposition, especially those who aid in dividing the Republican ranks must be considered apostates from principle. In abetting the enemy to break down those Republican Land marks, set up by Mr. Jefferson, sustained by Mr. Madison and contended for by myself, . . . those who claim to be advocates of popular rights take the most effectual, indeed, the only practicable means of destroying them. I have long believed, that it was only by preserving the identity of the Republican party as embodied and characterized by the principles introduced by Mr. Jefferson that the original rights of the states and the people could be maintained as contemplated by the Constitution. I have labored to reconstruct this great Party and bring the popular power to bear with full influence upon the Government, by securing its permanent ascendancy, and when victory is grasped, when the people have already tried successfully the experiment of a national convention of delegates direct from and chosen by themselves to maintain the democratic strength unbroken and thus perpetuate their power, it is truly mortifying, to see men who have hitherto sustained me in the course I have pursued and acknowledging its rectitude, all at once turn round and endeavor to destroy by diverting a portion of the Republican strength, to the service of those who have always made war against the cause of the people, all that I have accomplished during an anxious administration of two terms.

The daring and unprincipled Leaders north and south, who have conspired against the union and sought even the alliance of the foreign enemies of our Institutions in their eagerness to subvert them, the men who have attempted to build up a colossal monied power to corrupt and over shadow the government, springing from the will of the people, the men whose skilful intrigues once already made the Chief Magistracy a subject to be chaffered for, in the House of Reps. and who disposed of it against the public will, the men who at this moment defy the positive Instructions of their immediate constituents in various states of the union, these are the men who have called out Judge Whites sectional popularity in aid of their object, which is the overthrow of all the labors of my administration and the final subversion of Republican principles. That my old friend Judge White, should have permitted his professed friends but secret enemies to place him in this false position is a mortification to me and is one of the greatest misfortunes of his life. . . . They will first use and then abandon him, unless he consents to abandon the system of politics he has supported through life. And he will find himself in the situation of many others, who have abandoned those principles which had acquired the confidence of the people. The people will abandon him. They are too virtuous and intelligent to be hood-winked by politicians. . . .

I perceive among other artifices employed by those late adherents of the administration, who have turned against it, that it is now pretended that my policy is sustained, by the corrupt office holders! The truth is, the people have always sustained me both against the majority of the office holders, of the politicians, and of the public presses of the country. . . . The mass of the Office Holders, will allways cling to that party which would establish a life estate in office, give high salaries and exact small service. This party is the aristocracy and hence it is, that the Democratic party has, (although in the ascendancy for the greatest part of the time since the establishment of the Government) always been in the minority in the official corps. For the most part whenever a man obtains station, he adopts those principles calculated to make it lucrative and permanent, he grows jealous of the power of the people, which makes or seems to render his situation precarious, and imperceptibly and gradually all his feelings and political biases are surrendered to the leading men who would make Government in its great and minor officers independent altogether of the people. I consider it, therefore, an honorable testimonial for my administration, that I have been harassed by the clamor of officeholders from the beginning up to this hour.

But with these enemies in my camp and all the desertion which the seductions of the opposition can purchase I have no fear of the result. Mr. Jefferson in his most popular day would have lost the confidence of the people, if he had placed himself under the odious imputation of abandoning principle and the republican fold, for the sake of office. I would abandon my only and adopted son if he would permit himself to be placed in this attitude, and from the sentiments of my own bosom, I feel assured, that no personal or local consideration will ever vanquish the patriotic attachment felt by the great mass of the people, for the cause of the Republican party, which is indeed the cause of the Country. The late results in Connecticut, Rhode Island and Virginia must satisfy those who have sought so recently to sacrifice this cause, how imbecile are all the arts of political managers in conflict with the good sense and spirit which belongs to the american people.

I am with great respect

P.S. It has been my wish to keep out of the discussions in regard to my successor, not that I did not feel myself deeply mortified at the offensive uses which it is designed by my bitterest enemies to make of many whom, I have been in the habit of regarding as amongst my warmest friends, but because I thought that course more consistant with my official station. . . . But I trust all candid men will agree with me in opinion that it was requiring an unreasonable sacrafice to my position that I should submit in silence to being held up to the nation by a print in my immediate neighbourhood, and professing to speak as my friend, as countenancing if not encouraging a line of conduct which, situated as I am, and holding the opinions I do, would involve me in the double crime of apostacy, and ingratitude. Having placed myself in a right position in this regard, I am still desirous of taking as little part in the matter as is consistant with justice to myself and a due regard for the public interests so far as they may depend upon the stability and success of my administration. . . .

23

ANDREW JACKSON

Farewell Address

1837

George Washington had been the only previous president to issue a formal farewell address, but Jackson was determined to follow the example of "the Father of his Country." The following address was issued in pamphlet form on the day Martin Van Buren was inaugurated as Jackson's successor. Jackson used the occasion to summarize his political philosophy and to issue a series of warnings to posterity, including the famous injunction "eternal vigilance by the people is the price of liberty."

How would you describe the tone of the address? What are Jackson's leading themes? What is his purpose in issuing the address?

Jackson here stresses the importance of Union and "democracy," or government by the people themselves. How does he link these themes together? Why does he balance his defense of the Union by condemning those who "cast odium upon . . . [the] institutions" of other states?

The bulk of the address deals with tariffs, banking, and paper money. In

James D. Richardson, comp., *A Compilation of the Messages and Papers of the Presidents, 1789–1897,* 10 vols. (Washington, D.C.: Government Printing Office, 1897), 3: 292–308.

Jackson's view, what are the fundamental dangers that these fiscal policies hold for republican government? How did his ideas about federal aid for economic development change during his administration? What would Henry Clay say in rebuttal to the Farewell Address?

Fellow-Citizens: Being about to retire finally from public life, I beg leave to offer you my grateful thanks for the many proofs of kindness and confidence which I have received at your hands. . . . My public life has been a long one, and I can not hope that it has at all times been free from errors; but I have the consolation of knowing that if mistakes have been committed they have not seriously injured the country I so anxiously endeavored to serve, and at the moment when I surrender my last public trust I leave this great people prosperous and happy, in the full enjoyment of liberty and peace, and honored and respected by every nation of the world.

If my humble efforts have in any degree contributed to preserve to you these blessings, I have been more than rewarded by the honors you have heaped upon me. . . . And if I use the occasion to offer to you the counsels of age and experience, you will, I trust, receive them with the same indulgent kindness which you have so often extended to me, and will at least see in them an earnest desire to perpetuate in this favored land the blessings of liberty and equal law.

We have now lived almost fifty years under the Constitution framed by the sages and patriots of the Revolution. The conflicts in which the nations of Europe were engaged during a great part of this period, the spirit in which they waged war against each other, and our intimate commercial connections with every part of the civilized world rendered it a time of much difficulty for the Government of the United States. We have had our seasons of peace and of war, with all the evils which precede or follow a state of hostility with powerful nations. We encountered these trials with our Constitution yet in its infancy, and under the disadvantages which a new and untried government must always feel when it is called upon to put forth its whole strength without the lights of experience to guide it or the weight of precedents to justify its measures. But we have passed triumphantly through all these difficulties. Our Constitution is no longer a doubtful experiment, and at the end of nearly half a century we find that it has preserved unimpaired the liberties of the people, secured the rights of property, and that our country has improved and is flourishing beyond any former example in the history of nations.

In our domestic concerns there is everything to encourage us, and if you are true to yourselves nothing can impede your march to the highest point of national prosperity. The States which had so long been retarded in their improvement by the Indian tribes residing in the midst of them are at length relieved from the evil, and this unhappy race—the original dwellers in our land—are now placed in a situation where we may well hope that they will share in the blessings of civilization and be saved from that degradation and destruction to which they were rapidly hastening while they remained in the States; and while the safety and comfort of our own citizens have been greatly promoted by their removal, the philanthropist will rejoice that the remnant of that ill-fated race has been at length placed beyond the reach of injury or oppression, and that the paternal care of the General Government will hereafter watch over them and protect them. . . .

These cheering and grateful prospects and these multiplied favors we owe, under Providence, to the adoption of the Federal Constitution. It is no longer a question whether this great country can remain happily united and flourish under our present form of government. Experience, the unerring test of all human undertakings, has shown the wisdom and foresight of those who formed it, and has proved that in the union of these States there is a sure foundation for the brightest hopes of freedom and for the happiness of the people. At every hazard and by every sacrifice this Union must be preserved.

The necessity of watching with jealous anxiety for the preservation of the Union was earnestly pressed upon his fellow-citizens by the Father of his Country in his Farewell Address. He has there . . . cautioned us in the strongest terms against the formation of parties on geographical discriminations, as one of the means which might disturb our Union and to which designing men would be likely to resort.

The lessons contained in this invaluable legacy of Washington to his countrymen should be cherished in the heart of every citizen to the latest generation; and perhaps at no period of time could they be more usefully remembered than at the present moment. . . . Amid . . . [our] general prosperity and splendid success the dangers of which he warned us are becoming every day more evident, and the signs of evil are sufficiently apparent to awaken the deepest anxiety in the bosom of the patriot. We behold systematic efforts publicly made to sow the seeds of discord between different parts of the United States and to place party divisions directly upon geographical distinctions; to excite the *South* against the *North* and the *North* against the *South,* and to force into the controversy the most delicate and exciting topics—topics upon which it is impossible that a large portion of the Union can ever speak without strong emotion. Appeals, too, are constantly made to sectional interests in order to influence the election of the Chief Magistrate, as if it were desired that he should favor a particular quarter of the country instead of fulfilling the duties of his station with impartial justice to all; and the possible dissolution of the Union has at length become an ordinary and familiar subject of discussion. Has the warning voice of Washington been forgotten, or have designs already been formed to sever the Union? . . . The honorable feeling of State pride and local attachments finds a place in the bosoms of the most enlightened and pure. But while such men are conscious of their own integrity and honesty of purpose, they ought never to forget that the citizens of other States are their political brethren, and that however mistaken they may be in their views, the great body of them are equally honest and upright with themselves. Mutual suspicions and reproaches may in time create mutual hostility, and artful and designing men will always be found who are ready to foment these fatal divisions and to inflame the natural jealousies of different sections of the country. The history of the world is full of such examples, and especially the history of republics.

What have you to gain by division and dissension? Delude not yourselves with the belief that a breach once made may be afterwards repaired. If the Union is once severed, the line of separation will grow wider and wider, and the controversies which are now debated and settled in the halls of legislation will then be tried in fields of battle and determined by the sword. Neither should you deceive yourselves with the hope that the first line of separation would be the permanent one, and that nothing but harmony and concord would be found in the new associations formed upon the dissolution of this Union. . . . The first line of separation would not last for a single generation; new fragments would be torn off, new leaders would spring up, and this great and glorious Republic would soon be broken into a multitude of petty States, without commerce, without credit, jealous of one another, armed for mutual aggression, loaded with taxes to pay armies and leaders, seeking aid against each other from foreign powers, insulted and trampled upon by the nations of Europe, until, harassed with conflicts and humbled and debased in spirit, they would be ready to submit to the absolute dominion of any military adventurer and to surrender their liberty for the sake of repose. It is impossible to look on the consequences that would inevitably follow the destruction of this Government and not feel indignant when we hear cold calculations about the value of the Union and have so constantly before us a line of conduct so well calculated to weaken its ties.

There is too much at stake to allow pride or passion to influence your decision. Never for a moment believe that the great body of the citizens of any State or States can deliberately intend to do wrong. They may, under the influence of temporary excitement or misguided opinions, commit mistakes; they may be misled for a time by the suggestions of self-interest; but in a community so enlightened and patriotic as the people of the United States argument will soon make them sensible of their errors, and when convinced they will be ready to repair them. If they have no higher or better motives to govern them, they will at least perceive that their own interest requires them to be just to others, as they hope to receive justice at their hands.

But in order to maintain the Union unimpaired it is absolutely necessary that the laws passed by the constituted authorities should be faithfully executed in every part of the country, and that every good citizen should at all times stand ready to put down, with the combined force of the nation, every attempt at unlawful resistance, under whatever pretext it may be made or whatever shape it may assume. Unconstitutional or oppressive laws may no doubt be passed by Congress, either from erroneous views or the want of due consideration; if they are within the reach of judicial authority, the remedy is easy and peaceful; and if, from the character of the law, it is an abuse of power not within the control of the judiciary, then free discussion and calm appeals to reason and to the justice of the people will not fail to redress the wrong. But until the law shall be declared void by the courts or repealed by Congress no individual or combination of individuals can be justified in forcibly resisting its execution. It is impossible that any government can continue to exist upon any other principles. It would cease to be a government and be unworthy of the name if it had not the power to enforce the execution of its own laws within its own sphere of action.

It is true that cases may be imagined disclosing such a settled purpose of usurpation and oppression on the part of the Government as would justify an appeal to arms. These, however, are extreme cases, which we have no reason to apprehend in a government where the power is in the hands of a patriotic people. And no citizen who loves his country would in any case whatever resort to forcible resistance unless he clearly saw that the time had come when a freeman should prefer death to submission; for if such a struggle is once begun, and the citizens of one section of the country arrayed in arms against those of another in doubtful conflict, let the battle result as it may, there will be an end of the Union and with it an end to the hopes of freedom. The victory of the injured would not secure to them the blessings of liberty; it would avenge their wrongs, but they would themselves share in the common ruin.

But the Constitution can not be maintained nor the Union preserved, in opposition to public feeling, by the mere exertion of the coercive powers confided to the General Government. The foundations must be laid in the affections of the people, in the security it gives to life, liberty, character, and property in every quarter of the country, and in the fraternal attachment which the citizens of the several States bear to one another as members of one political family, mutually contributing to promote the happiness of each other. Hence the citizens of every State should studiously avoid everything calculated to wound the sensibility or offend the just pride of the people of other States, and they should frown upon any proceedings within their own borders likely to disturb the tranquillity of their political brethren in other portions of the Union. . . . Each State has the unquestionable right to regulate its own internal concerns according to its own pleasure, and while it does not interfere with the rights of the people of other States or the rights of the Union, every State must be the sole judge of the measures proper to secure the safety of its citizens and promote their happiness; and all efforts on the part of people of other States to cast odium upon their institutions, and all measures calculated to disturb their rights of property or to put in jeopardy their peace and internal tranquillity, are in direct opposition to the spirit in which the Union was formed, and must endanger its safety. Motives of philanthropy may be assigned for this unwarrantable interference, and weak men may persuade themselves for a moment that they are laboring in the cause of humanity and asserting the rights of the human race; but everyone, upon sober reflection, will see that nothing but mischief can come from these improper assaults upon the feelings and rights of others. Rest assured that the men found busy in this work of discord are not worthy of your confidence, and deserve your strongest reprobation.

In the legislation of Congress also, and in every measure of the General Government, justice to every portion of the United States should be faithfully observed. No free government can stand without virtue in the people and a lofty spirit of patriotism, and if the sordid feelings of mere selfishness shall usurp the place which ought to be filled by public spirit, the legislation of Congress will soon be converted into a scramble for personal and sectional advantages. . . . Justice—full and ample justice—to every portion of the United States should be the ruling principle of every freeman, and should guide the deliberations of every public body, whether it be State or national.

It is well known that there have always been those amongst us who wish to enlarge the powers of the General Government, and experience would seem to indicate that there is a tendency on the part of this Government to overstep the boundaries marked out for it by the Constitution. Its legitimate authority is abundantly sufficient for all the purposes for which it was created, and its powers being expressly enumerated, there can be no justification for claiming anything beyond them. . . . From the extent of our country, its diversified interests, different pursuits, and different habits, it is too obvious for argument that a single consolidated government would be wholly inadequate to watch over and protect its interests; and every friend of our free institutions should be always prepared to maintain unimpaired and in full vigor the rights and sovereignty of the States and to confine the action of the General Government strictly to the sphere of its appropriate duties.

There is, perhaps, no one of the powers conferred on the Federal Government so liable to abuse as the taxing power. The most productive and convenient sources of revenue were necessarily given to it, that it might be able to perform the important duties imposed upon it. . . . But . . . Congress has no right under the Constitution to take money from the people unless it is required to execute some one of the specific powers intrusted to the Government; and if they raise more than is necessary for such purposes, it is an abuse of the power of taxation, and unjust and oppressive. . . .

Plain as these principles appear to be, you will yet find there is a constant effort to induce the General Government to go beyond the limits of its taxing power and to impose unnecessary burdens upon the people. Many powerful interests are continually at work to procure heavy duties on commerce and to swell the revenue beyond the real necessities of the public service, and the country has already felt the injurious effects of their combined influence. They succeeded in obtaining a tariff of duties bearing most oppressively on the agricultural and laboring classes of society and producing a revenue that could not be usefully employed within the range of the powers conferred upon Congress, and in order to fasten upon the people this unjust and unequal system of taxation extravagant schemes of internal improvement were got up in various quarters to squander the money and to purchase support. Thus one unconstitutional measure was intended to be upheld by another, and the abuse of the power of taxation was to be maintained by usurping the power of expending the money in internal improvements. You can not have forgotten the severe and doubtful struggle through which we passed when the executive department of the Government by its veto endeavored to arrest this prodigal scheme of injustice and to bring back the legislation of Congress to the boundaries prescribed by the Constitution. The good sense and practical judgment of the people when the subject was brought before them sustained the course of the Executive, and this plan of unconstitutional expenditures for the purposes of corrupt influence is, I trust, finally overthrown.

The result of this decision has been felt in the rapid extinguishment of the public debt and the large accumulation of a surplus in the Treasury, notwithstanding the tariff was reduced and is now very far below the amount originally contemplated by its advocates. But, rely upon it, the design to collect an extravagant revenue and to burden you with taxes beyond the economical wants of the Government is not yet abandoned. The various interests which have combined together to impose a heavy tariff and to produce an overflowing Treasury are too strong and have too much at stake to surrender the contest. The corporations and wealthy individuals who are engaged in large manufacturing establishments desire a high tariff to increase their gains. Designing politicians will support it to conciliate their favor and to obtain the means of profuse expenditure for the purpose of purchasing influence in other quarters; . . . and the temptation will become irresistible to support a high tariff in order to obtain a surplus for distribution. Do not allow yourselves, my fellow-citizens, to be misled on this subject. . . . The surplus revenue will be drawn from the pockets of the people—from the farmer, the mechanic, and the laboring classes of society; but who will receive it when distributed among the States, where it is to be disposed of by leading State politicians, who have friends to favor and political partisans to gratify? It will certainly not be returned to those who paid it and who have most need of it and are honestly entitled to it. There is but one safe rule, and that is to confine the General Government rigidly within the sphere of its appropriate duties. It has no power to raise a revenue or impose taxes except for the purposes enumerated in the Constitution, and if its income is found to exceed these wants it should be forthwith reduced and the burden of the people so far lightened.

In reviewing the conflicts which have taken place between different interests in the United States and the policy pursued since the adoption of our present form of Government, we find nothing that has produced such deep-seated evil as the course of legislation in relation to the currency. The Constitution of the United States unquestionably intended to secure to the people a circulating medium of gold and silver. But the establishment of a national bank by Congress, with the privilege of issuing paper money receivable in the payment of the public dues, and the unfortunate course of legislation in the several States upon the same subject, drove from general circulation the constitutional currency and substituted one of paper in its place.

It was not easy for men engaged in the ordinary pursuits of business, . . . to foresee all the consequences of a currency exclusively of paper. . . . But experience has now proved the mischiefs and dangers of a paper currency, and it rests with you to determine whether the proper remedy shall be applied.

The paper system being founded on public confidence and having of itself no intrinsic value, it is liable to great and sudden fluctuations, thereby rendering property insecure and the wages of labor unsteady and uncertain. . . . In times of prosperity, when confidence is high, . . . [the banks] extend their issues of paper beyond the bounds of discretion and the reasonable demands of business; and when . . . public confidence is at length shaken, then a reaction takes place, and they immediately withdraw the credits they have given, suddenly curtail their issues, and produce an unexpected and ruinous contraction of the circulating medium, which is felt by the whole community. The banks by this means save themselves, and the mischievous consequences of their imprudence or cupidity are visited upon the public. Nor does the evil stop here. These ebbs and flows in the currency and these indiscreet extensions of credit naturally engender a spirit of speculation injurious to the habits and character of the people. . . . It is not by encouraging this spirit that we shall best preserve public virtue and promote the true interests of our country; but if your currency continues as exclusively paper as it now is, it will foster this eager desire to amass wealth without labor; it will multiply the number of dependents on bank accommodations and bank favors; the temptation to obtain money at any sacrifice will become stronger and stronger, and inevitably lead to corruption, which will find its way into your public councils and destroy at no distant day the purity of your Government. Some of the evils which arise from this system of paper press with peculiar hardship upon the class of society least able to bear it. . . . Frauds are most generally perpetrated in the smaller notes, which are used in the daily transactions of ordinary business, and the losses occasioned by them are commonly thrown upon the laboring classes of society, . . . whose daily wages are necessary for their subsistence. It is the duty of every government so to regulate its currency as to protect this numerous class, as far as practicable, from the impositions of avarice and fraud. . . . Yet it is evident that their interests can not be effectually protected unless silver and gold are restored to circulation. . . .

Recent events have proved that the paper-money system of this country may be used as an engine to undermine your free institutions, and that those who desire to engross all power in the hands of the few and to govern by corruption or force are aware of its power and prepared to employ it. Your banks now furnish your only circulating medium, and money is plenty or scarce according to the quantity of notes issued by them. While they have capitals not greatly disproportioned to each other, they are competitors in business, and no one of them can exercise dominion over the rest; and . . . they can not combine for the purposes of political influence. . . .

But when the charter for the Bank of the United States was obtained from Congress it perfected the schemes of the paper system. . . . The immense capital and peculiar privileges bestowed upon it enabled it to exercise despotic sway over the other banks in every part of the country. From its superior strength it could seriously injure, if not destroy, the business of any one of them which might incur its resentment; and it openly claimed for itself the power of regulating the currency throughout the United States. In other words, it asserted (and it undoubtedly possessed) the power to make money plenty or scarce at its pleasure, . . . by controlling the issues of other banks and permitting an expansion or compelling a general contraction of the circulating medium, according to its own will. The other banking institutions were sensible of its strength, and they soon generally became its obedient instruments, ready at all times to execute its mandates. . . . The result of the ill-advised legislation which established this great monopoly was to concentrate the whole moneyed power of the Union, with its boundless means of corruption and its numerous dependents, under the direction and command of one acknowledged head, . . . and enabling it to bring forward upon any occasion its entire and undivided strength to support or defeat any measure of the Government. In the hands of this formidable power, thus perfectly organized, was also placed unlimited dominion over the amount of the circulating medium, giving it the power to regulate the value of property and the fruits of labor in every quarter of the Union. . . .

We are not left to conjecture how the moneyed power, thus organized and with such a weapon in its hands, would be likely to use it. . . . No nation but the freemen of the United States could have come out victorious from such a contest; yet, if you had not conquered, the Government would have passed from the hands of the many to the hands of the few, and this organized money power from its secret conclave would have dictated the choice of your highest officers. . . . The forms of your Government might for a time have remained, but its living spirit would have departed from it.

The distress and sufferings inflicted on the people by the bank are some of the fruits of that system of policy which is continually striving to enlarge the authority of the Federal Government beyond the limits fixed by the Constitution. The powers enumerated in that instrument do not confer on Congress the right to establish such a corporation as the Bank of the United States, and the evil consequences which followed may warn us of the danger of departing from the true rule of construction. . . . Let us abide by the Constitution as it is written, or amend it in the constitutional mode if it is found to be defective.

The severe lessons of experience will, I doubt not, be sufficient to prevent Congress from again chartering such a monopoly, even if the Constitution did not present an insuperable objection to it. But you must remember, my fellow-citizens, that eternal vigilance by the people is the price of liberty, and that you must pay the price if you wish to secure the blessing. It behooves you, therefore, to be watchful in your States as well as in the Federal Government. . . .

It is one of the serious evils of our present system of banking that it enables one class of society—and that by no means a numerous one— by its control over the currency, to act injuriously upon the interests of all the others and to exercise more than its just proportion of influence in political affairs. The agricultural, the mechanical, and the laboring classes have little or no share in the direction of the great moneyed corporations, and from their habits and the nature of their pursuits they are incapable of forming extensive combinations to act together with united force. . . . The planter, the farmer, the mechanic, and the laborer all know that their success depends upon their own industry and economy, and that they must not expect to become suddenly rich by the fruits of their toil. Yet these classes of society form the great body of the people of the United States; they are the bone and sinew of the country—men who love liberty and desire nothing but equal rights and equal laws, and who, moreover, hold the great mass of our national wealth, although it is distributed in moderate amounts among the millions of freemen who possess it. But with overwhelming numbers and wealth on their side they are in constant danger of losing their fair influence in the Government, and with difficulty maintain their just rights against the incessant efforts daily made to encroach upon them. The mischief springs from the power which the moneyed interest derives from a paper currency which they are able to control, from the multitude of corporations with exclusive privileges which they have succeeded in obtaining in the different States, and which are employed altogether for their benefit; and unless you become more watchful in your States and check this spirit of monopoly and thirst for exclusive privileges you will in the end find that the most important powers of Government have been given or bartered away, and the control over your dearest interests has passed into the hands of these corporations.

. . . In your hands is rightfully placed the sovereignty of the country, and to you everyone placed in authority is ultimately responsible. It is always in your power to see that the wishes of the people are carried into faithful execution, and their will, when once made known, must sooner or later be obeyed; and while the people remain, as I trust they ever will, uncorrupted and incorruptible, and continue watchful and jealous of their rights, the Government is safe, and the cause of freedom will continue to triumph over all its enemies.

But it will require steady and persevering exertions on your part to rid yourselves of the iniquities and mischiefs of the paper system and to check the spirit of monopoly and other abuses which have sprung up with it, and of which it is the main support. So many interests are united to resist all reform on this subject that you must not hope the conflict will be a short one nor success easy. My humble efforts have not been spared during my administration of the Government to restore the constitutional currency of gold and silver, and something, I trust, has been done toward the accomplishment of this most desirable object; but enough yet remains to require all your energy and perseverance. The power, however, is in your hands, and the remedy must and will be applied if you determine upon it. . . .

In presenting to you, my fellow-citizens, these parting counsels, I have brought before you the leading principles upon which I endeavored to administer the Government in the high office with which you twice honored me. Knowing that the path of freedom is continually beset by enemies who often assume the disguise of friends, I have devoted the last hours of my public life to warn you of the dangers. The progress of the United States under our free and happy institutions has surpassed the most sanguine hopes of the founders of the Republic. Our growth has been rapid beyond all former example in numbers, in wealth, in knowledge, and all the useful arts which contribute to the comforts and convenience of man, and from the earliest ages of history to the present day there never have been thirteen millions of people associated in one political body who enjoyed so much freedom and happiness as the people of these United States. You have no longer any cause to fear danger from abroad; your strength and power are well known throughout the civilized world, as well as the high and gallant bearing of your sons. It is from within, among yourselves—from cupidity, from corruption, from disappointed ambition and inordinate thirst for power—that factions will be formed and liberty endangered. It is against such designs, whatever disguise the actors may assume, that you have especially to guard yourselves. You have the highest of human trusts committed to your care. Providence has showered on this favored land blessings without number, and has chosen you as the guardians of freedom, to preserve it for the benefit of the human race. May He who holds in His hands the destinies of nations make you worthy of the favors He has bestowed and enable you, with pure hearts and pure hands and sleepless vigilance, to guard and defend to the end of time the great charge He has committed to your keeping.

My own race is nearly run; advanced age and failing health warn me that before long I must pass beyond the reach of human events and cease to feel the vicissitudes of human affairs. I thank God that my life has been spent in a land of liberty and that He has given me a heart to love my country with the affection of a son. And filled with gratitude for your constant and unwavering kindness, I bid you a last and affectionate farewell.

24

Whig Campaign Platform of 1844

Democratic methods of party organization proved so effective at the state and local levels that the Whigs were forced to imitate them, even though the Whigs continued to feel distaste for the dictatorial and dogmatic aspects of party discipline. The National Republicans had held a national nominating convention in 1832 to give their blessing to the presidential candidacy of Henry Clay, but it was the Democrats who raised the nominating convention to a supreme tool of party organization. At the local, state, and national levels,

Reprinted in Arthur M. Schlesinger, Jr., and Fred L. Israel, eds., *History of American Presidential Elections, 1789–1968,* 4 vols. (New York: Chelsea House, 1971), 1: 807.

Democratic conventions tried to hold party activists to strict discipline and required all good Democrats to work for success of all "regular" party nominees, regardless of the individual's own preferences. Under the banner of party unity, Democrats tried to present themselves as the true voice of the whole American people, steadfast against a tiny coterie of elitists. The Whigs used a convention to nominate William Henry Harrison for president in 1840 and Henry Clay in 1844. In Clay's case, they made no effort to bind the candidate to a long and detailed platform, but they did adopt a series of resolutions that expressed the party's overall governing philosophy.

Read the platform carefully. Is it consistent with Henry Clay's previous political philosophy? Are there significant differences between this Whig platform and the ideas of Jackson's Farewell Address (see Document 23)? How does the Whig Party support Clay's American System?

What does the platform say about Theodore Frelinghuysen? Would the Whigs have endorsed his ideas of Indian removal (see Document 13)? Why do you think the platform tries to link him with the American Revolution and religious benevolence and reform?

Resolved, That, in presenting to the country the names of Henry Clay for president, and of Theodore Frelinghuysen for vice-president of the United States, this Convention is actuated by the conviction that all the great principles of the Whig party—principles inseparable from the public honor and prosperity—will be maintained and advanced by these candidates.

Resolved, That these principles may be summed as comprising, a well-regulated currency; a tariff for revenue to defray the necessary expenses of the government, and discriminating with special reference to the protection of the domestic labor of the country; the distribution of the proceeds of the sales of the public lands; a single term for the presidency; a reform of executive usurpations;—and, generally—such an administration of the affairs of the country as shall impart to every branch of the public service the greatest practicable efficiency, controlled by a well regulated and wise economy.

Resolved, That the name of Henry Clay needs no eulogy; the history of the country since his first appearance in public life is his history; its brightest pages of prosperity and success are identified with the principles which he has upheld, as its darkest and more disastrous pages are with every material departure in our public policy from those principles.

Resolved, That in Theodore Frelinghuysen we present a man pledged alike by his revolutionary ancestry and his own public course to every measure calculated to sustain the honor and interest of the country. Inheriting the principles as well as the name of a father who, with Washington, on the fields of Trenton and of Monmouth,[1] perilled life in the contest for liberty, and afterwards, as a senator of the United States, acted with Washington in establishing and perpetuating that liberty, Theodore Frelinghuysen, by his course as Attorney-General of the State of New Jersey for twelve years, and subsequently as a senator of the United States for several years, was always strenuous on the side of law, order, and the constitution, while as a private man, his head, his hand, and his heart have been given without stint to the cause of morals, education, philanthropy, and religion.

[1]Frederick Frelinghuysen, father of Theodore Frelinghuysen, played a distinguished role as an American military officer in the Battle of Trenton (1776) and in the Battle of Monmouth (1778), two important engagements of the American Revolution.

25

HENRY CLAY

Resolutions and Speech on the Proposed Compromise of 1850

January 29 and
February 5 and 6, 1850

American victory in the Mexican War of 1846–48 led to the annexation of a vast territory that included all or most of the modern states of California, Arizona, New Mexico, Nevada, Colorado, and Utah. Congress immediately began to quarrel over the future of slavery in these new territories. Party lines melted as southerners demanded the right to take their slave property everywhere in the common territories of the United States and as northerners closed ranks to prevent the spread of slavery. By early 1850, the government was nearly at a standstill because neither side would allow the transaction of the simplest congressional business until the issues had been resolved.

Calvin Colton, ed., *The Life, Correspondence, and Speeches of Henry Clay,* 6 vols. (New York: Barnes, 1857), 3: 301–45.

As he had done in the dispute over the admission of Missouri in 1820 and the nullification controversy in 1833, Henry Clay favored a compromise of these issues to preserve the union. On January 29, 1850, he introduced eight resolutions in the Senate that proposed a resolution of all the major questions facing the country over the future of slavery, particularly in the formerly Mexican territories but also in the District of Columbia and in the interstate slave trade. He supported these resolutions in a lengthy speech delivered a few days later. Clay was already seventy-two, and his delivery in the Senate was so painful that his Whig colleagues often begged him to stop speaking and rest, but the Great Compromiser pressed on and completed his eloquent appeal for the preservation of the Union.

After fighting for his plan for most of the spring and summer of 1850, Clay finally gave up the struggle to pass all his proposals in a single package that would commit all sides to its support. Instead, Congress passed the Compromise of 1850 as a series of individual laws, each one supported by a different coalition. The country recognized the compromise as Clay's handiwork, however, and praised it as the senior statesman's last and greatest public service.

What are the most important elements of Clay's proposed Compromise of 1850? How do they fit together? How well do they address the specific disputes that had paralyzed the government and threatened to bring about secession? What arguments does Clay use to persuade the North and South to compromise on their differences? How are his ideas about the Union different from Andrew Jackson's?

How does Clay's speech continue to reflect his old ideas about economic development? In what way was the existing party debate over democracy and development relevant to the dispute over slavery in the territories?

Why was Clay's compromise not sufficient in the long run to preserve the Union?

Resolutions Introduced in the Senate of the United States, by Mr. Clay, January 29, 1850.

PREAMBLE.—It being desirable for the peace, concord, and harmony of the Union of these States, to settle and adjust amicably all questions of controversy between them arising out of the institution of Slavery, upon a fair equality and just basis, therefore—

1st. *Resolved,* That California, with suitable boundaries, ought, upon her application, to be admitted as one of the States of this Union, without the imposition by Congress of any restriction to the exclusion or introduction of slavery within those boundaries.

2d. *Resolved,* That as slavery does not exist by law, and is not likely to be introduced into any of the territory acquired by the United States from the Republic of Mexico, it is inexpedient for Congress to provide, by law, either for its introduction into, or its exclusion from, any part of the said territory; and that appropriate territorial Governments ought to be established by Congress, in all of the said territory not assigned as the boundaries of the proposed State of California, without the addition of any restriction or condition on the subject of slavery.

3d. *Resolved,* That the western boundary of the State of Texas ought to be fixed on the Rio del Norte, commencing one marine league from its mouth, and running up that river to the southern line of New Mexico, thence with that line eastwardly, and continuing in the same direction, to the line as established between the United States and Spain, excluding any portion of New Mexico, whether lying on the east or west of that river.

4th. *Resolved,* That it be proposed to the State of Texas that the United States will provide for the payment of all that portion of all the legitimate and bonâ fide public debts of that State, contracted prior to its annexation to the United States, and for which the duties on foreign imports were pledged by the said State to its creditors, not exceeding the sum of _____ dollars, in consideration of the duties, as pledged, having been no longer applicable to that object after the said annexation, but having thenceforward become payable to the United States, and upon the condition also that the said State shall, by some solemn and authentic act of her Legislature, or of a convention, relinquish to the United States any claim which it has to any part of New Mexico.

5th. *Resolved,* That it is inexpedient to abolish slavery in the District of Columbia, while that institution continues to exist in the State of Maryland, without the consent of that State, without the consent of the people of the District, and without just compensation to the owners of slaves within the District.

6th. *Resolved,* That it is expedient to prohibit within the District the trade in slaves brought into it from States or places beyond the limits of the District, either to be sold therein, as merchandise, or to be transported to other markets without the District of Columbia.

7th. *Resolved,* That more effectual provision ought to be made by law according to the requirements of the Constitution, for the restitution and delivery of persons bound to service or labor, in any State, who may escape into any other State or Territory of this Union.

8th. *Resolved,* That Congress has no power to prohibit or obstruct the trade in slaves between the slaveholding States, and that the admission or exclusion of slaves brought from one into another of them, depends exclusively upon their own particular law.

Speech of Mr. Clay
on the Foregoing Resolutions,
Delivered February 5th and 6th, 1850.

Mr. President, never on any former occasion have I risen under feelings of such painful solicitude. I have seen many periods of great anxiety, of peril, and of danger in this country, and I have never before risen to address any assemblage so oppressed, so appalled, and so anxious; and sir, I hope it will not be out of place to do here, what again and again I have done in my private chamber, to implore of Him who holds the destinies of nations and individuals in His hands, to bestow upon our country His blessing, to calm the violence and rage of party, to still passion, to allow reason once more to resume its empire. And may I not ask of Him too, sir, to bestow on his humble servant, now before him, the blessing of his smiles, and of strength and ability to perform the work which now lies before him? Sir, I have said that I have seen other anxious periods in the history of our country, and if I were to venture, Mr. President, to trace to their original source the cause of all our present dangers, difficulties, and distraction, I should ascribe it to the violence and intemperance of party spirit. To party spirit! Sir, in the progress of this session we have had the testimony of two senators here, who, however they may differ on other matters, concur in the existence of that cause in originating the unhappy differences which prevail throughout the country, on the subject of the institution of slavery.

Parties, in their endeavors to obtain, the one ascendency over the other, catch at every passing or floating plank in order to add strength and power to each. We have been told by the two senators to whom I have referred, that each of the parties at the North, in its turn, has moved and endeavored to obtain the assistance of a small party called Abolitionists, in order that the scale in its favor might preponderate against that of its adversary. And all around us, every where, we see too many evidences of the existence of the spirit and intemperance of party. . . . During this very session one whole week has been exhausted—I think about a week—in the vain endeavor to elect a doorkeeper of the House.

And, Mr. President, what was the question in this struggle to elect a doorkeeper? It was not as to the man or the qualities of the man, or who is best adapted to the situation. It was whether the doorkeeper entertained opinions upon certain national measures coincident with this or that side of the House. That was the sole question which prevented the election of a doorkeeper for about the period of a week. Sir, I make no reproaches—none, to either portion of that House; I state the fact; and I state the fact to draw from it the conclusion and to express the hope that there will be an endeavor to check this violence of party. . . .

But, sir, it is impossible for us to be blind to the facts which are daily transpiring before us. It is impossible for us not to perceive that party spirit and future elevation mix more or less in all our affairs, in all our deliberations. At a moment when the White House itself is in danger of conflagration, instead of all hands uniting to extinguish the flames, we are contending about who shall be its next occupant. When a dreadful *crevasse* has occurred, which threatens inundation and destruction to all around it, we are contending and disputing about the profits of an estate which is threatened with total submersion.

Mr. President, it is passion, passion—party, party, and intemperance—that is all I dread in the adjustment of the great questions which unhappily at this time divide our distracted country. . . . Two months ago all was calm in comparison to the present moment. All now is uproar, confusion, and menace to the existence of the Union, and to the happiness and safety of this people. Sir, I implore senators . . . but to listen to their own reason, their own judgment, their own good sense, in determining upon what is best to be done for our country in the actual posture in which we find her. Sir, to this great object have my efforts been directed during the whole session.

I have cut myself off from all the usual enjoyments of social life, I have confined myself almost entirely, with very few exceptions, to my own chamber, and from the beginning of the session to the present time my thoughts have been anxiously directed to the object of finding some plan, of proposing some mode of accommodation, which would once more restore the blessings of concord, harmony and peace to this great country. . . .

Sir, when I came to consider this subject, there were two or three general purposes which it seemed to me to be most desirable, if possible, to accomplish. The one was, to settle all the controverted questions arising out of the subject of slavery. It seemed to me to be doing very little, if we settled one question and left other distracting questions unadjusted, . . . if we stopped one leak only in the ship of State, and left other leaks capable of producing danger, if not destruction, to the vessel. I therefore turned my attention to every subject connected with the institution of slavery, and out of which controverted questions had sprung, to see if it were possible or practicable to accommodate and adjust the whole of them. Another principal object which attracted my attention was, to endeavor to form such a scheme of accommodation that neither of the two classes of States into which our country is so unhappily divided should make any sacrifice of any great principle. I believe, sir, the series of resolutions which I have had the honor to present to the Senate accomplishes that object.

Sir, another purpose which I had in view was this: I was aware of the difference of opinion prevailing between these two classes of States. I was aware that, while one portion of the Union was pushing matters, as it seemed to me, to the greatest extremity, another portion of the Union was pushing them to an opposite, perhaps not less dangerous extremity. It appeared to me . . . that if any arrangement . . . could be made . . . that adjustment . . . could only be successful and effectual by extracting from both parties some concessions—not of principle, . . . but of feeling, of opinion, in relation to matters in controversy between them. Sir, I believe the resolutions which I have prepared fulfill that object. . . . I think every one of these characteristics which I have assigned, and the measures which I proposed, is susceptible of clear and satisfactory demonstration by an attentive perusal and critical examination of the resolutions themselves. . . .

[Clay proceeded here to discuss each individual resolution in a speech that continued for two days.]

Sir, I am taxing both the physical and intellectual powers which a kind Providence has bestowed upon me . . .—though I beg to be permitted, if the Senate will have patience with me, to conclude what I have to say, for I do not desire to trespass another day upon your time and patience, as I am approaching, though I have not yet nearly arrived at the conclusion.

Mr. Mangum—If the senator will permit me, I will move an adjournment.

Mr. Clay—No, sir, no; I will conclude. . . .

Sir, this Union is threatened with subversion. I want, Mr. President, to take a very rapid glance at the course of public measures in this Union presently. I want, however, before I do that, to ask the Senate to look back upon the career which this country has run since the adoption of this Constitution down to the present day. Was there ever a nation upon which the sun of heaven has shone that has exhibited so much of prosperity? At the commencement of this Government our population amounted to about four millions; it has now reached upward of twenty millions. Our territory was limited chiefly and principally to the border upon the Atlantic Ocean, and that which includes the southern shores of the interior lakes of our country.

Our country now extends from the Northern provinces of Great Britain to the Rio Grande and the Gulf of Mexico on one side, and from the Atlantic Ocean to the Pacific on the other side—the largest extent of territory under any Government that exists on the face of the earth, with only two solitary exceptions. . . .

Sir, our prosperity is unbounded—nay, Mr. President, I sometimes fear that it is in the wantonness of that prosperity that many of the threatening ills of the moment have arisen. . . . At this moment . . . all is prosperity and peace, and the nation is rich and powerful. Our country has grown to a magnitude, to a power and greatness, such as to command the respect, if it does not awe the apprehensions, of the powers of the earth, with whom we come in contact.

. . . And now, sir, let me go a little into detail with respect to sway in the councils of the nation, whether from the North or the South, during the sixty years of unparalleled prosperity that we have enjoyed. During the first twelve years of the administration of the Government Northern counsels rather prevailed; and out of them sprang the Bank of the United States, the assumption of the State debts, bounties to the fisheries, protection to our domestic manufactures—I allude to the act of 1789—neutrality in the wars of Europe, Jay's treaty, the alien and sedition laws, and war with France. I do not say, sir, that these, the leading and prominent measures which were adopted during the administrations of Washington and the elder Adams, were carried exclusively by Northern counsels—they could not have been—but mainly by the ascendency which Northern counsels had obtained in the affairs of the nation. So, sir, of the later period—for the last fifty years.

. . . During that fifty years, or nearly that period, in which Southern counsels have preponderated, the embargo and other commercial restrictions of non-intercourse and non-importation were imposed; war with Great Britain, the Bank of the United States overthrown, protection enlarged and extended to domestic manufactures—I allude to the passage of the act of 1815 or 1816—the Bank of the United States reestablished, the same bank put down, re-established by Southern counsels and put down by Southern counsels, Louisiana acquired, Florida bought, Texas annexed, war with Mexico, California and other territories acquired from Mexico by conquest and purchase, protection superseded, and free trade established, Indians removed west of the Mississippi, and fifteen new States admitted into the Union. It is very possible, sir, that in this enumeration I may have omitted some of the important measures which have been adopted during this later period of time—the last fifty years—but these I believe to be the most prominent ones.

Now, sir, I do not deduce from the enumeration of the measures adopted by the one side or the other any just cause of reproach either upon one side or the other; though one side or the other has predominated in the two periods to which I have referred. These measures were, to say the least, the joint work of both parties, and neither of them have any just cause to reproach the other. But, sir, I must say, in all kindness and sincerity, that least of all ought the South to reproach the North, when we look at the long list of measures which, under her sway in the counsels of the nation, have been adopted; when we reflect that even opposite doctrines have been from time to time advanced by her; that the establishment of the Bank of the United States, which was done under the administration of Mr. Madison, met with the co-operation of the South. . . . It was during Mr. Madison's administration that the Bank of the United States was established. My friend, . . . (Mr. Calhoun), was the chairman of the committee, and carried the measure through Congress. I voted for it with all my heart. Although I had been instrumental with other Southern votes in putting down the Bank of the United States, I changed my opinion and co-operated in the establishment of the Bank of 1816. The same bank was again put down by Southern counsels, with General Jackson at their head, at a later period. Again, with respect to the policy of protection. The South in 1815—I mean the prominent Southern men, the lamented Lowndes, Mr. Calhoun, and others—united in extending a certain measure of protection to domestic manufactures as well as the North.

We find a few years afterward the South interposing most serious objections to this policy, and one member of the South, threatening on that occasion, a dissolution of the Union or separation. . . . What have been the territorial acquisitions made by this country, and to what interests have they conduced? Florida, where slavery exists, has been introduced; Louisiana . . . I say, with the exception of that which lies north of 36° 30′, including Oregon, to which we obtained title mainly on the ground of its being a part of the acquisition of Louisiana; all Texas; all the territories which have been acquired by the Government of the United States during its sixty years' operation have been slave territories, the theater of slavery. . . .

And here, in the case of a war made essentially by the South—growing out of the annexation of Texas, which was a measure proposed by the South in the councils of the country, and which led to the war with Mexico . . . and the war with Mexico led to the acquisition of those territories which now constitute the bone of contention between the different members of the Confederacy. And now, sir, for the first time after the three great acquisitions of Texas, Florida, and Louisiana have been made and have redounded to the benefit of the South—now, for the first time, when three territories are attempted to be introduced without the institution of slavery, I put it to the hearts of my countrymen of the South, if it is right to press matters to the disastrous consequences which have been indicated no longer ago than this very morning, on the occasion of the presentation of certain resolutions—even extending to a dissolution of the Union. Mr. President, I can not believe it.

Mr. Underwood—Will the Senator give way for an adjournment?

Mr. Clay—Oh, no; if I do not weary the patience of the Senate, I prefer to go on. I think I can begin to see land. I shall soon come to the conclusion of what I have to say. Such is the Union, and such are the glorious fruits which are now threatened with subversion and destruction. Well, sir, the first question which naturally arises is, supposing the Union to be dissolved for any of the causes or grievances which are complained of, how far will dissolution furnish a remedy for those grievances? If the Union is to be dissolved for any existing cause, it will be because slavery is interdicted or not allowed to be introduced into the ceded territories; or because slavery is threatened to be abolished in the District of Columbia; or because fugitive slaves are not restored, as in my opinion they ought to be, to their masters. . . . Let us suppose the Union dissolved; what remedy does it, in a severed state, furnish for the grievances complained of in its united condition? Will you be able at the South to push slavery into the ceded territory? How are you to do it, supposing the North, or all the States north of the Potomac, in possession of the navy and army of the United States? Can you expect, I say, under these circumstances, that if there is a dissolution of the Union you can carry slavery into California and New Mexico? Sir, you can not dream of such an occurrence.

If it were abolished in the District of Columbia and the Union were dissolved, would the dissolution of the Union restore slavery in the District of Columbia? Is your chance for the recovery of your fugitive slaves safer in a state of dissolution or of severance of the Union than when in the Union itself? . . . Sir, there is . . . some remedy while you are a part of the Union for the recovery of your slaves, and some indemnification for their loss. What would you have, if the Union was severed? Why, then the several parts would be independent of each other—foreign countries—and slaves escaping from one to the other would be like slaves escaping from the United States to Canada. There would be no right of extradition, no right to demand your slaves; no right to appeal to the courts of justice to indemnify you for the loss of your slaves. Where one slave escapes now by running away from his master, hundreds and thousands would escape if the Union were dissevered—I care not how or where you run the line, or whether independent sovereignties be established. . . .

And, sir, I must take occasion here to say that in my opinion there is no right on the part of any one or more of the States to secede from the Union. War and dissolution of the Union are identical and inevitable, in my opinion. There can be a dissolution of the Union only by consent or by war. . . . If consent were given—if it were possible that we were to be separated by one great line—in less than sixty days after such consent was given war would break out between the slaveholding and non-slaveholding portions of this Union—between the two independent parts into which it would be erected in virtue of the act of separation. In less than sixty days, I believe, our slaves from Kentucky, flocking over in numbers to the other side of the river, would be pursued by their owners. . . . They would pursue their slaves into the adjacent free States; they would be repelled, and the consequence would be that, in less than sixty days, war would be blazing in every part of this now happy and peaceful land. . . .

Mr. President, I am directly opposed to any purpose of secession or separation. I am for staying within the Union, and defying any portion of this Confederacy to expel me or drive me out of the Union. . . . Here I am within it, and here I mean to stand and die, as far as my individual wishes or purposes can go—within it to protect my property and defend myself, defying all the power on earth to expel me or drive me from the situation in which I am placed. And would there not be more safety in fighting within the Union than out of it? . . . You can vindicate your rights within the Union better than if expelled from the Union, and driven from it without ceremony and without authority.

. . . The Constitution of the United States was made not merely for the generation that then existed, but for posterity—unlimited, undefined, endless, perpetual posterity. And every State that then came into the Union, and every State that has since come into the Union, came into it binding itself, by indissoluble bands, to remain within the Union itself, and to remain within it by its posterity forever. Like another of the sacred connections, in private life, it is a marriage which no human authority can dissolve or divorce the parties from. And if I may be allowed to refer to some examples in private life, let me say to the North and to the South, what husband and wife say to each other. We have mutual faults; neither of us is perfect; nothing in the form of humanity is perfect; let us, then, be kind to each other—forbearing, forgiving each other's faults—and above all, let us live in happiness and peace together.

Mr. President, I have said, what I solemnly believe, that dissolution of the Union and war are identical and inevitable; and they are convertible terms; and such a war as it would be, following a dissolution of the Union! Sir, we may search the pages of history, and none so ferocious, so bloody, so implacable, so exterminating—not even the wars of Greece, including those of the Commoners of England and the revolutions of France—none, none of them all would rage with such violence, or be characterized with such bloodshed and enormities as would the war which must succeed, if that event ever happens, the dissolution of the Union. And what would be its termination? . . . Exterminating wars would ensue, until, after the struggles and exhaustion of both parties, some Philip or Alexander, some Cæsar or Napoleon, would arise and cut the Gordian knot, and solve the problem of the capacity of man for self-government, and crush the liberties of both the severed portions of this common empire. Can you doubt it?

. . . The final disposition of the whole would be some despot treading down the liberties of the people—the final result would be the extinction of this last and glorious light which is leading all mankind, who are gazing upon it, in the hope and anxious expectation that the liberty which prevails here will sooner or later be diffused throughout the whole of the civilized world. Sir, can you lightly contemplate these consequences? Can you yield yourself to the tyranny of passion, amid dangers which I have depicted in colors far too tame of what the result would be if that direful event to which I have referred should ever occur? Sir, I implore gentlemen, I adjure them, whether from the South or the North, by all that they hold dear in this world—by all their love of liberty—by all their veneration for their ancestors—by all their regard for posterity—by all their gratitude to Him who has bestowed on them such unnumbered and countless blessings—by all the duties which they owe to mankind—and by all the duties which they owe to themselves, to pause, solemnly to pause at the edge of the precipice, before the fearful and dangerous leap be taken into the yawning abyss below, from which none who ever take it shall return in safety.

Finally, Mr. President, and in conclusion, I implore, as the best blessing which Heaven can bestow upon me, upon earth, that if the direful event of the dissolution of this Union is to happen, I shall not survive to behold the sad and heart-rending spectacle.

An Andrew Jackson and
Henry Clay Chronology

1767

March 15: Andrew Jackson born in the Waxhaws community on the North Carolina and South Carolina border.
Father dies shortly after Jackson's birth.

1777

April 12: Henry Clay born in Hanover County, Virginia.
Father dies when Clay is young.

1780–1781

Jackson serves in American Revolution. His mother and brothers die.

1787

Jackson licensed to practice law.

1788

Jackson moves to Nashville in future state of Tennessee.
Jackson practices law privately and as public prosecutor.
Jackson purchases first slave and fights first duel.

1793

Connecticut tutor Eli Whitney invents cotton gin.

1796

Jackson elected Tennessee's first representative to U.S. House of Representatives and serves one term.

1797

Jackson elected by Tennessee legislature to U.S. Senate and serves six months.
Clay licensed to practice law and moves to Lexington, Kentucky.

1798

April 16: Slaveholder Clay, as "Scaevola," calls for state constitutional reform that would allow legislature to abolish slavery.

1801

Thomas Jefferson elected president by U.S. House of Representatives.

1802

Jackson appointed major general in Tennessee state militia.
Jackson spends most of next decade building up the Hermitage, his plantation near Nashville.

1803

Louisiana Purchase signed by Jefferson.
Clay elected to Kentucky legislature.

1810

February 22: War Hawk Clay, in Senate speech, advocates war with Great Britain.
Clay elected to his first term in U.S. House of Representatives.

1811

Freshman representative Clay elected Speaker of the House.
Charter of first Bank of the United States expires.
General William Henry Harrison defeats Tecumseh at the Battle of Tippecanoe.

1812

Creek War and War of 1812 begin.

1813

Jackson undertakes grueling march to Natchez and back to Tennessee, earning soldiers' loyalty and nickname Old Hickory.
Jackson first leads troops into battle (against Creeks).

1814

Jackson appointed major general in U.S. Army and retains position until 1821.
Jackson defeats Creeks at Battle of Horseshoe Bend.
Clay, with John Quincy Adams and three others, travels to Belgium to negotiate Treaty of Ghent, ending War of 1812.

1815

January 8: Jackson defeats British at Battle of New Orleans.

1817

Jackson invades Florida in First Seminole War.

1819

January 20: Clay leads unsuccessful move in Congress to censure Jackson for invading Florida.
United States purchases Florida from Spain in Adams-Onís Treaty.
Monroe appoints Jackson governor of Florida territory.
Panic of 1819.
Missouri applies for statehood.

1820

Speaker Clay leads House to pass Missouri Compromise and earns reputation as Great Compromiser.

1821

Clay resigns from Congress and pursues farming and law, often as counsel for Bank of the United States.

1823

Clay reclaims his House seat and Speakership.
Jackson elected U.S. senator.

1824

Jackson leads in presidential balloting, with John Quincy Adams second, William H. Crawford third, and Henry Clay fourth, but no man wins a majority.

1825

U.S. House of Representatives elects John Quincy Adams president with Clay's support.
Adams appoints Clay secretary of state, prompting charges of "corrupt bargain."

1828

Congressional Jacksonians pass "Tariff of Abominations."
Jackson elected president over John Quincy Adams.

1830

Jackson signs Indian Removal Act.
Jackson vetoes Maysville Road.

1831

Clay, on return to U.S. Senate, nominated for president by National Republican convention.
Nat Turner leads slave rebellion in Virginia.

1832

July 10: Jackson vetoes recharter of Bank of the United States. Jackson signs Tariff of 1832.
November: Jackson defeats Clay for second term as president. South Carolina nullifies Tariffs of 1828 and 1832.
December 10: Jackson denounces tariff nullification in Proclamation to South Carolina.

1833

February 12: Clay advocates Compromise Tariff to end nullification crisis.
March: Jackson signs Compromise Tariff. Inaugurated for second term. South Carolina rescinds its Ordinance of Nullification.
September: Jackson explains to his cabinet removal of federal deposits from Bank of the United States. Removes William J. Duane as secretary of the Treasury and replaces him with Attorney General Roger B. Taney. Taney deposits government funds in five regional "pet" banks.

1836

December: Charter of second Bank of the United States expires.

1837

March 4: Jackson's Farewell Address issued in pamphlet form. Martin Van Buren inaugurated as president.
Spring: Panic of 1837.

1840

Whig General William Henry Harrison ("Old Tippecanoe") defeats Martin Van Buren in "Log Cabin and Hard Cider" campaign.

1841

Harrison dies in office.
Clay leads fight over "American System" against Harrison's unorthodox Whig successor, John Tyler.

1844

Clay wins Whig nomination for president.
Democrat and former Tennessee governor James K. Polk defeats Clay for president by pressing for territorial expansion.

1845

Texas annexed.
June 8: Andrew Jackson dies at age seventy-eight. Buried at the Hermitage.

1846–1848

U.S.–Mexican War.

1848

Clay seeks Whig nomination for presidency but loses to General Winfield Scott.

1849

Clay returns to Senate.

1850

February 5–6: Clay proposes Compromise of 1850 in two-day speech to Senate.

1852

Clay dies in Washington, D.C., at age seventy-five. Buried in Lexington, Kentucky.

Selected Bibliography

Aron, Stephen. *How the West Was Lost: The Transformation of Kentucky from Daniel Boone to Henry Clay.* Baltimore: Johns Hopkins University Press, 1996.

Ashworth, John. *"Agrarians" and "Aristocrats": Political Party Ideology in the United States, 1837–1846.* London: Royal Historical Society.

Ashworth, John. *Slavery, Capitalism, and Politics in the Antebellum Republic.* Vol. 1, *Commerce and Compromise, 1820–1850.* Cambridge: Cambridge University Press, 1995.

Bassett, John Spencer, ed. *The Correspondence of Andrew Jackson.* 7 vols. Washington: Carnegie Institution of Washington, 1926–1935.

Blau, Joseph L., ed. *Social Theories of Jacksonian Democracy: Representative Writings of the Period 1825–1850.* New York: The Liberal Arts Press, 1954.

Cashin, Joan E. *A Family Venture: Men and Women on the Southern Frontier.* New York: Oxford University Press, 1991.

Cole, Donald B. *The Presidency of Andrew Jackson.* Lawrence: University Press of Kansas, 1993.

Dawley, Alan. *Class and Community: The Industrial Revolution in Lynn.* Cambridge, Mass.: Harvard University Press, 1976.

de Tocqueville, Alexis. *Democracy in America,* trans. Henry Reeve, rev. Francis Bowen, and ed. Phillips Bradley. New York: Knopf, 1945.

Dupre, Daniel S. *Transforming the Cotton Frontier: Madison County, Alabama, 1800–1840.* Baton Rouge: Louisiana State University Press, 1997.

Eaton, Clement. *Henry Clay and the Art of American Politics.* Boston: Little, Brown, 1957.

Elkins, Stanley, and Eric McKitrick. *The Age of Federalism.* New York: Oxford University Press, 1993.

Ellis, Richard E. *The Union at Risk: Jacksonian Democracy, States' Rights, and the Nullification Crisis.* New York: Oxford University Press, 1987.

Feller, Daniel. *The Jacksonian Promise: America, 1815–1840.* Baltimore: Johns Hopkins University Press, 1995.

Foreman, Grant. *Indian Removal: The Emigration of the Five Civilized Tribes of Indians.* Norman: University of Oklahoma Press, 1932.

Freehling, William W., ed. *The Nullification Era: A Documentary Record.* New York: Harper & Row, 1967.

Freehling, William W. *Prelude to Civil War: The Nullification Controversy in South Carolina, 1816–1836.* New York: Harper & Row, 1966.

Gouge, William M. *A Short History of Paper Money and Banking in the United States.* Philadelphia: T. W. Ustick, 1833. (Reprint, with an introduction by Joseph Dorfman, New York: A. M. Kelley, 1968.)

Harris, J. William. *Plain Folk and Gentry in a Slave Society: White Liberty and Black Slavery in Augusta's Hinterlands.* Hanover, N.H.: Wesleyan University Press [University Press of New England], 1985.

Hofstadter, Richard. *The Idea of a Party System: The Rise of Legitimate Opposition in the United States, 1780–1840.* Berkeley: University of California Press, 1972.

Holt, Michael F. *The Political Crisis of the 1850s.* New York: Wiley, 1978.

Howe, Daniel Walker. *The Political Culture of the American Whigs.* Chicago: University of Chicago Press, 1980.

John, Richard R. *Spreading the News: The American Postal System from Franklin to Morse.* Cambridge, Mass.: Harvard University Press, 1995.

Johnson, Paul E. *A Shopkeeper's Millennium: Society and Revivals in Rochester, New York, 1815–1837.* New York: Hill & Wang, 1978.

Jordan, Winthrop. *White over Black: American Attitudes toward the Negro, 1550–1812.* Chapel Hill: University of North Carolina Press, 1968.

Kohl, Lawrence Frederick. *The Politics of Individualism: Parties and the American Character in the Jacksonian Era.* New York: Oxford University Press, 1989.

Latner, Richard B. *The Presidency of Andrew Jackson: White House Politics, 1829–1837.* Athens: University of Georgia Press, 1979.

Lockridge, Kenneth A. "Land, Population and the Evolution of New England Society, 1630–1790." *Past and Present* 39 (1968): 62–80.

McCormick, Richard P. *The Second American Party System: Party Formation in the Jacksonian Era.* Chapel Hill: University of North Carolina Press, 1966.

Meyers, Marvin. *The Jacksonian Persuasion: Politics and Belief.* Stanford, Calif.: Stanford University Press, 1957.

Nelson, John R. *Liberty and Property: Political Economy and Policymaking in the New Nation, 1789–1812.* Baltimore: Johns Hopkins University Press, 1987.

Parton, James. *Life of Andrew Jackson.* 3 vols. New York: Mason Brothers, 1861.

Peterson, Merrill D. *The Great Triumvirate: Webster, Clay, and Calhoun.* New York: Oxford University Press, 1987.

Peterson, Merrill D. *Olive Branch and Sword: The Compromise of 1833.* Baton Rouge: Louisiana State University Press, 1982.

Poage, George R. *Henry Clay and the Whig Party.* Chapel Hill: University of North Carolina Press, 1936.

Remini, Robert V. *Andrew Jackson and the Course of American Empire, 1767–1821.* Vol. I. New York: Harper & Row, 1977.

Remini, Robert V. *Andrew Jackson and the Course of American Freedom.* Vol. II. New York: Harper & Row, 1981.

Remini, Robert V. *Andrew Jackson and the Course of American Democracy.* Vol. III. New York: Harper & Row, 1984.

Remini, Robert V. *The Election of Andrew Jackson.* Philadelphia: Lippincott, 1963.

Remini, Robert V. *Henry Clay: Statesman for the Union.* New York: Norton, 1991.

Remini, Robert V. *The Legacy of Andrew Jackson: Essays on Democracy, Indian Removal, and Slavery.* Baton Rouge: Louisiana State University Press, 1988.

Remini, Robert V. *The Life of Andrew Jackson.* New York: Harper & Row, 1988.

Roediger, David R. *The Wages of Whiteness: Race and the Making of the American Working Class.* London: Verso, 1991.

Rogin, Michael Paul. *Fathers and Children: Andrew Jackson and the Subjugation of the American Indian.* New York: Knopf, 1975.

Satz, Ronald N. *American Policy in the Jacksonian Era.* Lincoln: University of Nebraska Press, 1975.

Schlesinger, Arthur M. Jr. *The Age of Jackson.* Boston: Little, Brown, 1945.

Schlesinger, Arthur M. Jr., ed. *History of U.S. Political Parties.* 4 vols. New York: Chelsea House, 1973.

Schlesinger, Arthur M. Jr., and Fred L. Israel, eds. *History of American Presidential Elections, 1789–1968.* 4 vols. New York: Chelsea House, 1971.

Sellers, Charles. *The Market Revolution: Jacksonian America, 1815–1846.* New York: Oxford University Press, 1991.

Smith, Sam B., and Harriet Chappell Owsley, eds. *The Papers of Andrew Jackson.* 5 vols to date. Knoxville: University of Tennessee Press, 1980–.

Taylor, George Rogers. *The Transportation Revolution, 1815–1860.* New York: Holt, Rinehart, and Winston, 1951.

Temin, Peter. *The Jacksonian Economy.* New York: Norton, 1969.

Thornton, J. Mills, III. *Politics and Power in a Slave Society: Alabama, 1800–1860.* Baton Rouge: Louisiana State University Press, 1978.

Ward, John William. *Andrew Jackson: Symbol for an Age.* New York: Oxford University Press, 1955.

Watson, Harry L. *Jacksonian Politics and Community Conflict: The Emergence of the Second American Party System in Cumberland County, North Carolina.* Baton Rouge: Louisiana State University Press, 1981.

Watson, Harry L. *Liberty and Power: The Politics of Jacksonian America.* New York: Hill & Wang, 1990.

Welter, Rush. *The Mind of America, 1820–1860.* New York: Columbia University Press, 1975.

White, Leonard D. *The Jacksonians: A Study in Administrative History, 1829–1861.* New York: Macmillan, 1954.

Wiebe, Robert H. *The Opening of American Society: From the Adoption of the Constitution to the Eve of Disunion.* New York: Knopf, 1984.

Wilentz, Sean. *Chants Democratic: New York City and the Rise of the American Working Class, 1788–1850.* New York: Oxford University Press, 1984.

Williamson, Chilton. *American Suffrage from Property to Democracy.* Princeton: Princeton University Press, 1960.

Wilson, Major L. *Space, Time, and Freedom: The Quest for Nationality and the Irrepressible Conflict, 1815–1860.* Westport, Conn.: Greenwood Press, 1974.

Wood, Gordon S. *The Radicalism of the American Revolution.* New York: Knopf, 1991.

Wyatt-Brown, Bertram. *Southern Honor: Ethics and Behavior in the Old South.* New York: Oxford University Press, 1982.

(*Continued from p. iv*)

Scaevola [Henry Clay], "To the Electors of Fayette County," April 16, 1798. Reprinted from *The Papers of Henry Clay*, edited by James F. Hopkins et al., by permission of University Press of Kentucky. Copyright © 1959–1992 University Press of Kentucky.

Henry Clay, "On the Proposed Repeal of the Non-Intercourse Act," February 22, 1810. Reprinted from *The Papers of Henry Clay*, edited by James F. Hopkins et al., by permission of University Press of Kentucky. Copyright © 1959–1992 University Press of Kentucky.

Henry Clay, "On the Seminole War," January 20, 1819. Reprinted from *The Papers of Henry Clay*, edited by James F. Hopkins et al., by permission of University Press of Kentucky. Copyright © 1959–1992 University Press of Kentucky.

Henry Clay, "On the Tariff," March 30–31, 1824. Reprinted from *The Papers of Henry Clay*, edited by James F. Hopkins et al., by permission of University Press of Kentucky. Copyright © 1959–1992 University Press of Kentucky.

"Edward Patchell to Andrew Jackson," August 7, 1824. Reprinted from *The Correspondence of Andrew Jackson*, edited by John Spencer Bassett, by permission of the Carnegie Institution of Washington. Copyright © 1926–1935 Carnegie Institution of Washington.

"Andrew Jackson to L.H. Coleman," April 26, 1824. Reprinted from *The Correspondence of Andrew Jackson*, edited by John Spencer Bassett, by permission of the Carnegie Institution of Washington. Copyright © 1926–1935 Carnegie Institution of Washington.

"Henry Clay to Francis T. Brooke," January 28, 1825. Reprinted from *The Papers of Henry Clay*, edited by James F. Hopkins et al., by permission of University Press of Kentucky. Copyright © 1959–1992 University Press of Kentucky.

"Andrew Jackson to Samuel Swartwout," February 22, 1825. Reprinted from *The Correspondence of Andrew Jackson*, edited by John Spencer Bassett, by permission of the Carnegie Institution of Washington. Copyright © 1926–1935 Carnegie Institution of Washington.

"Andrew Jackson to Tilghman A. Howard," August 20, 1833. Reprinted from *The Correspondence of Andrew Jackson*, edited by John Spencer Bassett, by permission of the Carnegie Institution of Washington. Copyright © 1926–1935 Carnegie Institution of Washington.

"Andrew Jackson to Joseph Conn Guild," April 24, 1835. Reprinted from *The Correspondence of Andrew Jackson*, edited by John Spencer Bassett, by permission of the Carnegie Institution of Washington. Copyright © 1926–1935 Carnegie Institution of Washington.

"Whig Campaign Platform of 1844." Reprinted from *History of American Presidential Elections, 1789–1897*, edited by Arthur M. Schlesinger Jr. and Fred L. Israel, with permission from Chelsea House Publishers. Copyright © 1971 by Chelsea House Publishers, an imprint of Infobase Learning.

ILLUSTRATIONS

Figure 2. Jackson as General. National Portrait Gallery, Smithsonian Institution/Art Resource, NY.

Figure 4. Henry Clay, by John Neagle. Courtesy of the Abraham Lincoln Foundation of the Union League of Philadelphia.

Figure 5. The Jackson Ticket. Reproduced courtesy of the Collections of the Library of Congress.

Figure 6. The Coffin Handbill. Reproduced courtesy of the Collections of the Library of Congress.

Figure 7. King Andrew the First. Reproduced courtesy of The New-York Historical Society. Copyright © collection of The New-York Historical Society.

Figure 8. The County Election, 1851–1852, by George Caleb Bingham. Courtesy of the Saint Louis Art Museum.

Figure 9. Clay on the Floor of the U.S. Senate, 1850. Art Resource, NY.

Index